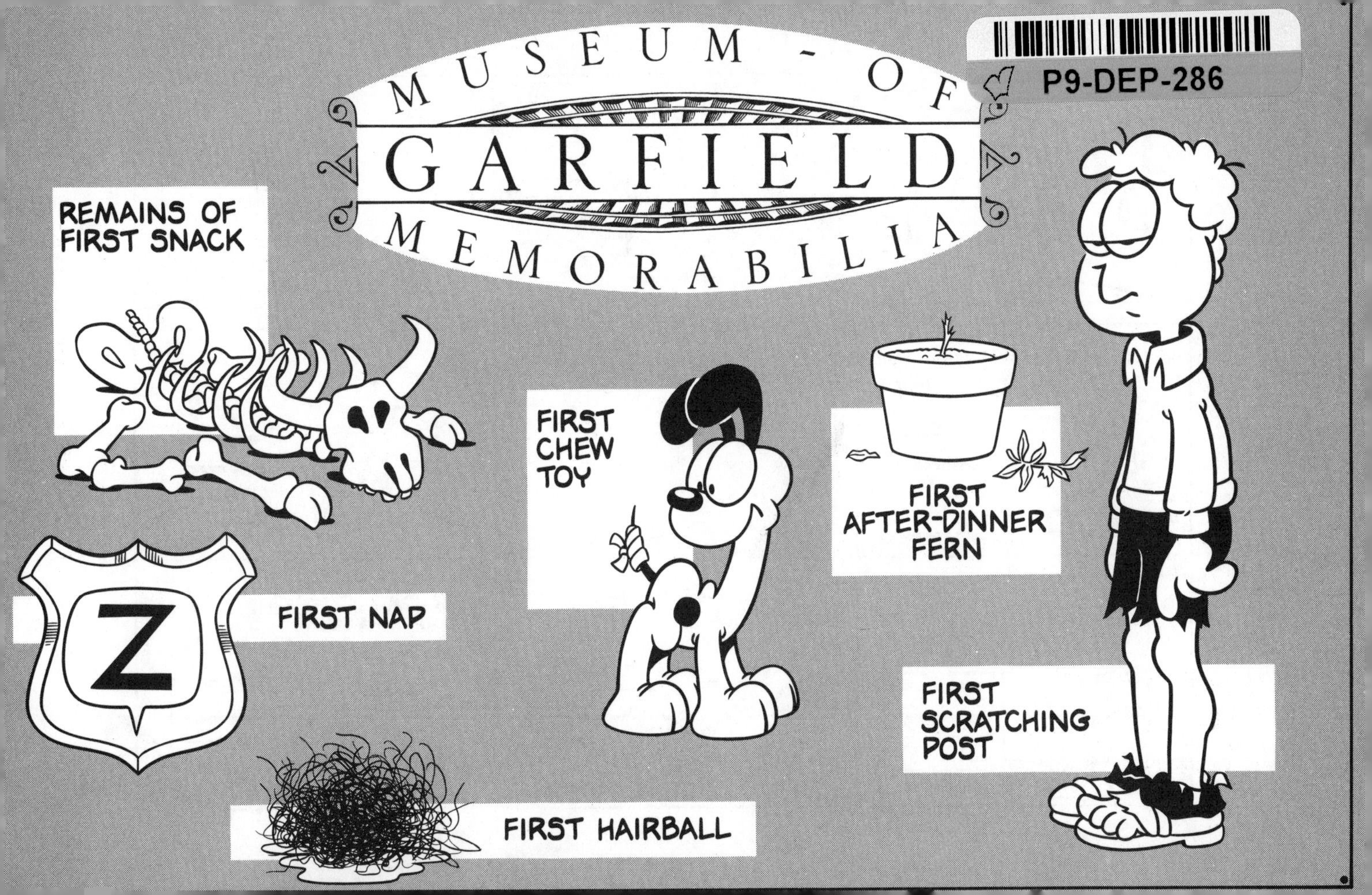
MUSEUM - OF
GARFIELD
MEMORABILIA
REMAINS OF FIRST SNACK
FIRST CHEW TOY
FIRST AFTER-DINNER FERN
FIRST NAP
Z
FIRST SCRATCHING POST
FIRST HAIRBALL

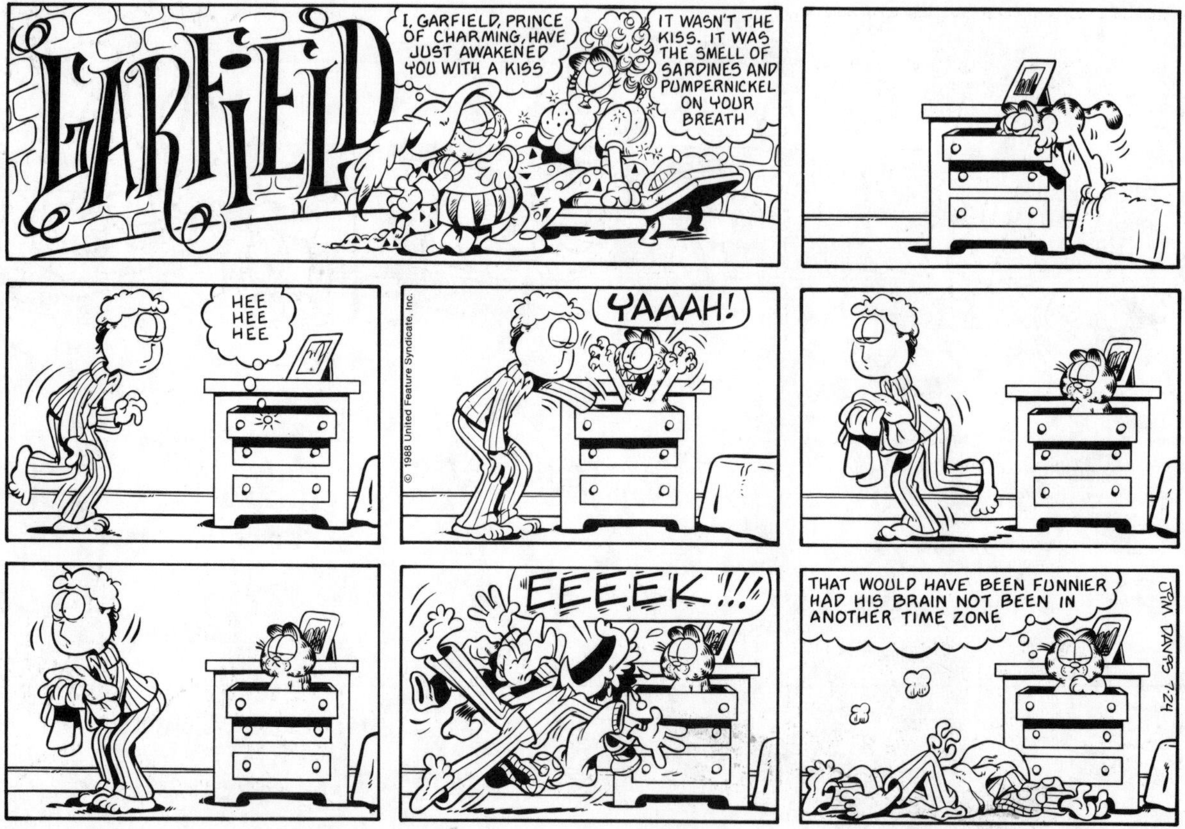
GARFIELD
I, GARFIELD, PRINCE OF CHARMING, HAVE JUST AWAKENED YOU WITH A KISS
IT WASN'T THE KISS. IT WAS THE SMELL OF SARDINES AND PUMPERNICKEL ON YOUR BREATH
HEE HEE HEE
© 1988 United Feature Syndicate, Inc.
YAAAH!
EEEEK!!!
THAT WOULD HAVE BEEN FUNNIER HAD HIS BRAIN NOT BEEN IN ANOTHER TIME ZONE
JIM DAVIS 7-24

Garfield goes to waist

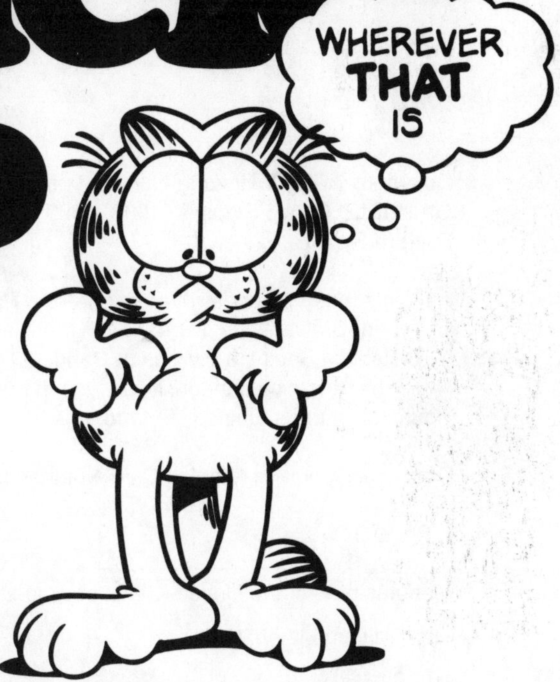
WHEREVER THAT IS

BY: JIM DAVIS

BALLANTINE BOOKS • NEW YORK

Copyright © 1990 United Feature Syndicate, Inc.
GARFIELD Comic Strips: © 1988, 1989   United
Feature Syndicate, Inc.

All rights reserved under International and Pan-American
Copyright Conventions. Published in the United States
by Ballantine Books, a division of Random House, Inc.,
New York, and simultaneously in Canada by Random
House of Canada Limited, Toronto.

Library of Congress Catalog Card Number: 89-90930

ISBN: 0-345-36430-9

Manufactured in the United States of America

First Edition: March 1990

10 9 8 7 6 5 4 3 2 1

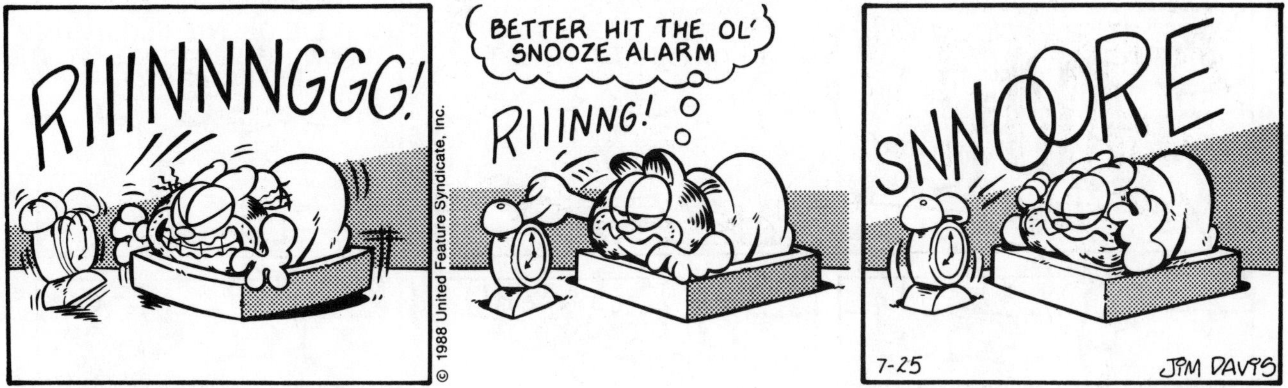
RIIINNNGGG!
BETTER HIT THE OL' SNOOZE ALARM
RIIINNG!
SNNOORE
© 1988 United Feature Syndicate, Inc.
7-25
JIM DAVIS

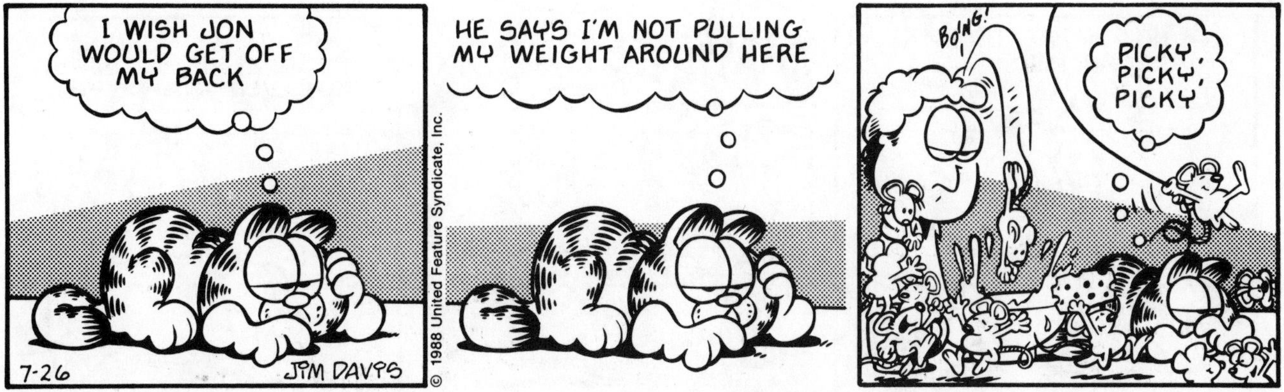
I WISH JON WOULD GET OFF MY BACK
HE SAYS I'M NOT PULLING MY WEIGHT AROUND HERE
BOING!
PICKY, PICKY, PICKY
© 1988 United Feature Syndicate, Inc.
7-26
JIM DAVIS

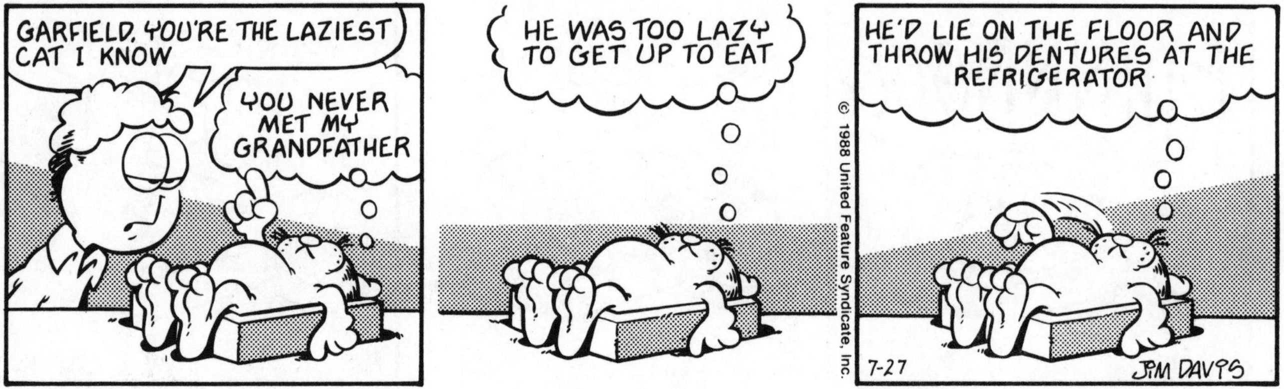
GARFIELD, YOU'RE THE LAZIEST CAT I KNOW
YOU NEVER MET MY GRANDFATHER
HE WAS TOO LAZY TO GET UP TO EAT
HE'D LIE ON THE FLOOR AND THROW HIS DENTURES AT THE REFRIGERATOR
© 1988 United Feature Syndicate, Inc.
7-27
JIM DAVIS

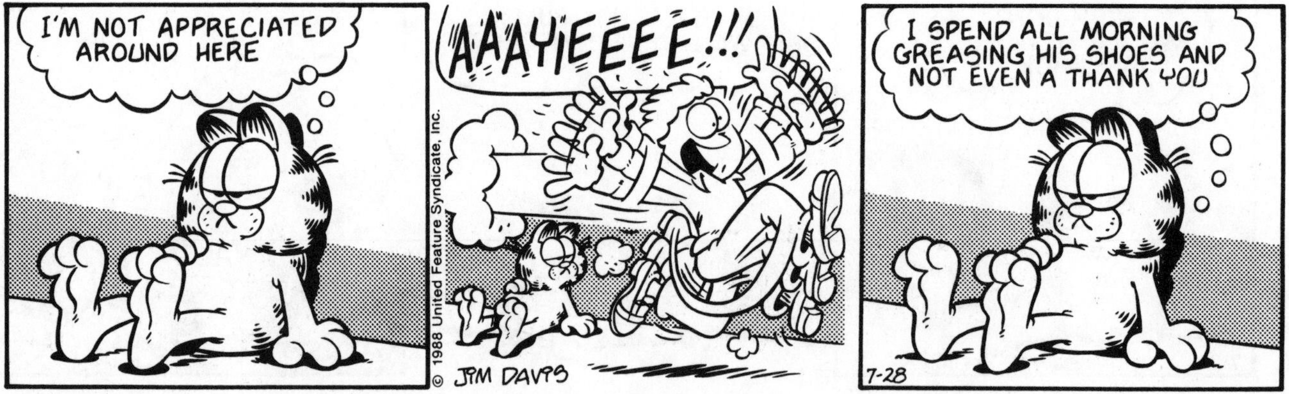
I'M NOT APPRECIATED AROUND HERE
AAAYIEEEEE!!!
© 1988 United Feature Syndicate, Inc.
JIM DAVIS
I SPEND ALL MORNING GREASING HIS SHOES AND NOT EVEN A THANK YOU
7-28

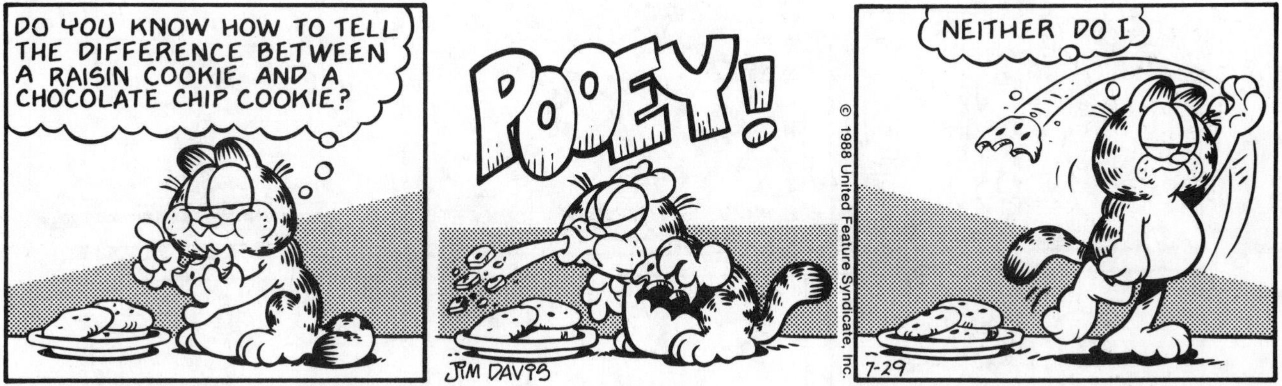
DO YOU KNOW HOW TO TELL THE DIFFERENCE BETWEEN A RAISIN COOKIE AND A CHOCOLATE CHIP COOKIE?
POOEY!
JIM DAVIS
© 1988 United Feature Syndicate, Inc.
NEITHER DO I
7-29

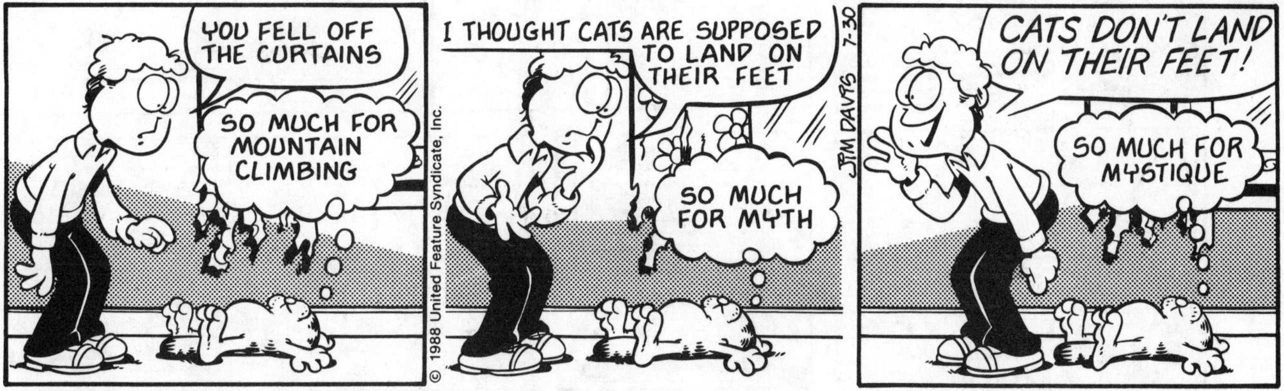
YOU FELL OFF THE CURTAINS
SO MUCH FOR MOUNTAIN CLIMBING
© 1988 United Feature Syndicate, Inc.
I THOUGHT CATS ARE SUPPOSED TO LAND ON THEIR FEET
SO MUCH FOR MYTH
7-30
JIM DAVIS
CATS DON'T LAND ON THEIR FEET!
SO MUCH FOR MYSTIQUE

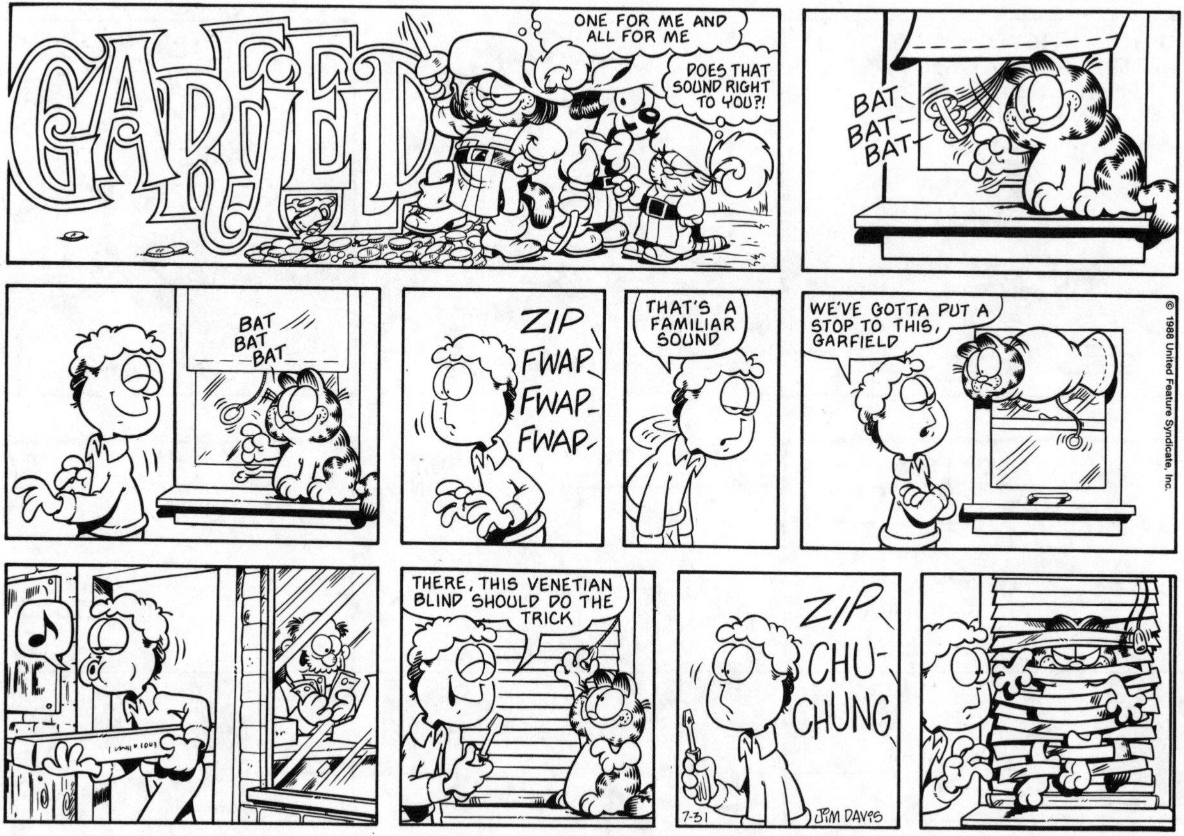
GARFIELD
ONE FOR ME AND ALL FOR ME
DOES THAT SOUND RIGHT TO YOU?!
BAT BAT BAT
BAT BAT BAT
ZIP FWAP FWAP FWAP
THAT'S A FAMILIAR SOUND
WE'VE GOTTA PUT A STOP TO THIS, GARFIELD
THERE, THIS VENETIAN BLIND SHOULD DO THE TRICK
ZIP CHU-CHUNG
7-31
JIM DAVIS

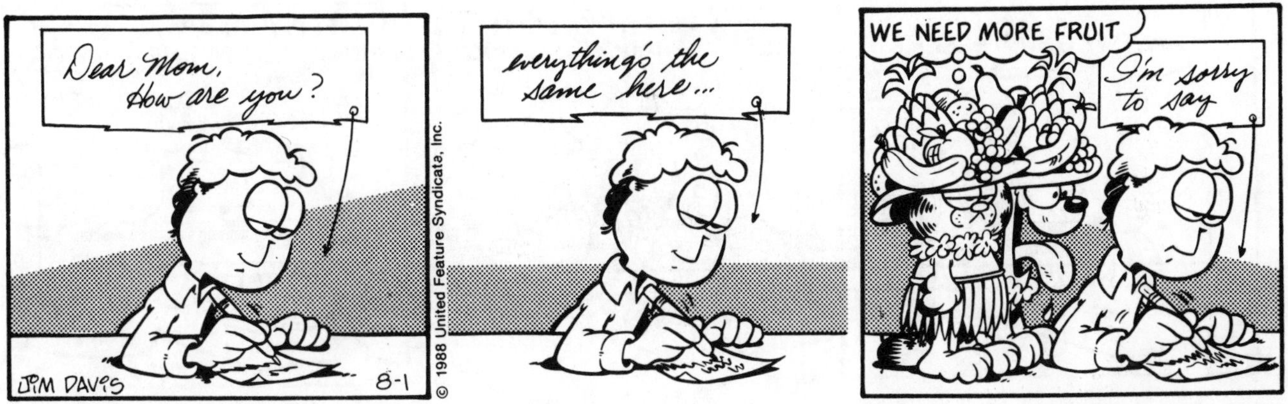
Dear Mom,
How are you?
everything's the same here...
WE NEED MORE FRUIT
I'm sorry to say
JIM DAVIS 8-1
© 1988 United Feature Syndicate, Inc.

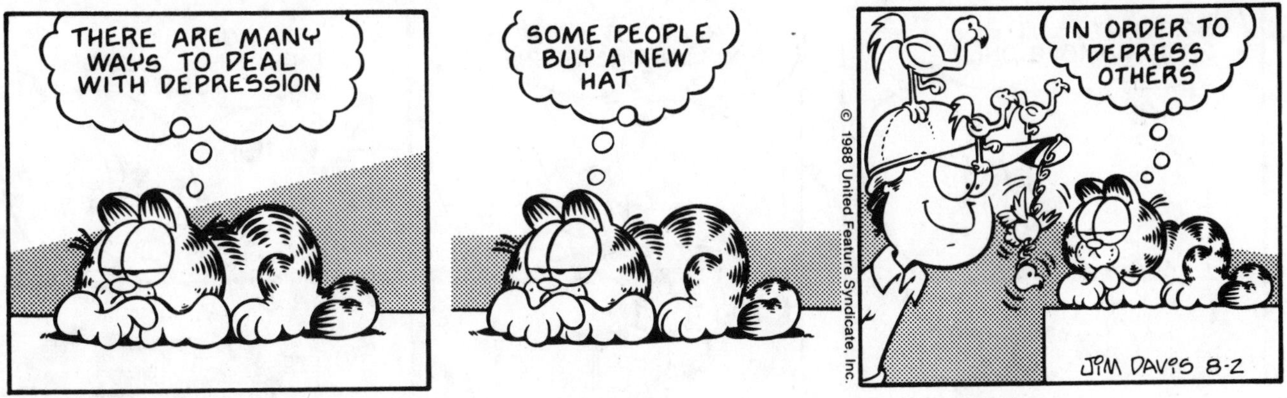
THERE ARE MANY WAYS TO DEAL WITH DEPRESSION
SOME PEOPLE BUY A NEW HAT
IN ORDER TO DEPRESS OTHERS
JIM DAVIS 8-2
© 1988 United Feature Syndicate, Inc.

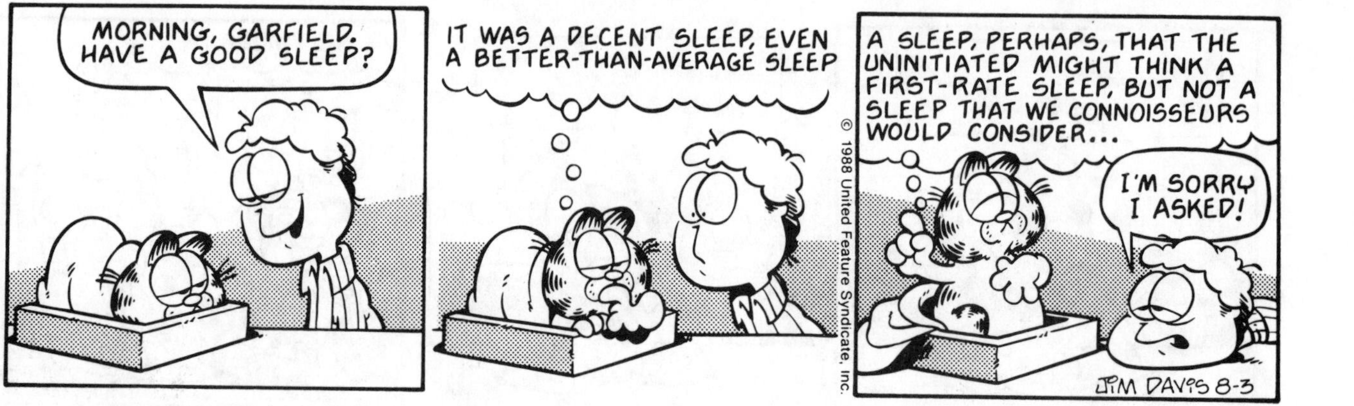
MORNING, GARFIELD. HAVE A GOOD SLEEP?
IT WAS A DECENT SLEEP, EVEN A BETTER-THAN-AVERAGE SLEEP
A SLEEP, PERHAPS, THAT THE UNINITIATED MIGHT THINK A FIRST-RATE SLEEP, BUT NOT A SLEEP THAT WE CONNOISSEURS WOULD CONSIDER...
I'M SORRY I ASKED!
JIM DAVIS 8-3
© 1988 United Feature Syndicate, Inc.

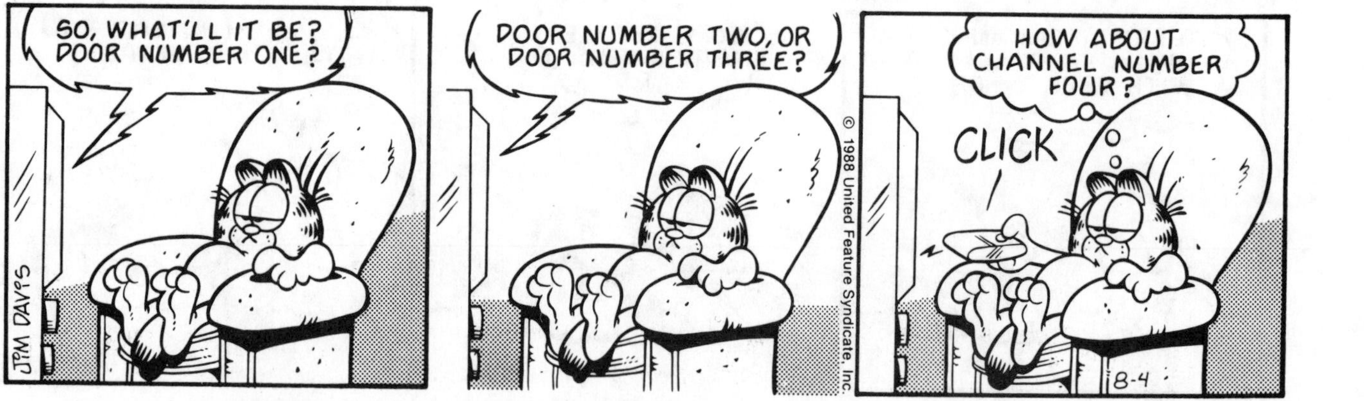
SO, WHAT'LL IT BE? DOOR NUMBER ONE?
DOOR NUMBER TWO, OR DOOR NUMBER THREE?
HOW ABOUT CHANNEL NUMBER FOUR?
CLICK
JIM DAVIS
8-4
© 1988 United Feature Syndicate, Inc.

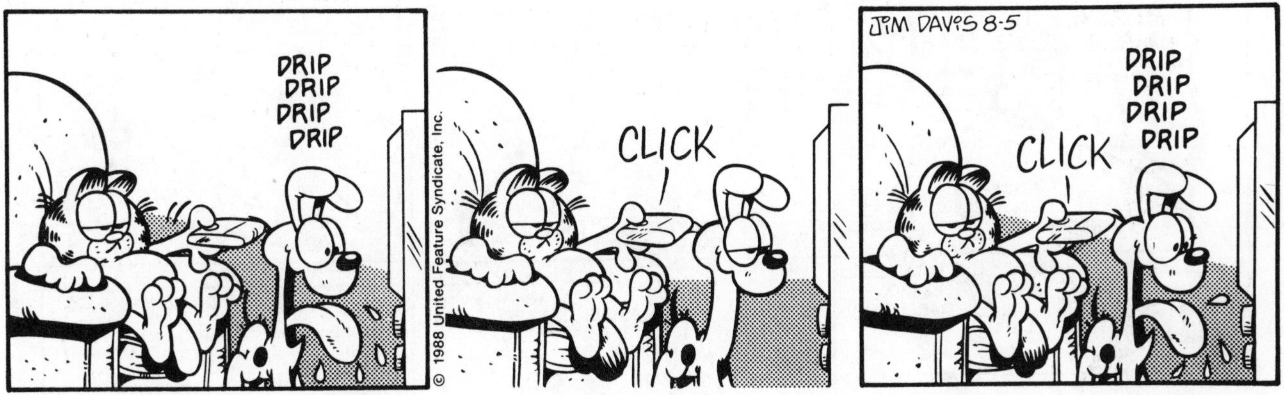
DRIP
DRIP
DRIP
DRIP
© 1988 United Feature Syndicate, Inc.
CLICK
JIM DAVIS 8-5
CLICK
DRIP
DRIP
DRIP
DRIP

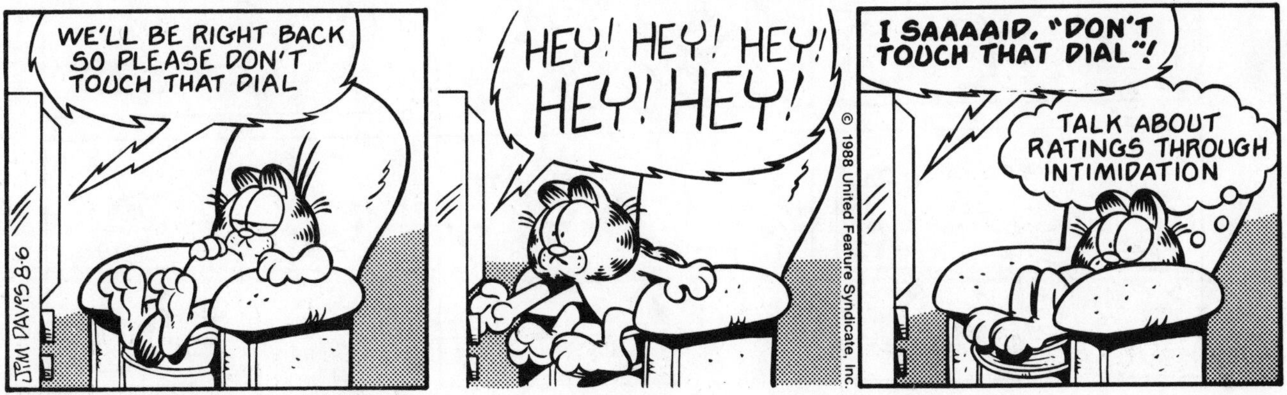
WE'LL BE RIGHT BACK SO PLEASE DON'T TOUCH THAT DIAL
JIM DAVIS 8-6
HEY! HEY! HEY! HEY! HEY!
© 1988 United Feature Syndicate, Inc.
I SAAAAID, "DON'T TOUCH THAT DIAL"!
TALK ABOUT RATINGS THROUGH INTIMIDATION

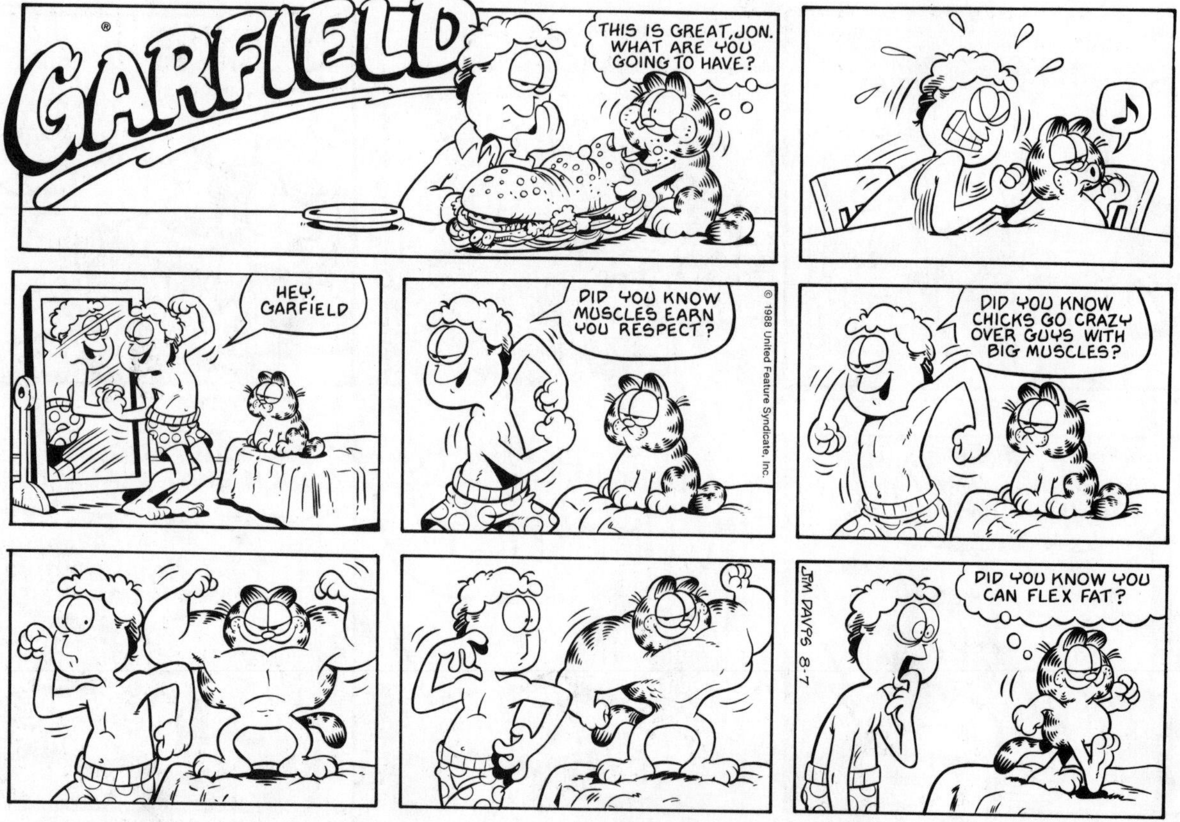
GARFIELD®
THIS IS GREAT, JON. WHAT ARE YOU GOING TO HAVE?
♪
HEY, GARFIELD
DID YOU KNOW MUSCLES EARN YOU RESPECT?
© 1988 United Feature Syndicate, Inc.
DID YOU KNOW CHICKS GO CRAZY OVER GUYS WITH BIG MUSCLES?
JIM DAVIS 8-7
DID YOU KNOW YOU CAN FLEX FAT?

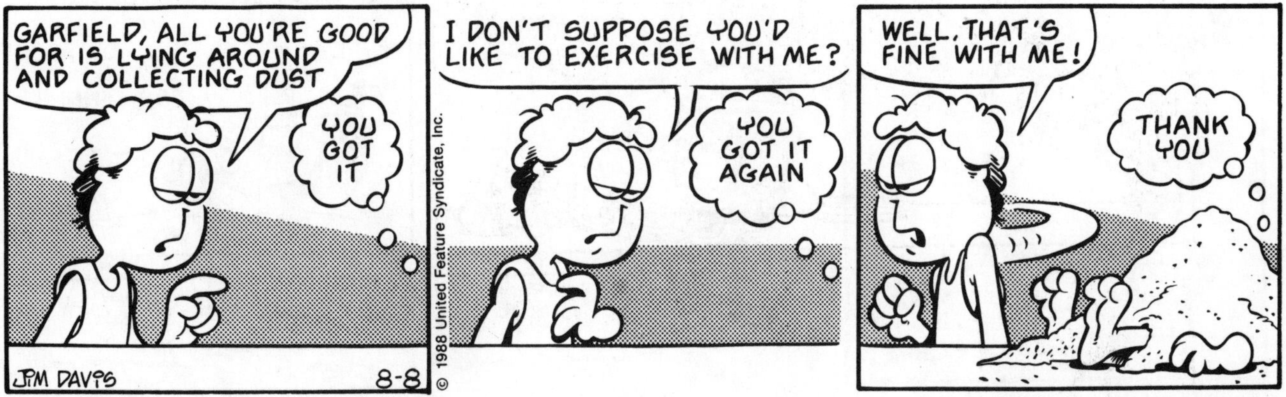
GARFIELD, ALL YOU'RE GOOD FOR IS LYING AROUND AND COLLECTING DUST
YOU GOT IT
JIM DAVIS
8-8
I DON'T SUPPOSE YOU'D LIKE TO EXERCISE WITH ME?
YOU GOT IT AGAIN
© 1988 United Feature Syndicate, Inc.
WELL, THAT'S FINE WITH ME!
THANK YOU

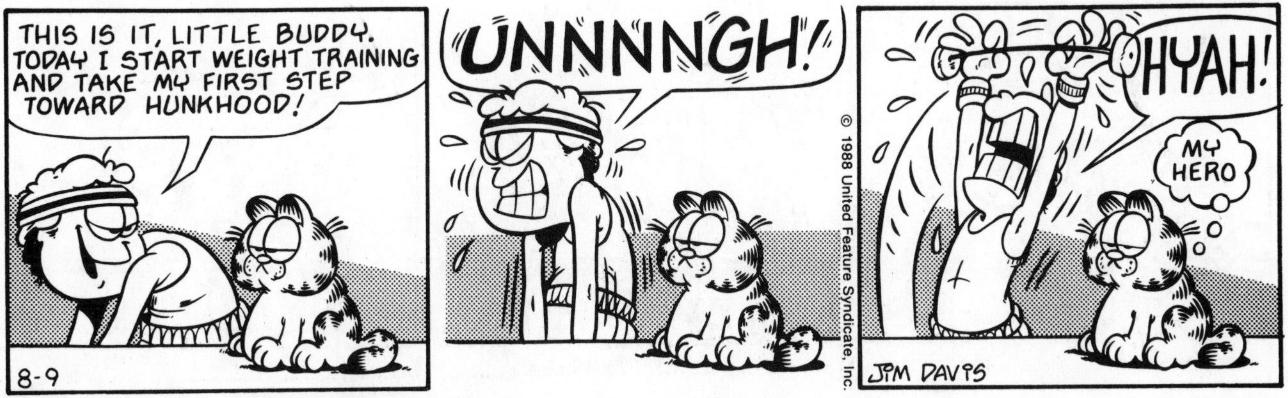
THIS IS IT, LITTLE BUDDY. TODAY I START WEIGHT TRAINING AND TAKE MY FIRST STEP TOWARD HUNKHOOD!
8-9
UNNNNGH!
© 1988 United Feature Syndicate, Inc.
HYAH!
MY HERO
JIM DAVIS

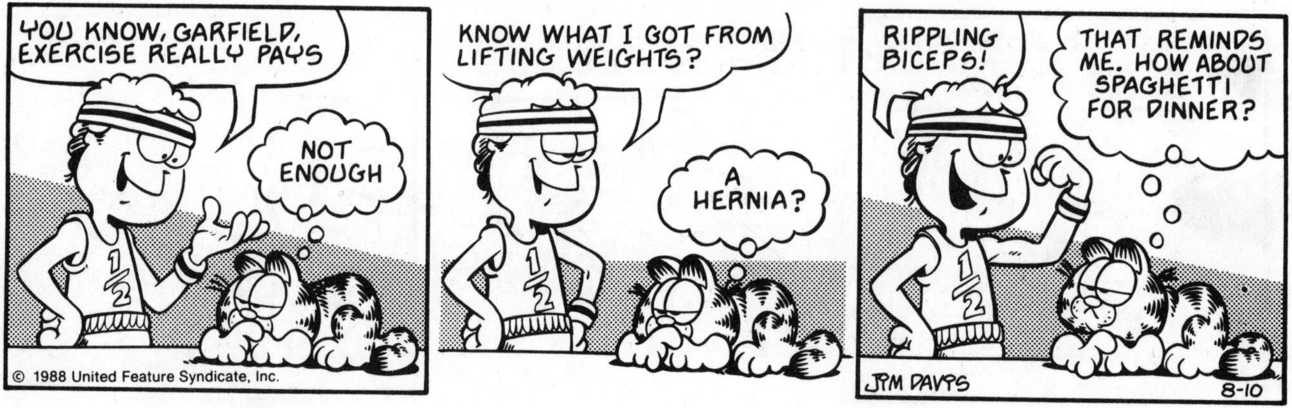
YOU KNOW, GARFIELD, EXERCISE REALLY PAYS
NOT ENOUGH
KNOW WHAT I GOT FROM LIFTING WEIGHTS?
A HERNIA?
RIPPLING BICEPS!
THAT REMINDS ME. HOW ABOUT SPAGHETTI FOR DINNER?
JIM DAVIS
8-10

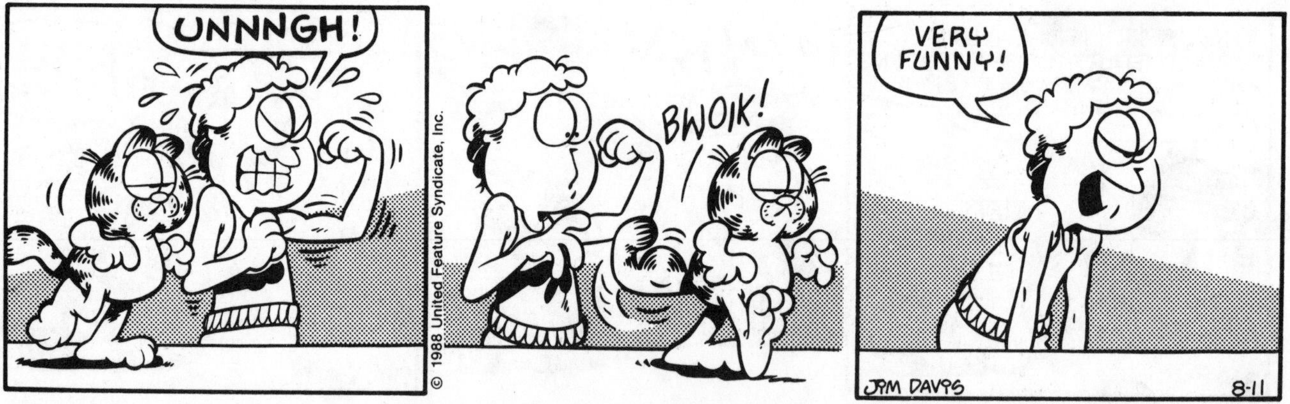
UNNNGH!
BWOIK!
VERY FUNNY!
JIM DAVIS
8-11

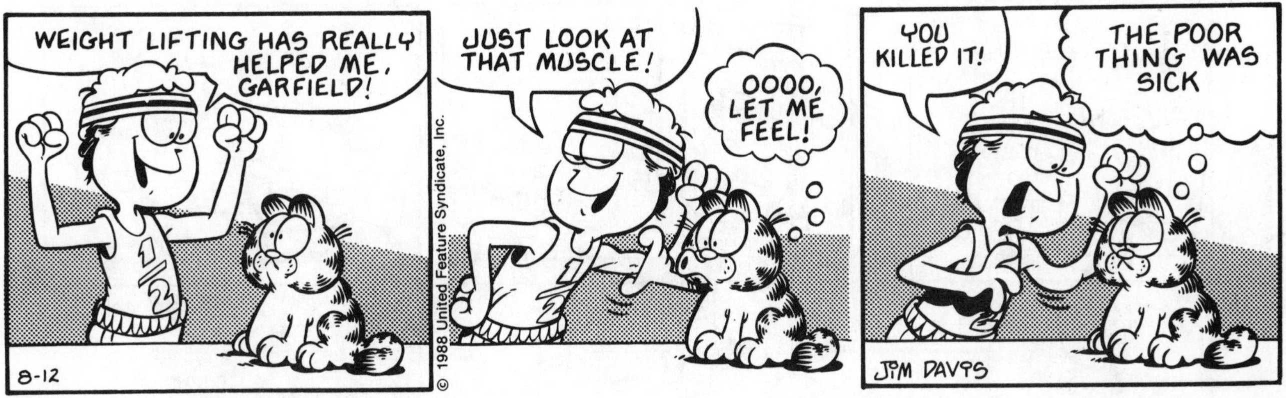

WEIGHT LIFTING HAS REALLY HELPED ME, GARFIELD!
8-12
JUST LOOK AT THAT MUSCLE!
OOOO, LET ME FEEL!
© 1988 United Feature Syndicate, Inc.
YOU KILLED IT!
THE POOR THING WAS SICK
JIM DAVIS

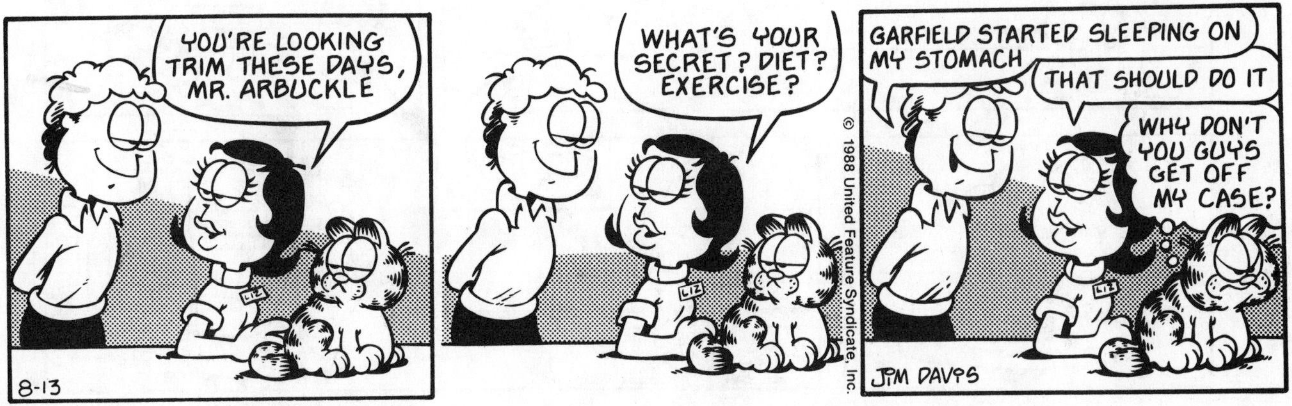

YOU'RE LOOKING TRIM THESE DAYS, MR. ARBUCKLE
8-13
WHAT'S YOUR SECRET? DIET? EXERCISE?
© 1988 United Feature Syndicate, Inc.
GARFIELD STARTED SLEEPING ON MY STOMACH
THAT SHOULD DO IT
WHY DON'T YOU GUYS GET OFF MY CASE?
JIM DAVIS

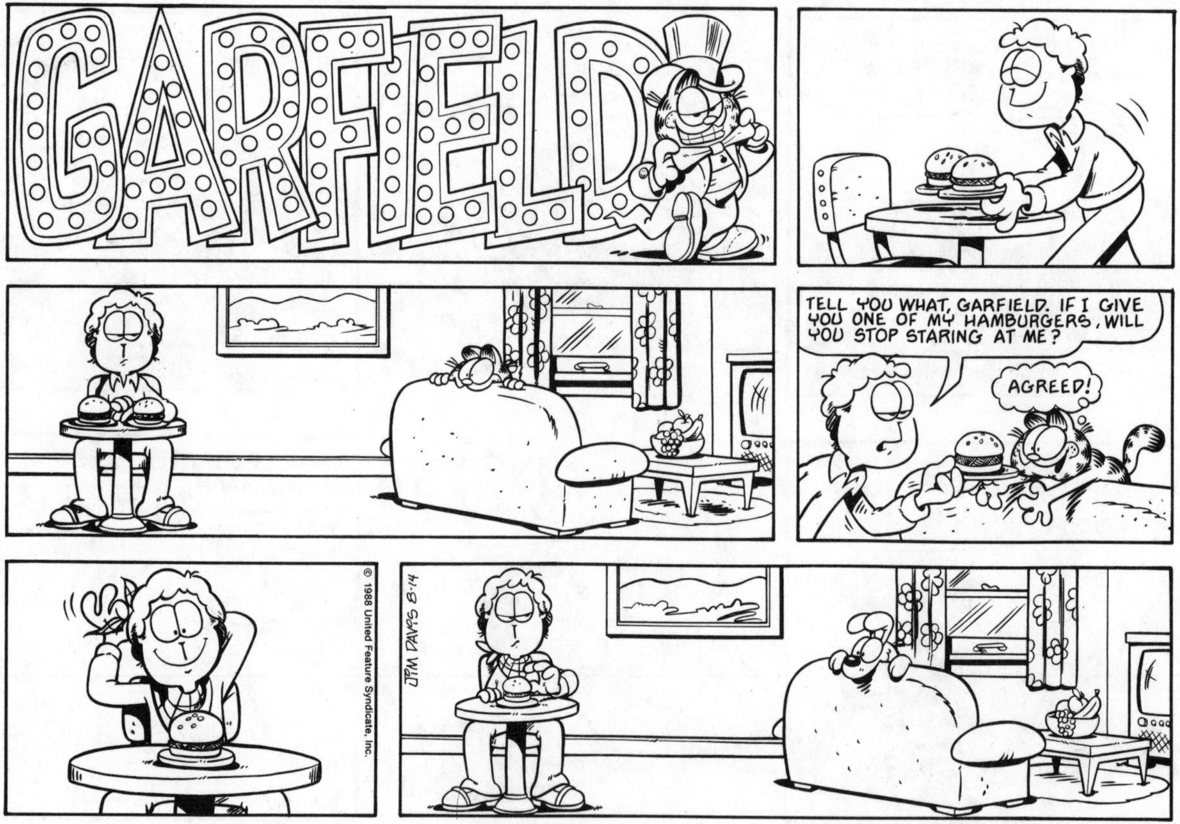
GARFIELD
TELL YOU WHAT, GARFIELD. IF I GIVE YOU ONE OF MY HAMBURGERS, WILL YOU STOP STARING AT ME?
AGREED!
© 1988 United Feature Syndicate, Inc.
JIM DAVIS 8-14

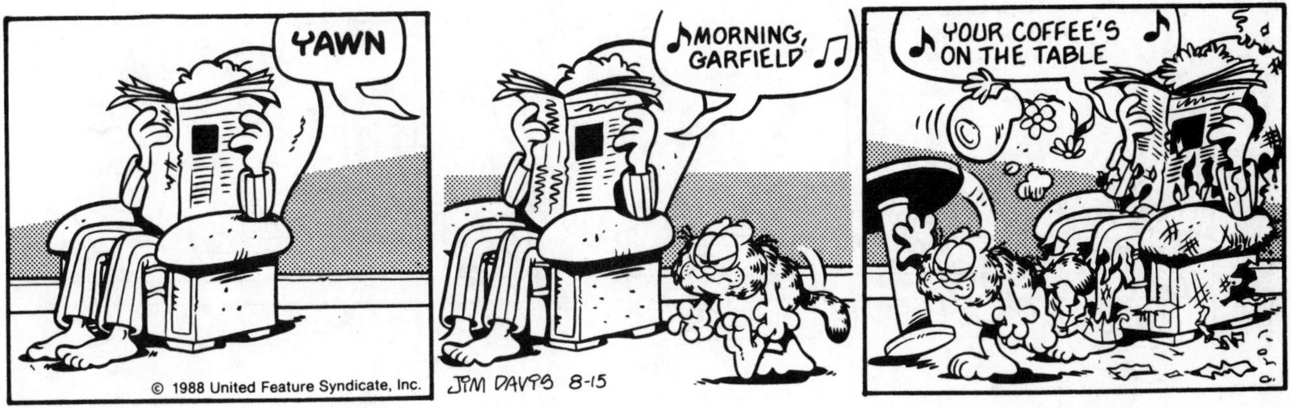
YAWN
♪MORNING, GARFIELD ♫
♪ YOUR COFFEE'S ON THE TABLE ♪
© 1988 United Feature Syndicate, Inc.
JIM DAVIS 8-15

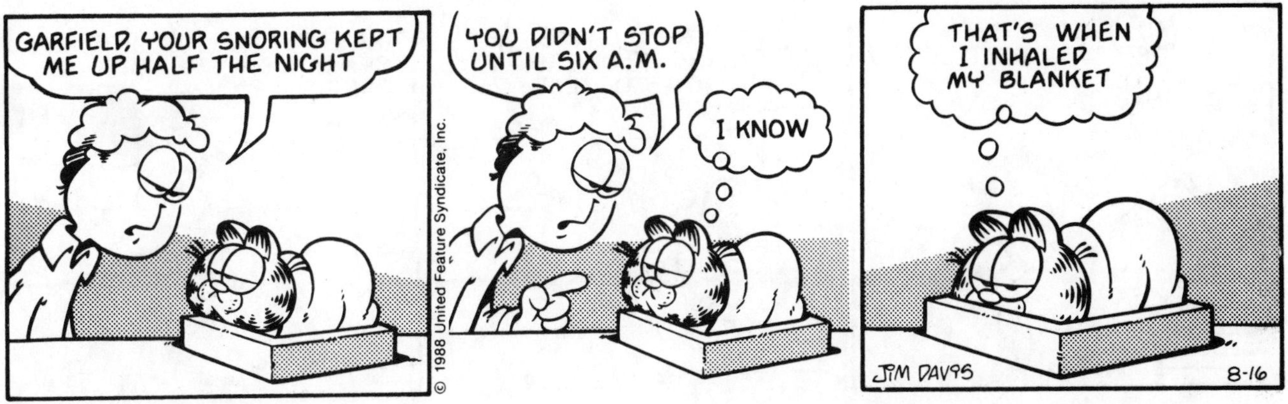
GARFIELD, YOUR SNORING KEPT ME UP HALF THE NIGHT
YOU DIDN'T STOP UNTIL SIX A.M.
I KNOW
THAT'S WHEN I INHALED MY BLANKET
© 1988 United Feature Syndicate, Inc.
JIM DAVIS 8-16

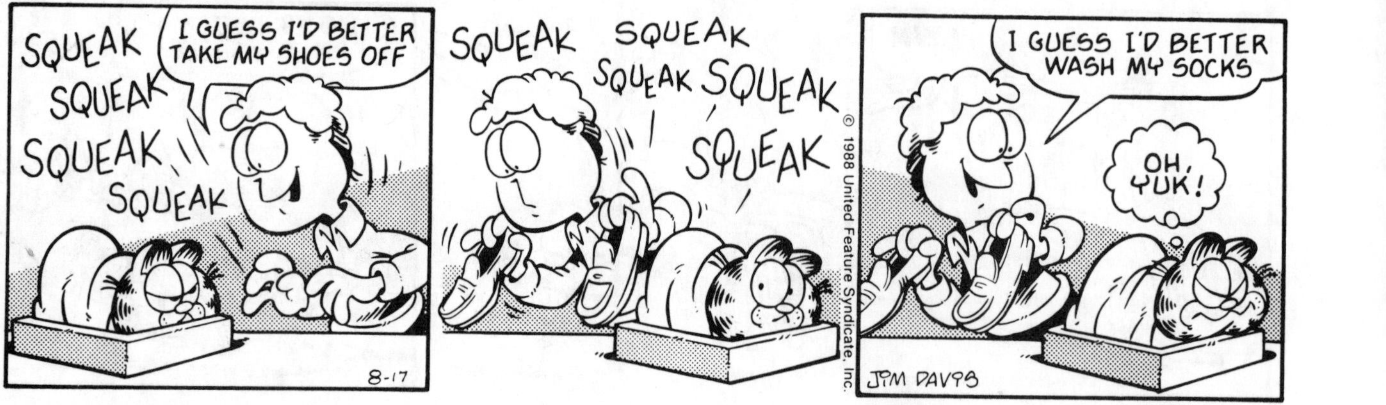
SQUEAK
SQUEAK
SQUEAK
SQUEAK
I GUESS I'D BETTER TAKE MY SHOES OFF
8-17
SQUEAK SQUEAK
SQUEAK SQUEAK
SQUEAK
© 1988 United Feature Syndicate, Inc.
I GUESS I'D BETTER WASH MY SOCKS
OH, YUK!
JIM DAVIS

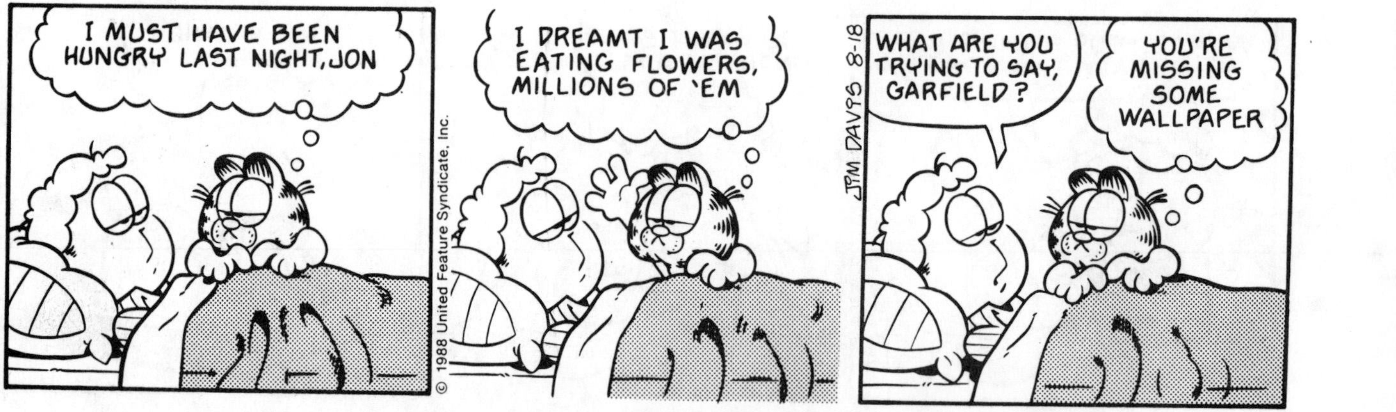
I MUST HAVE BEEN HUNGRY LAST NIGHT, JON
© 1988 United Feature Syndicate, Inc.
I DREAMT I WAS EATING FLOWERS, MILLIONS OF 'EM
JIM DAVIS 8-18
WHAT ARE YOU TRYING TO SAY, GARFIELD?
YOU'RE MISSING SOME WALLPAPER

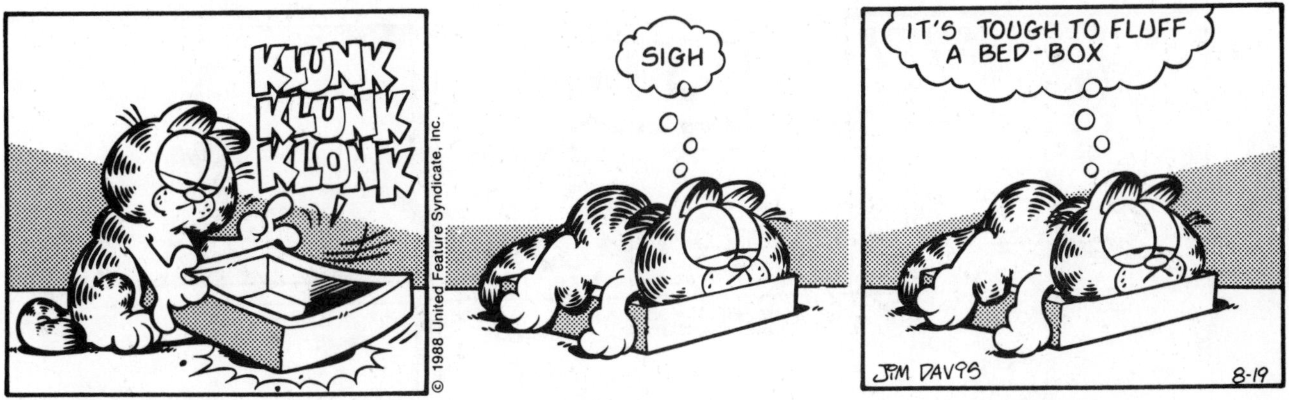
KLUNK KLUNK KLONK
© 1988 United Feature Syndicate, Inc.
SIGH
IT'S TOUGH TO FLUFF A BED-BOX
JIM DAVIS
8-19

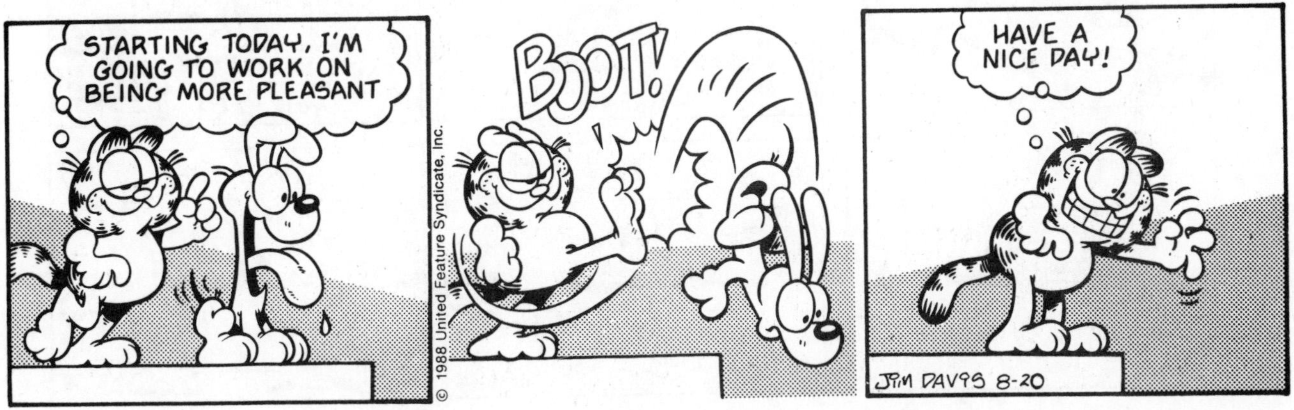
STARTING TODAY, I'M GOING TO WORK ON BEING MORE PLEASANT
© 1988 United Feature Syndicate, Inc.
BOOT!
HAVE A NICE DAY!
JIM DAVIS 8-20

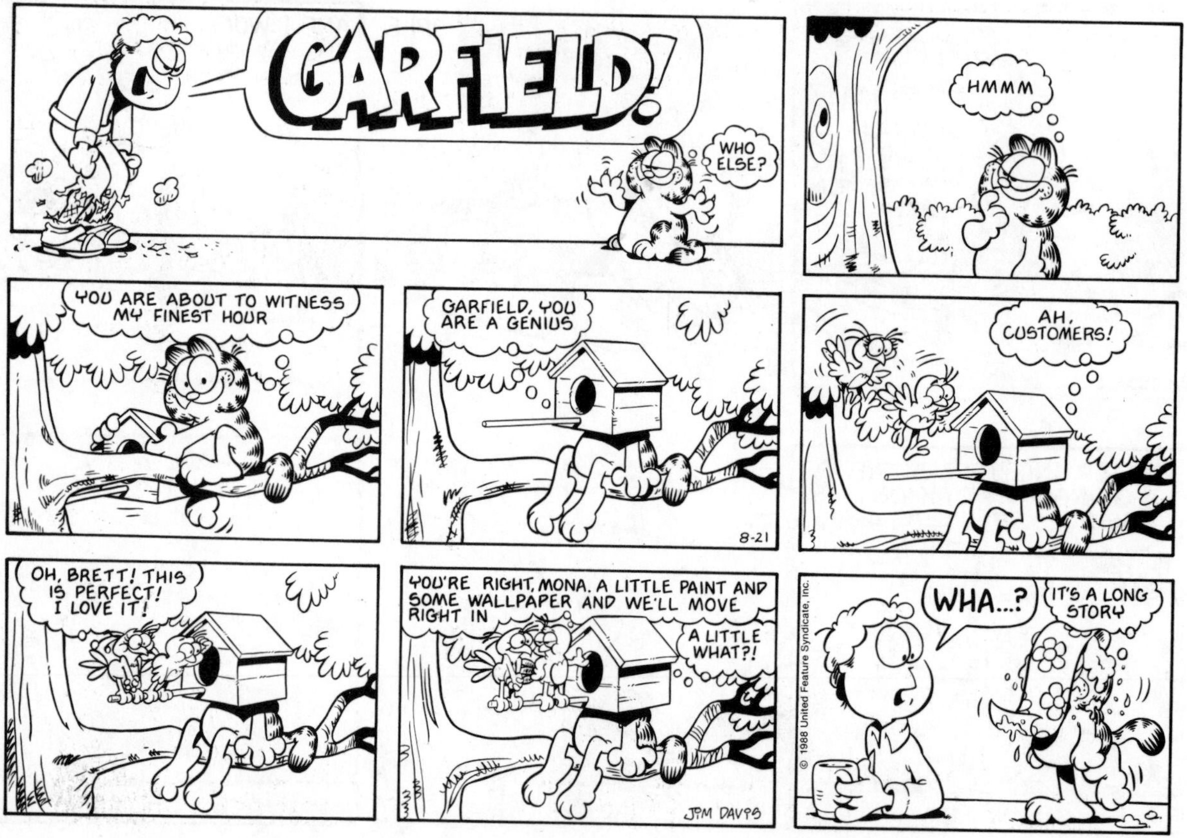
GARFIELD!
WHO ELSE?
HMMM
YOU ARE ABOUT TO WITNESS MY FINEST HOUR
GARFIELD, YOU ARE A GENIUS
8-21
AH, CUSTOMERS!
OH, BRETT! THIS IS PERFECT! I LOVE IT!
YOU'RE RIGHT, MONA. A LITTLE PAINT AND SOME WALLPAPER AND WE'LL MOVE RIGHT IN
A LITTLE WHAT?!
JIM DAVIS
© 1988 United Feature Syndicate, Inc.
WHA...?
IT'S A LONG STORY

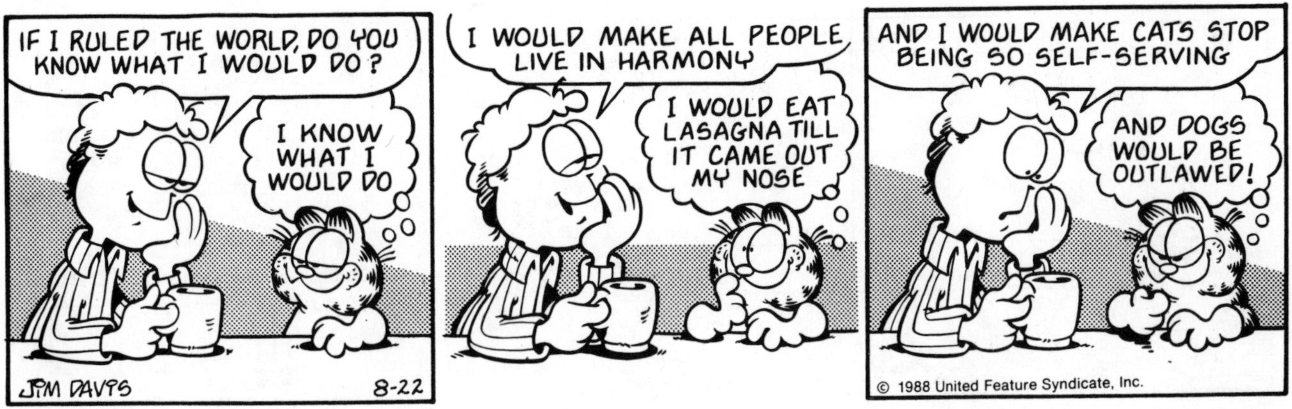
IF I RULED THE WORLD, DO YOU KNOW WHAT I WOULD DO?
I KNOW WHAT I WOULD DO
JIM DAVIS
8-22
I WOULD MAKE ALL PEOPLE LIVE IN HARMONY
I WOULD EAT LASAGNA TILL IT CAME OUT MY NOSE
AND I WOULD MAKE CATS STOP BEING SO SELF-SERVING
AND DOGS WOULD BE OUTLAWED!
© 1988 United Feature Syndicate, Inc.

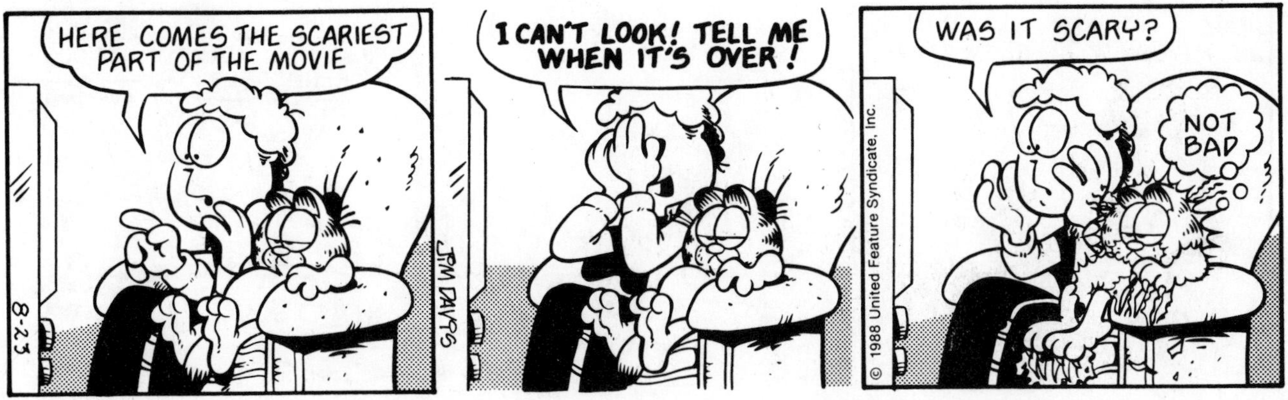
HERE COMES THE SCARIEST PART OF THE MOVIE
8-23
JIM DAVIS
I CAN'T LOOK! TELL ME WHEN IT'S OVER!
WAS IT SCARY?
NOT BAD
© 1988 United Feature Syndicate, Inc.

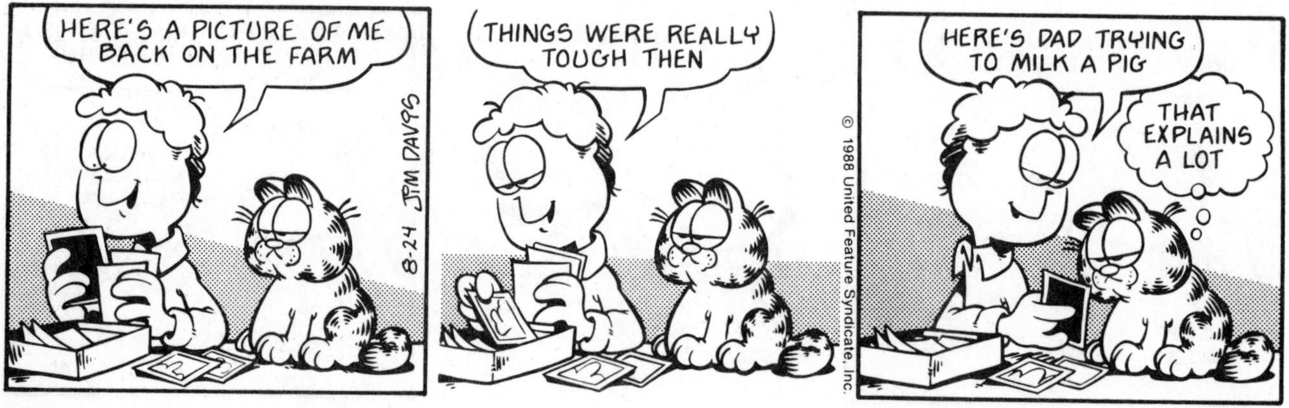
HERE'S A PICTURE OF ME BACK ON THE FARM
JIM DAVIS 8-24
THINGS WERE REALLY TOUGH THEN
© 1988 United Feature Syndicate, Inc.
HERE'S DAD TRYING TO MILK A PIG
THAT EXPLAINS A LOT

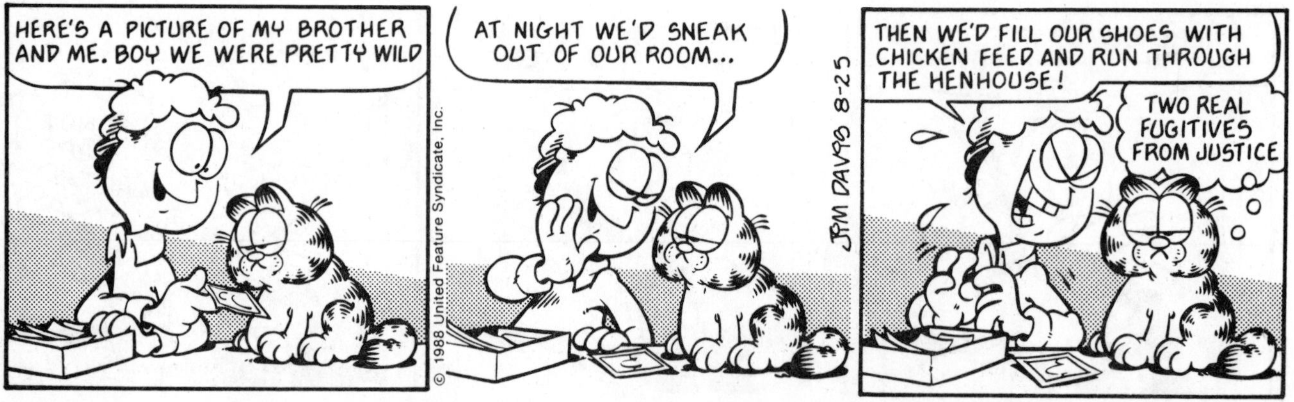
HERE'S A PICTURE OF MY BROTHER AND ME. BOY WE WERE PRETTY WILD
© 1988 United Feature Syndicate, Inc.
AT NIGHT WE'D SNEAK OUT OF OUR ROOM...
JIM DAVIS 8-25
THEN WE'D FILL OUR SHOES WITH CHICKEN FEED AND RUN THROUGH THE HENHOUSE!
TWO REAL FUGITIVES FROM JUSTICE

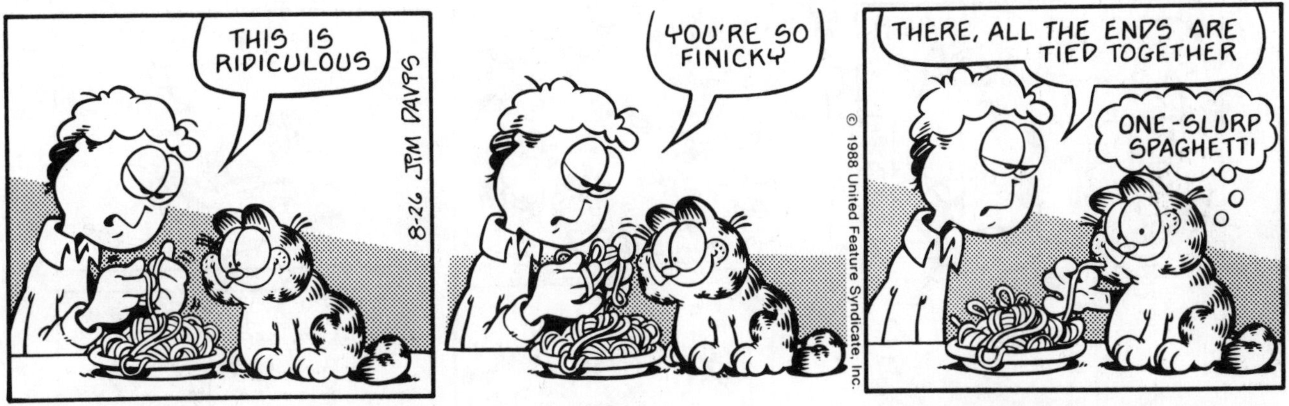
THIS IS RIDICULOUS
8-26 JIM DAVIS
YOU'RE SO FINICKY
© 1988 United Feature Syndicate, Inc.
THERE, ALL THE ENDS ARE TIED TOGETHER
ONE-SLURP SPAGHETTI

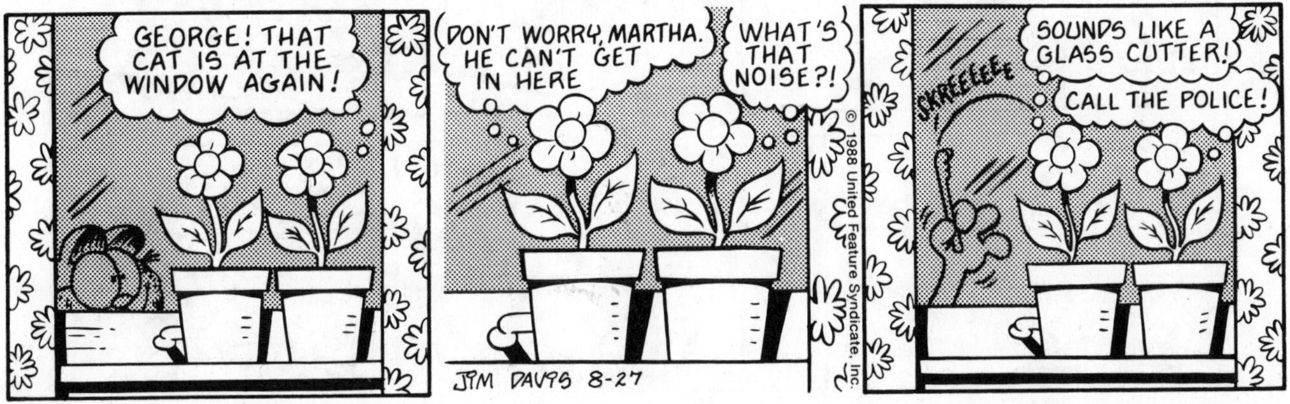
GEORGE! THAT CAT IS AT THE WINDOW AGAIN!
DON'T WORRY, MARTHA. HE CAN'T GET IN HERE
WHAT'S THAT NOISE?!
JIM DAVIS 8-27
© 1988 United Feature Syndicate, Inc.
SKREEEEEE
SOUNDS LIKE A GLASS CUTTER!
CALL THE POLICE!

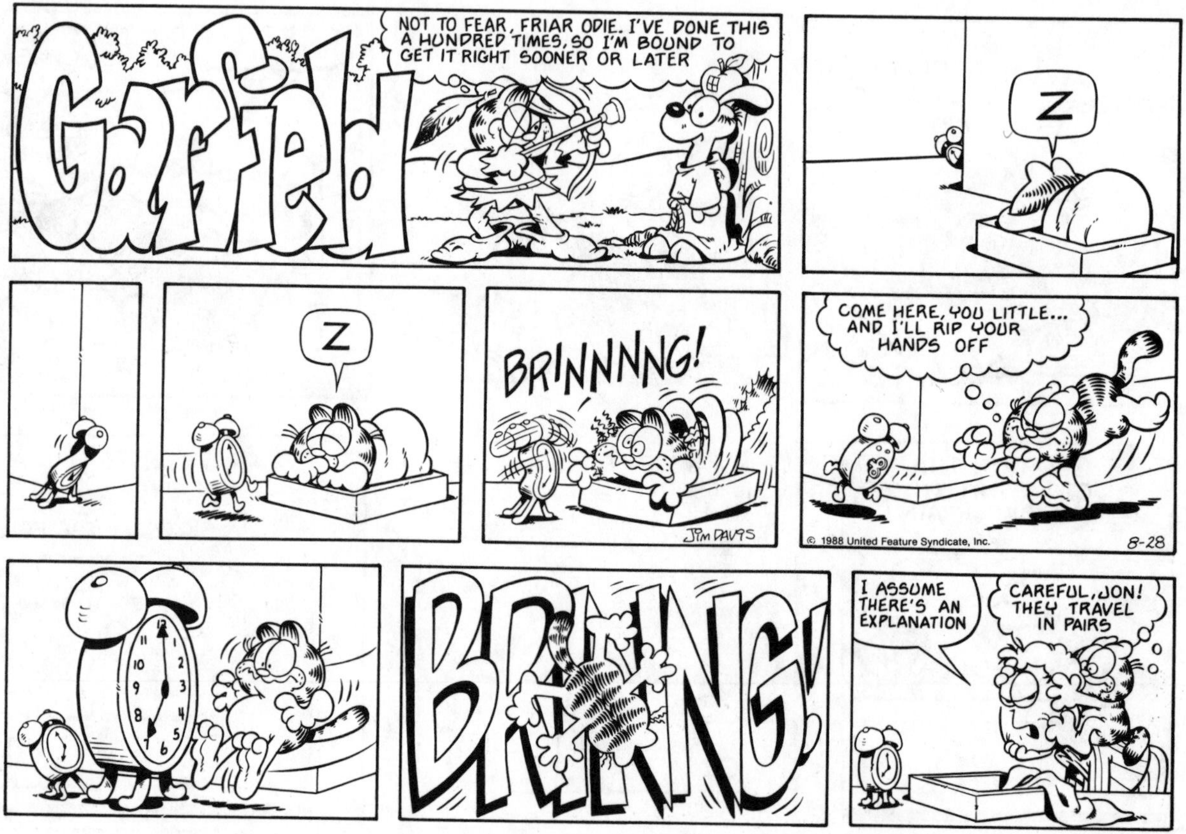

Garfield
NOT TO FEAR, FRIAR ODIE. I'VE DONE THIS A HUNDRED TIMES, SO I'M BOUND TO GET IT RIGHT SOONER OR LATER
Z
Z
BRINNNNG!
JIM DAVIS
COME HERE, YOU LITTLE... AND I'LL RIP YOUR HANDS OFF
© 1988 United Feature Syndicate, Inc.
8-28
BRINNG!
I ASSUME THERE'S AN EXPLANATION
CAREFUL, JON! THEY TRAVEL IN PAIRS

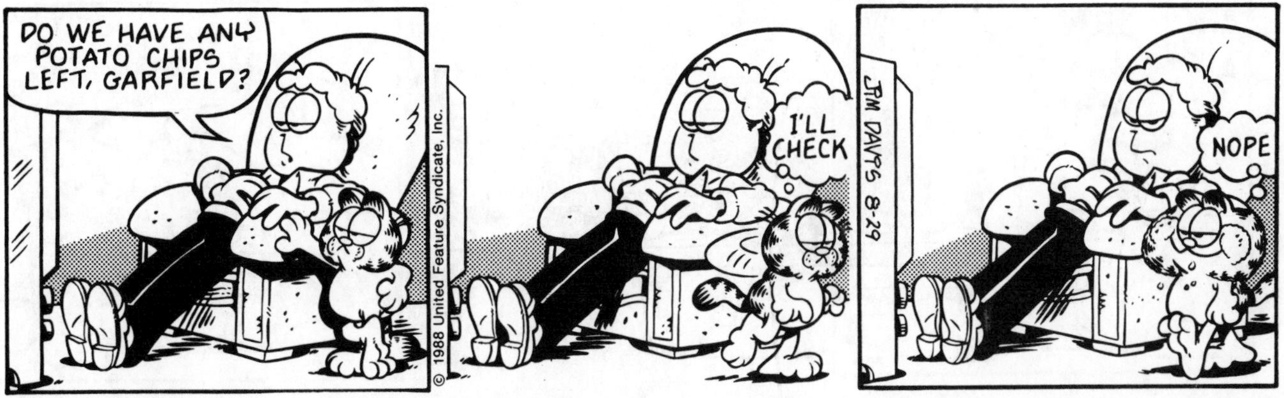
DO WE HAVE ANY POTATO CHIPS LEFT, GARFIELD?
© 1988 United Feature Syndicate, Inc.
I'LL CHECK
JIM DAVIS 8-29
NOPE

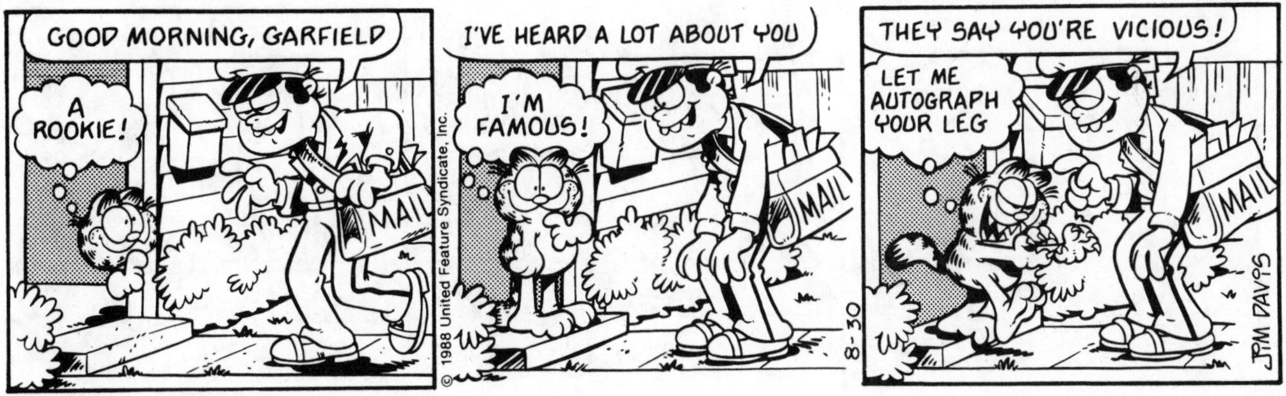
GOOD MORNING, GARFIELD
A ROOKIE!
© 1988 United Feature Syndicate, Inc.
I'VE HEARD A LOT ABOUT YOU
I'M FAMOUS!
MAIL
8-30
THEY SAY YOU'RE VICIOUS!
LET ME AUTOGRAPH YOUR LEG
MAIL
JIM DAVIS

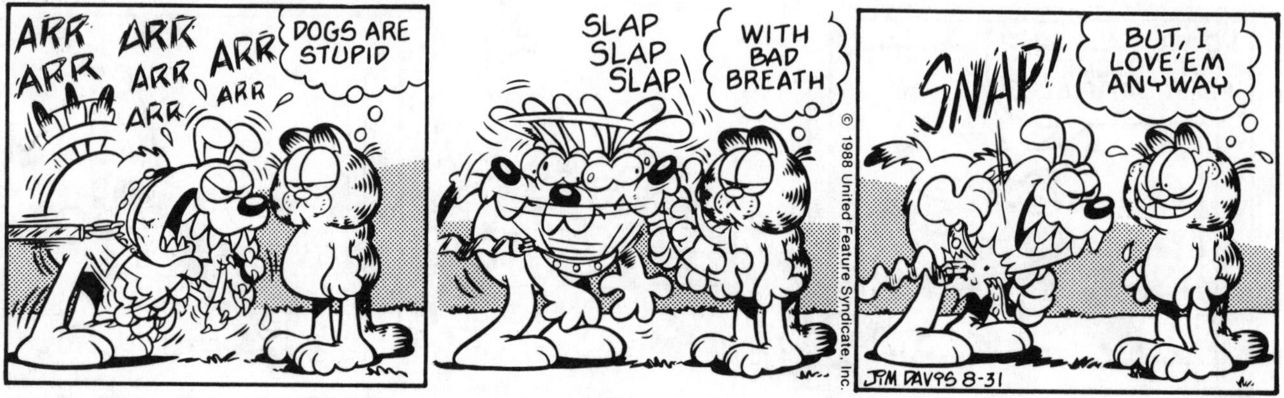
ARR ARR ARR ARR ARR ARR ARR
DOGS ARE STUPID
SLAP SLAP SLAP
WITH BAD BREATH
SNAP!
BUT, I LOVE'EM ANYWAY
JIM DAVIS 8-31
© 1988 United Feature Syndicate, Inc.

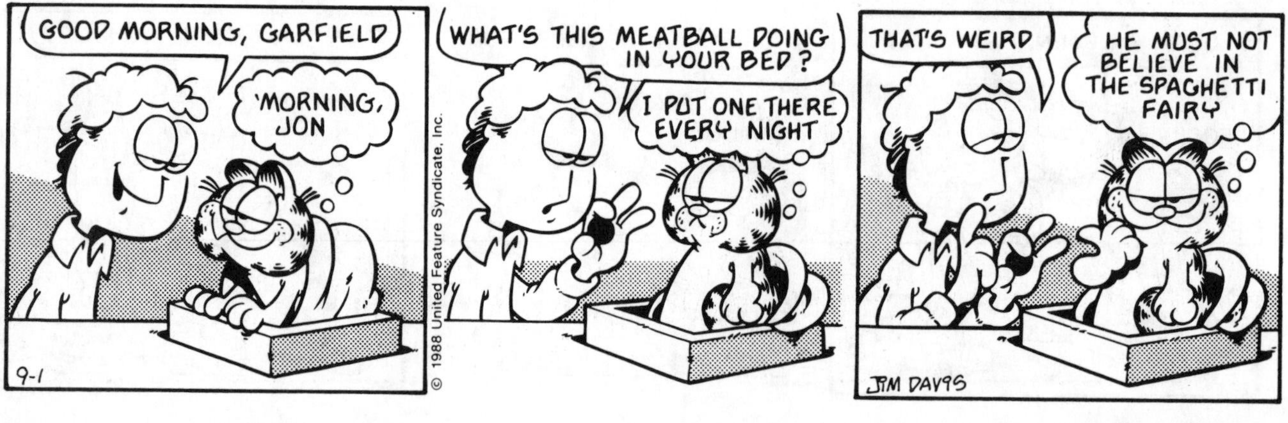
GOOD MORNING, GARFIELD
'MORNING, JON
9-1
© 1988 United Feature Syndicate, Inc.
WHAT'S THIS MEATBALL DOING IN YOUR BED?
I PUT ONE THERE EVERY NIGHT
THAT'S WEIRD
HE MUST NOT BELIEVE IN THE SPAGHETTI FAIRY
JIM DAVIS

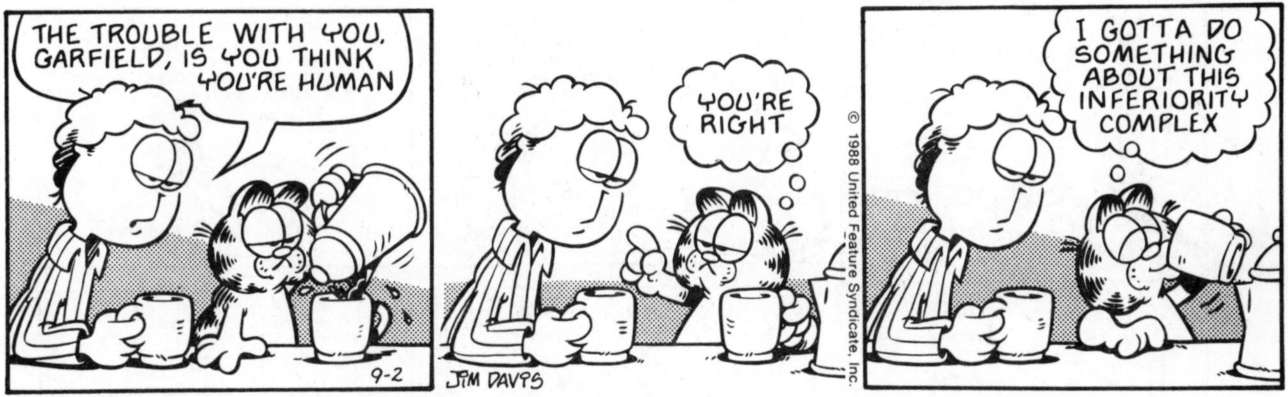
THE TROUBLE WITH YOU, GARFIELD, IS YOU THINK YOU'RE HUMAN
9-2
JIM DAVIS
YOU'RE RIGHT
© 1988 United Feature Syndicate, Inc.
I GOTTA DO SOMETHING ABOUT THIS INFERIORITY COMPLEX

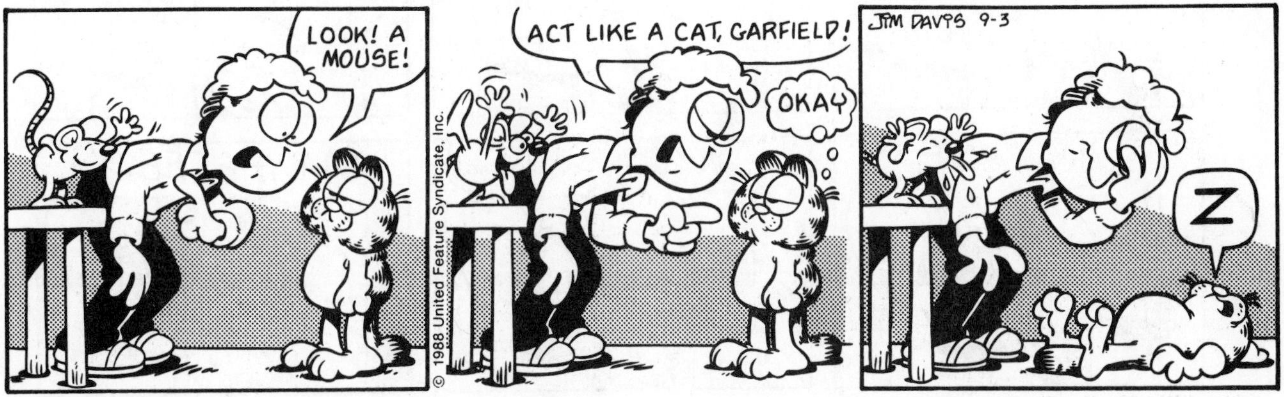
LOOK! A MOUSE!
© 1988 United Feature Syndicate, Inc.
ACT LIKE A CAT, GARFIELD!
OKAY
JIM DAVIS 9-3
Z

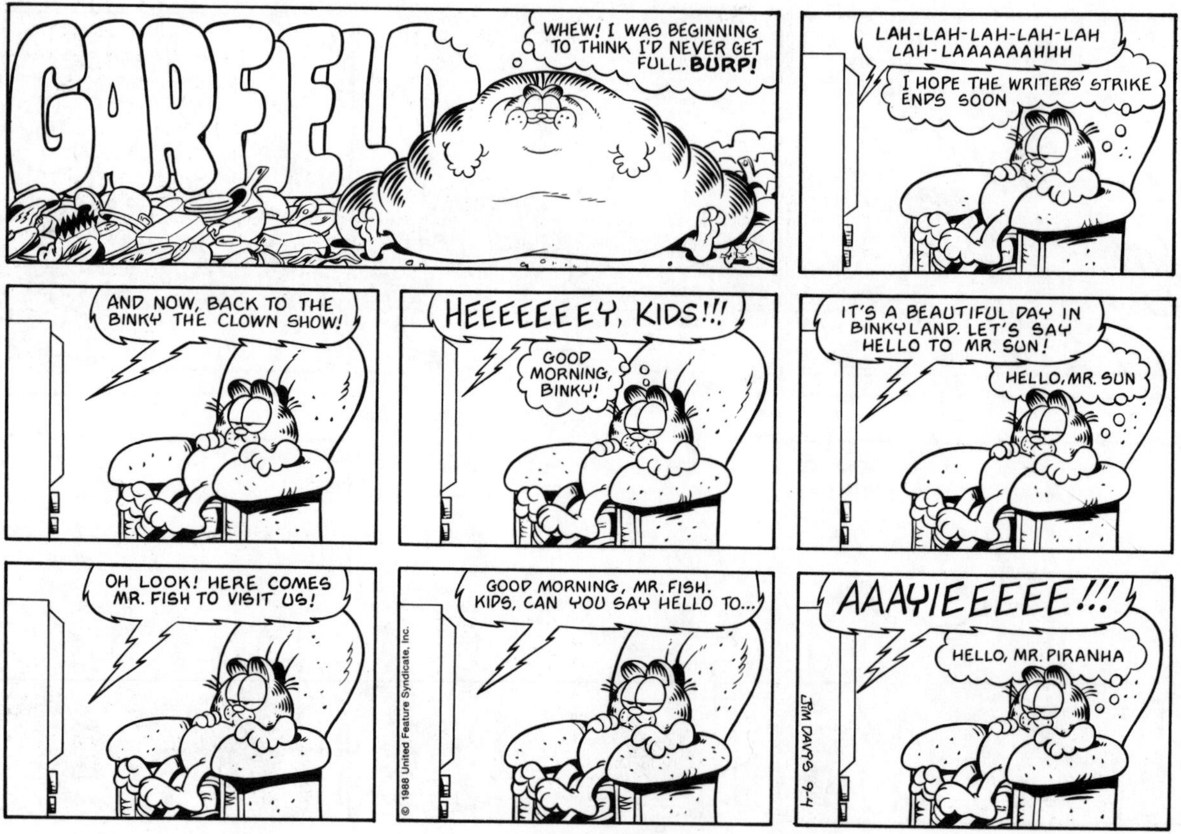
GARFIELD
WHEW! I WAS BEGINNING TO THINK I'D NEVER GET FULL. BURP!
LAH-LAH-LAH-LAH-LAH LAH-LAAAAAAHHH
I HOPE THE WRITERS' STRIKE ENDS SOON
AND NOW, BACK TO THE BINKY THE CLOWN SHOW!
HEEEEEEEY, KIDS!!!
GOOD MORNING, BINKY!
IT'S A BEAUTIFUL DAY IN BINKYLAND. LET'S SAY HELLO TO MR. SUN!
HELLO, MR. SUN
OH LOOK! HERE COMES MR. FISH TO VISIT US!
GOOD MORNING, MR. FISH. KIDS, CAN YOU SAY HELLO TO...
© 1988 United Feature Syndicate, Inc.
JIM DAVIS 9-4
AAAYIEEEEE!!!
HELLO, MR. PIRANHA

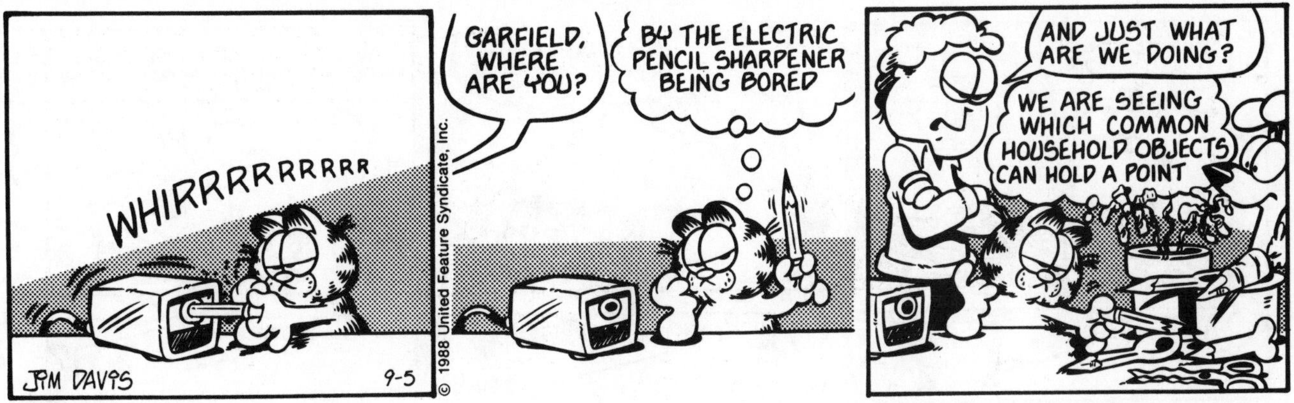
WHIRRRRRRRRR
JIM DAVIS
9-5
© 1988 United Feature Syndicate, Inc.
GARFIELD, WHERE ARE YOU?
BY THE ELECTRIC PENCIL SHARPENER BEING BORED
AND JUST WHAT ARE WE DOING?
WE ARE SEEING WHICH COMMON HOUSEHOLD OBJECTS CAN HOLD A POINT

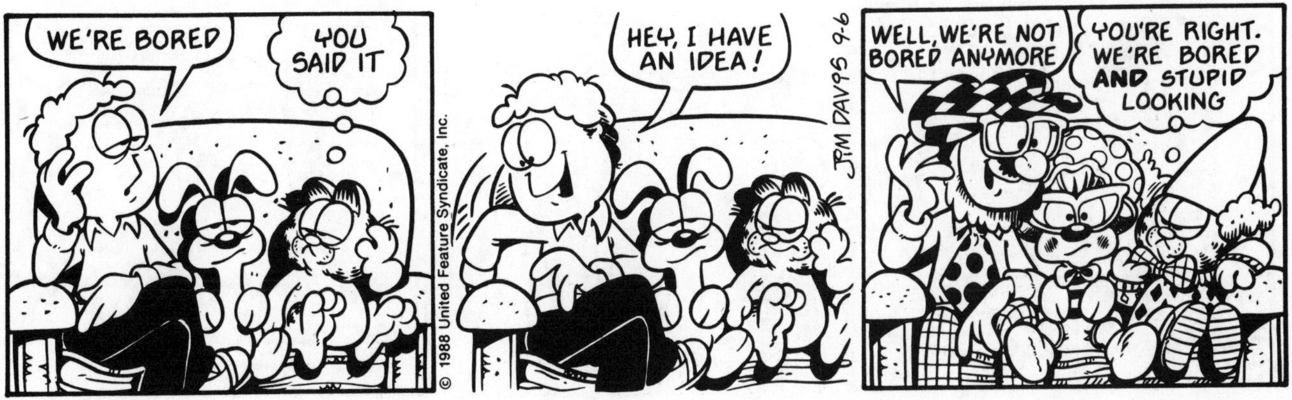
WE'RE BORED
YOU SAID IT
© 1988 United Feature Syndicate, Inc.
HEY, I HAVE AN IDEA!
JIM DAVIS 9-6
WELL, WE'RE NOT BORED ANYMORE
YOU'RE RIGHT. WE'RE BORED **AND** STUPID LOOKING

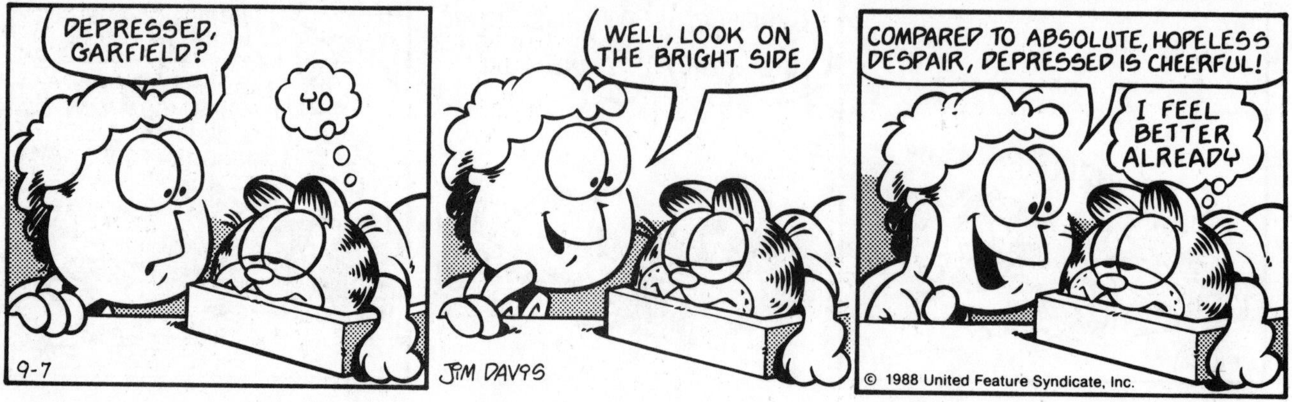
DEPRESSED, GARFIELD?
YO
WELL, LOOK ON THE BRIGHT SIDE
COMPARED TO ABSOLUTE, HOPELESS DESPAIR, DEPRESSED IS CHEERFUL!
I FEEL BETTER ALREADY
9-7
JIM DAVIS
© 1988 United Feature Syndicate, Inc.

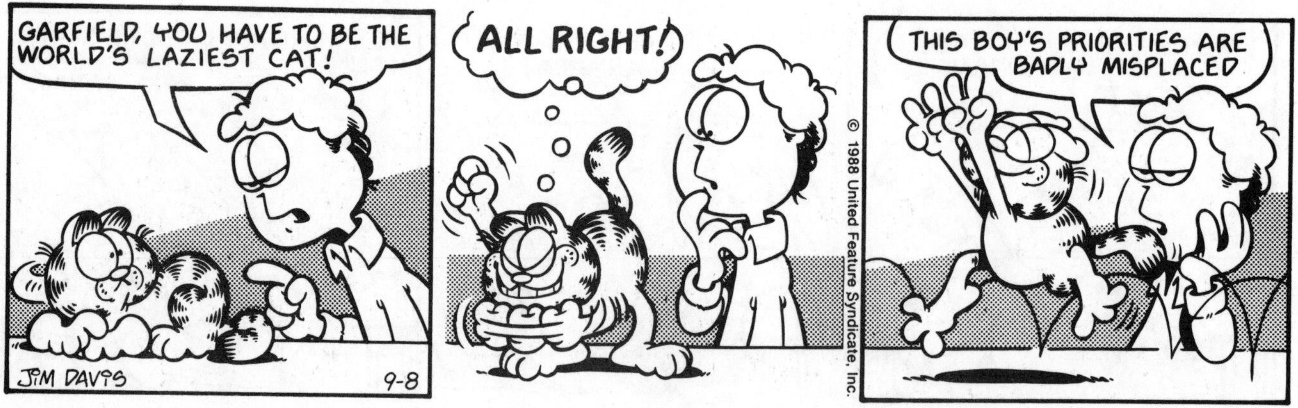
GARFIELD, YOU HAVE TO BE THE WORLD'S LAZIEST CAT!
ALL RIGHT!
THIS BOY'S PRIORITIES ARE BADLY MISPLACED
JIM DAVIS
9-8
© 1988 United Feature Syndicate, Inc.

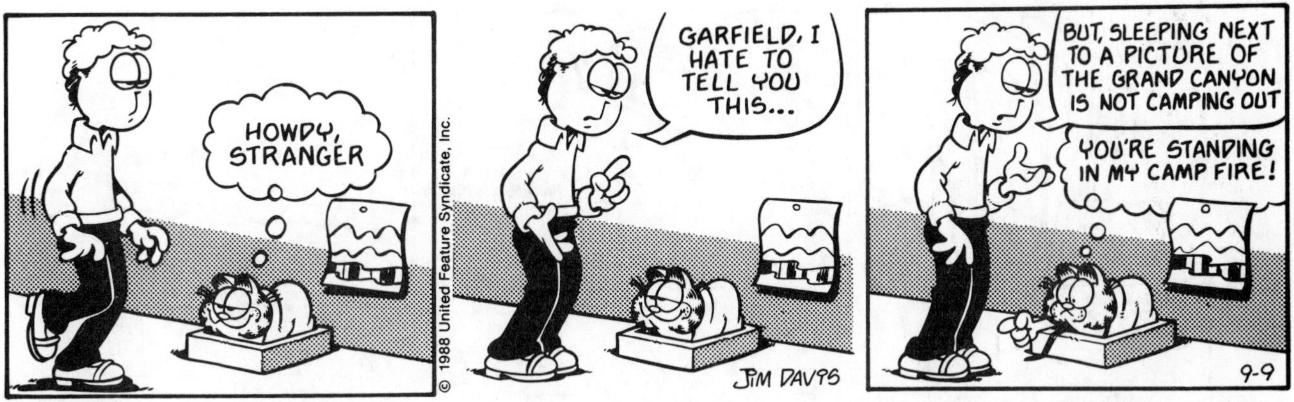
HOWDY, STRANGER
GARFIELD, I HATE TO TELL YOU THIS...
BUT, SLEEPING NEXT TO A PICTURE OF THE GRAND CANYON IS NOT CAMPING OUT
YOU'RE STANDING IN MY CAMP FIRE!
© 1988 United Feature Syndicate, Inc.
JIM DAVIS
9-9

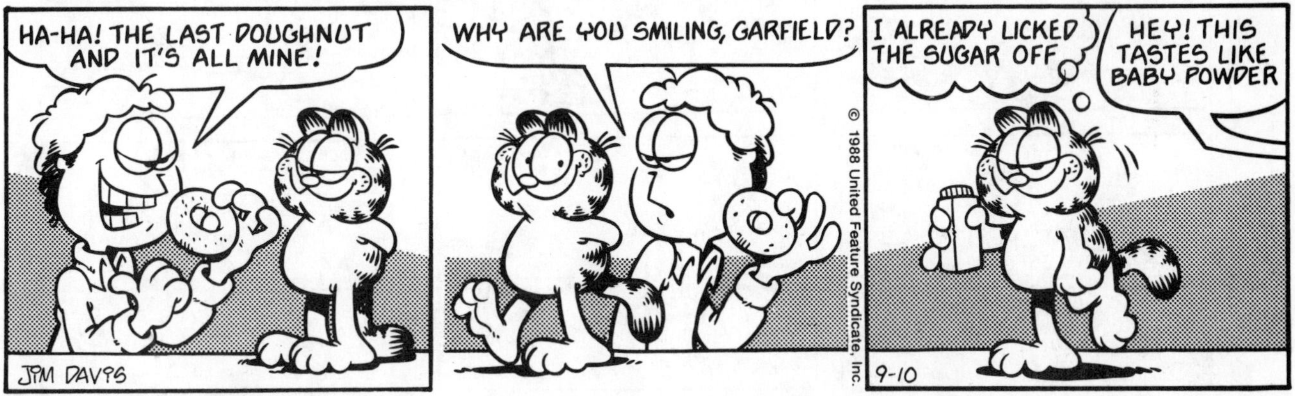
HA-HA! THE LAST DOUGHNUT AND IT'S ALL MINE!
WHY ARE YOU SMILING, GARFIELD?
I ALREADY LICKED THE SUGAR OFF
HEY! THIS TASTES LIKE BABY POWDER
© 1988 United Feature Syndicate, Inc.
JIM DAVIS
9-10

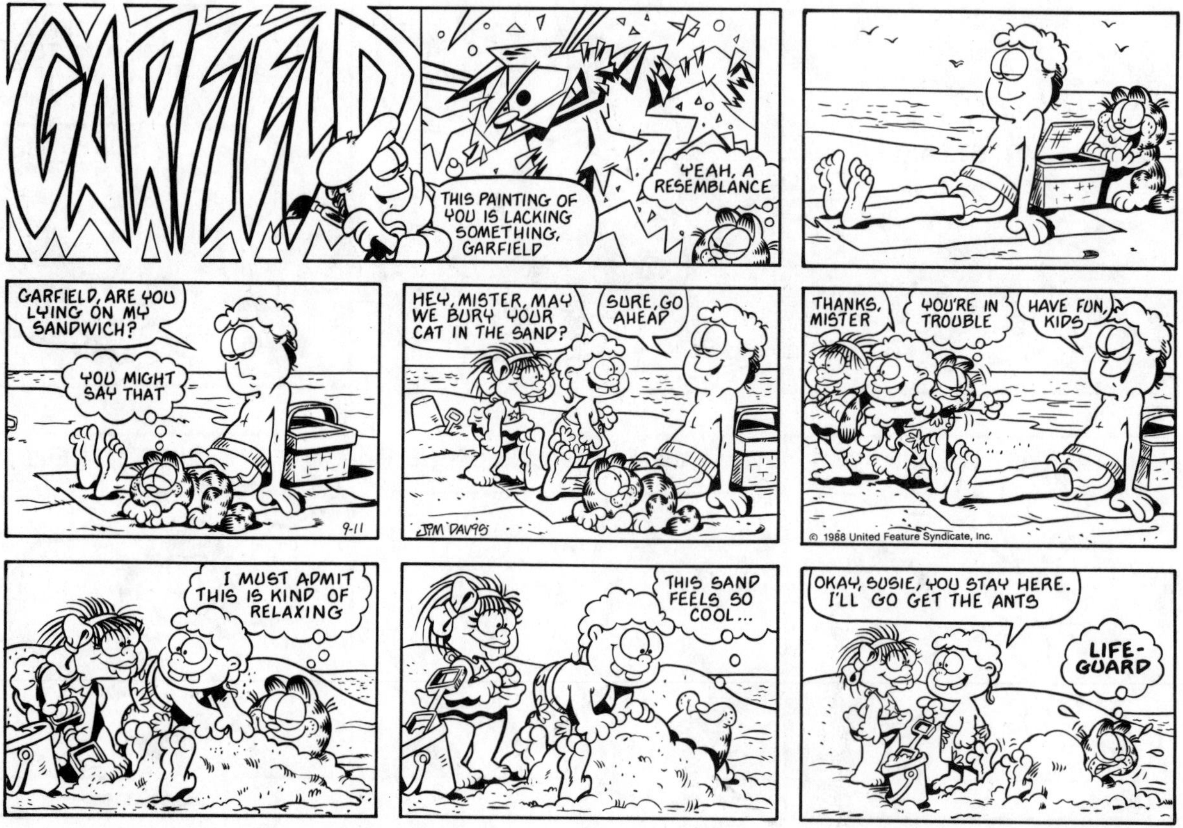
GARFIELD
THIS PAINTING OF YOU IS LACKING SOMETHING, GARFIELD
YEAH, A RESEMBLANCE
GARFIELD, ARE YOU LYING ON MY SANDWICH?
YOU MIGHT SAY THAT
9-11
HEY, MISTER, MAY WE BURY YOUR CAT IN THE SAND?
SURE, GO AHEAD
JPM DAVIS
THANKS, MISTER
YOU'RE IN TROUBLE
HAVE FUN, KIDS
© 1988 United Feature Syndicate, Inc.
I MUST ADMIT THIS IS KIND OF RELAXING
THIS SAND FEELS SO COOL...
OKAY, SUSIE, YOU STAY HERE. I'LL GO GET THE ANTS
LIFE-GUARD

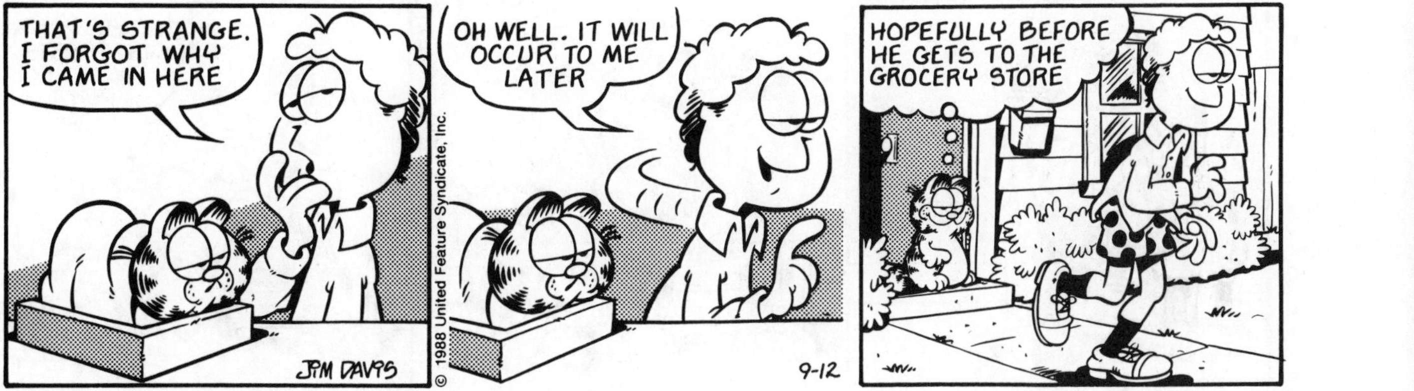
THAT'S STRANGE. I FORGOT WHY I CAME IN HERE
JIM DAVIS
© 1988 United Feature Syndicate, Inc.
OH WELL. IT WILL OCCUR TO ME LATER
9-12
HOPEFULLY BEFORE HE GETS TO THE GROCERY STORE

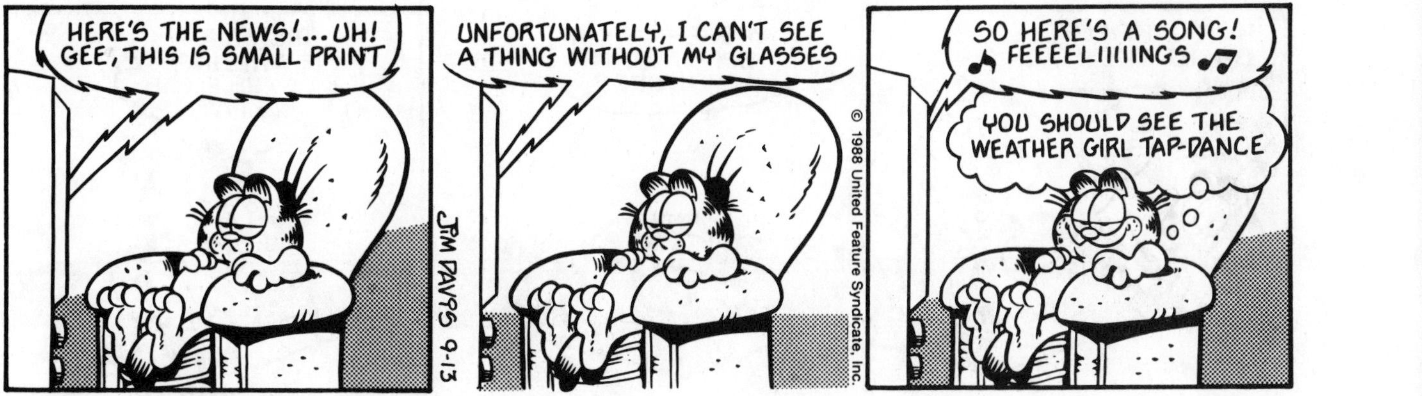
HERE'S THE NEWS!...UH! GEE, THIS IS SMALL PRINT
JIM DAVIS 9-13
UNFORTUNATELY, I CAN'T SEE A THING WITHOUT MY GLASSES
© 1988 United Feature Syndicate, Inc.
SO HERE'S A SONG! FEEEELIIIIIINGS
YOU SHOULD SEE THE WEATHER GIRL TAP-DANCE

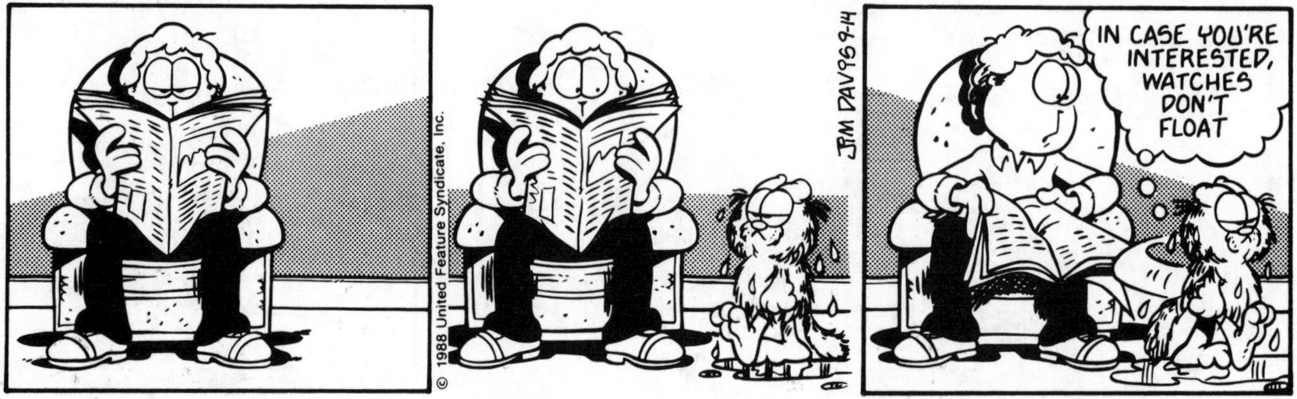
© 1988 United Feature Syndicate, Inc.
JIM DAVIS 9-14
IN CASE YOU'RE INTERESTED, WATCHES DON'T FLOAT

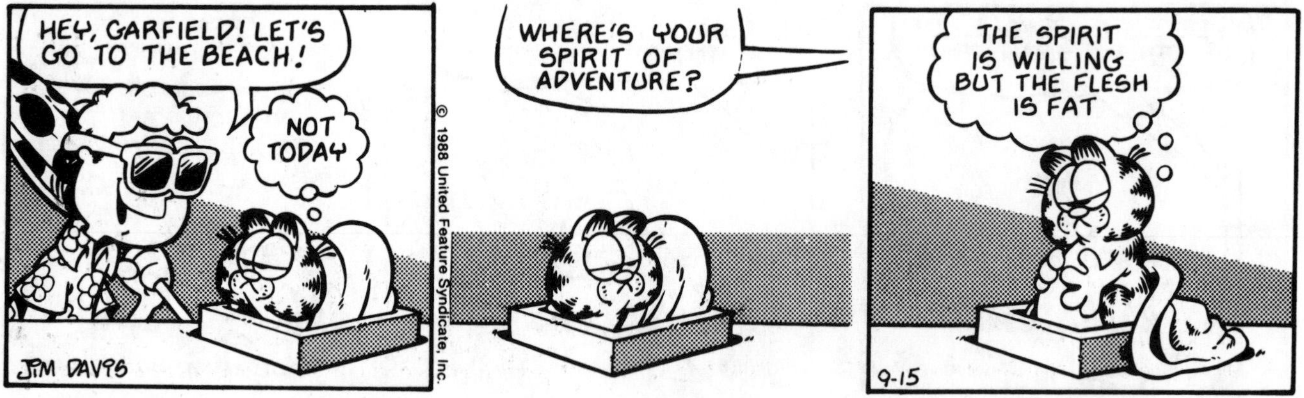
HEY, GARFIELD! LET'S GO TO THE BEACH!
NOT TODAY
JIM DAVIS
© 1988 United Feature Syndicate, Inc.
WHERE'S YOUR SPIRIT OF ADVENTURE?
THE SPIRIT IS WILLING BUT THE FLESH IS FAT
9-15

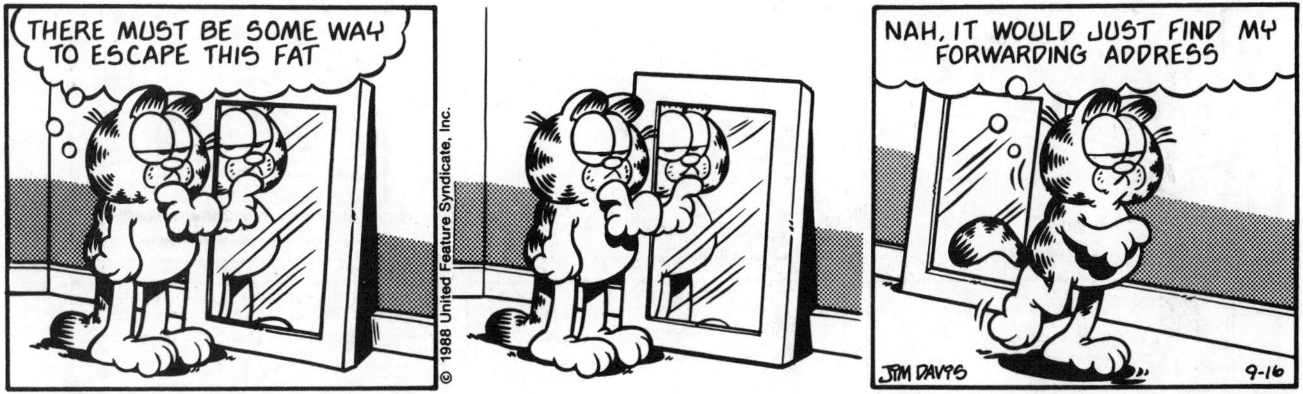
THERE MUST BE SOME WAY TO ESCAPE THIS FAT
© 1988 United Feature Syndicate, Inc.
NAH, IT WOULD JUST FIND MY FORWARDING ADDRESS
JIM DAVIS
9-16

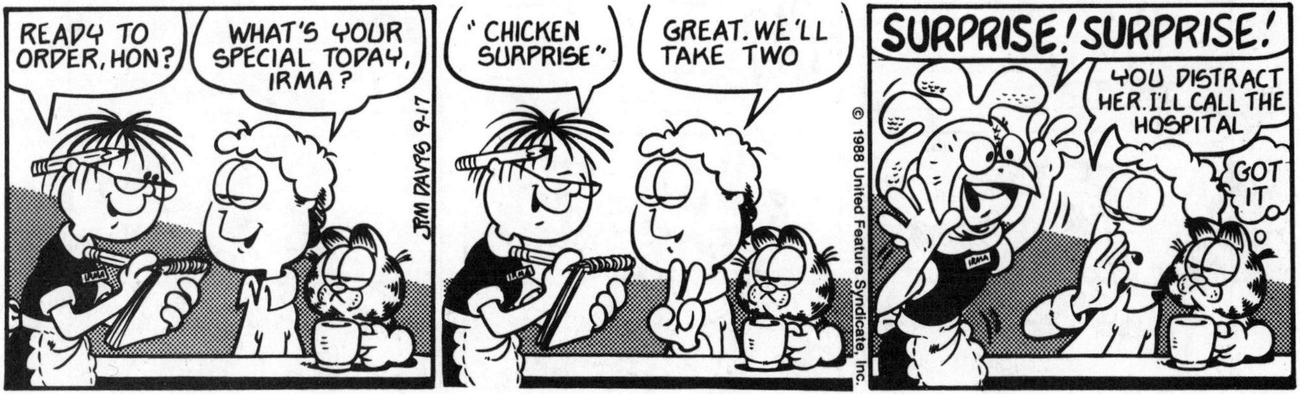
READY TO ORDER, HON?
WHAT'S YOUR SPECIAL TODAY, IRMA?
JIM DAVIS 9-17
"CHICKEN SURPRISE"
GREAT. WE'LL TAKE TWO
© 1988 United Feature Syndicate, Inc.
SURPRISE! SURPRISE!
YOU DISTRACT HER. I'LL CALL THE HOSPITAL
GOT IT

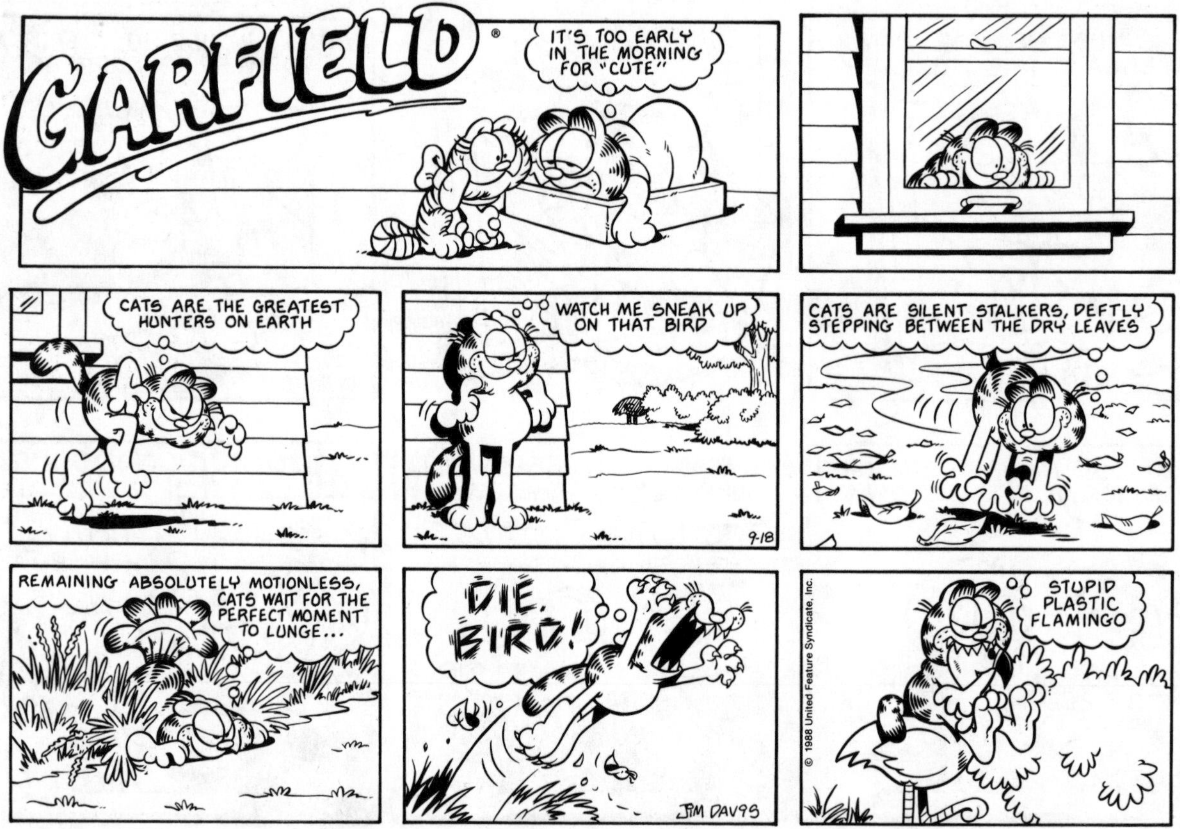
GARFIELD®
IT'S TOO EARLY IN THE MORNING FOR "CUTE"
CATS ARE THE GREATEST HUNTERS ON EARTH
WATCH ME SNEAK UP ON THAT BIRD
9-18
CATS ARE SILENT STALKERS, DEFTLY STEPPING BETWEEN THE DRY LEAVES
REMAINING ABSOLUTELY MOTIONLESS, CATS WAIT FOR THE PERFECT MOMENT TO LUNGE...
DIE, BIRD!
JIM DAVIS
© 1988 United Feature Syndicate, Inc.
STUPID PLASTIC FLAMINGO

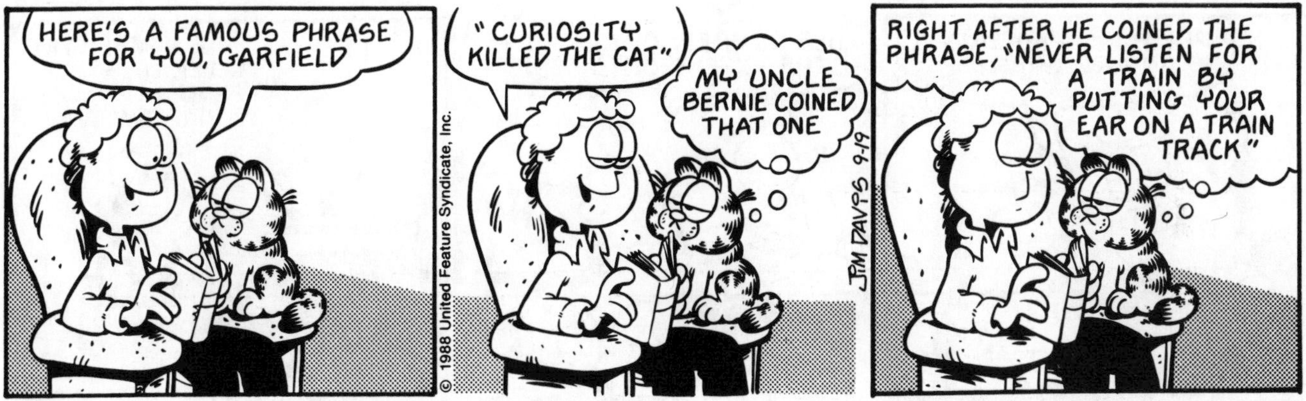
HERE'S A FAMOUS PHRASE FOR YOU, GARFIELD
"CURIOSITY KILLED THE CAT"
MY UNCLE BERNIE COINED THAT ONE
RIGHT AFTER HE COINED THE PHRASE, "NEVER LISTEN FOR A TRAIN BY PUTTING YOUR EAR ON A TRAIN TRACK"
© 1988 United Feature Syndicate, Inc.
JIM DAVIS 9-19

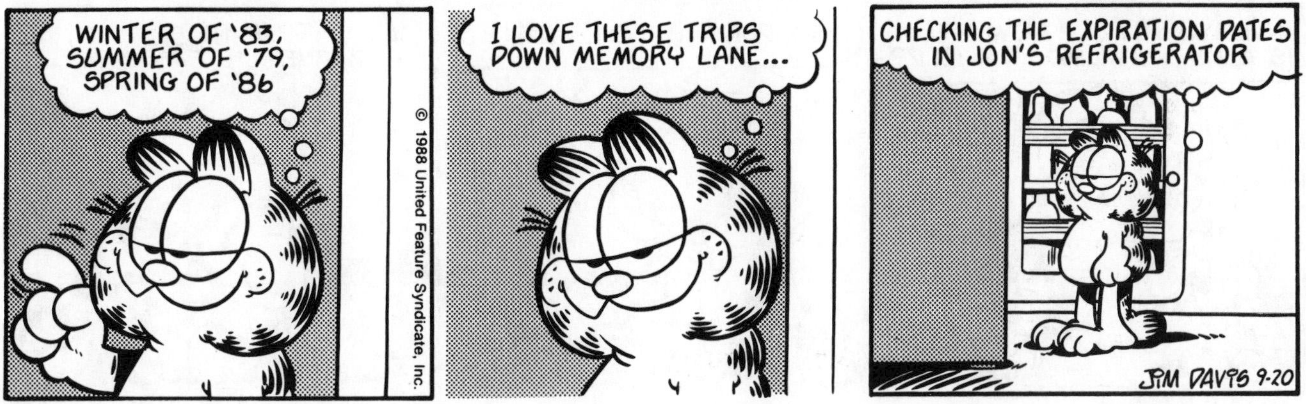
WINTER OF '83, SUMMER OF '79, SPRING OF '86
I LOVE THESE TRIPS DOWN MEMORY LANE...
CHECKING THE EXPIRATION DATES IN JON'S REFRIGERATOR
© 1988 United Feature Syndicate, Inc.
JIM DAVIS 9-20

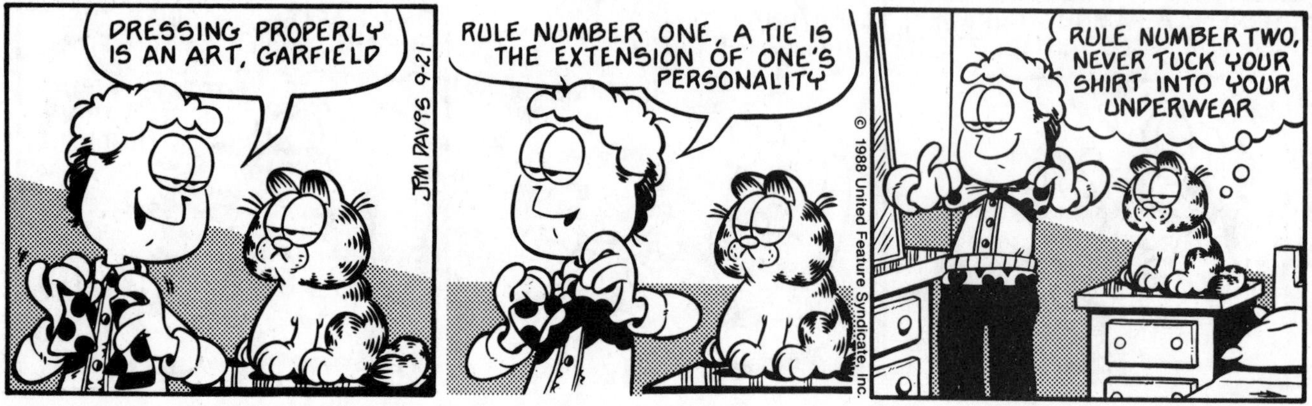
DRESSING PROPERLY IS AN ART, GARFIELD
JPM DAVPS 9-21
RULE NUMBER ONE, A TIE IS THE EXTENSION OF ONE'S PERSONALITY
© 1988 United Feature Syndicate, Inc.
RULE NUMBER TWO, NEVER TUCK YOUR SHIRT INTO YOUR UNDERWEAR

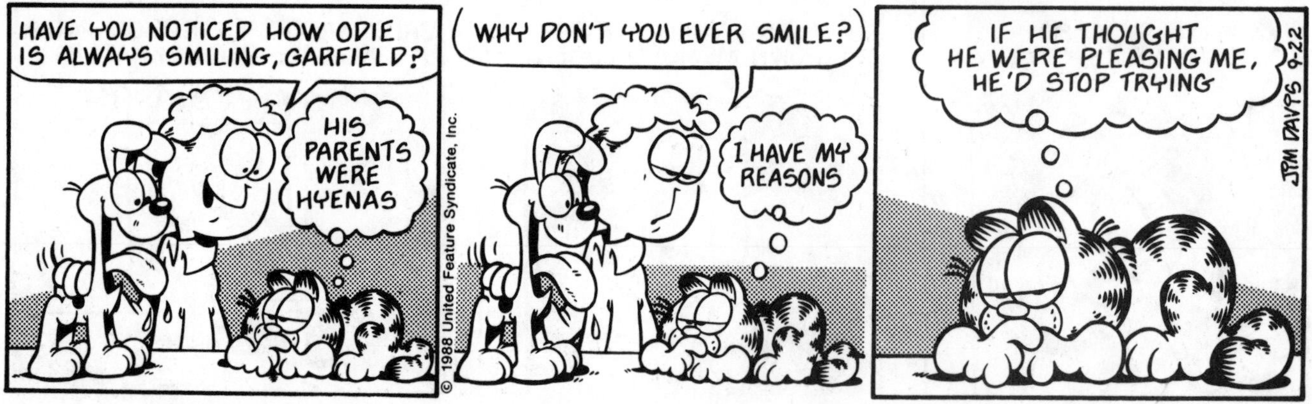
HAVE YOU NOTICED HOW ODIE IS ALWAYS SMILING, GARFIELD?
HIS PARENTS WERE HYENAS
© 1988 United Feature Syndicate, Inc.
WHY DON'T YOU EVER SMILE?
I HAVE MY REASONS
IF HE THOUGHT HE WERE PLEASING ME, HE'D STOP TRYING
JPM DAVPS 9-22

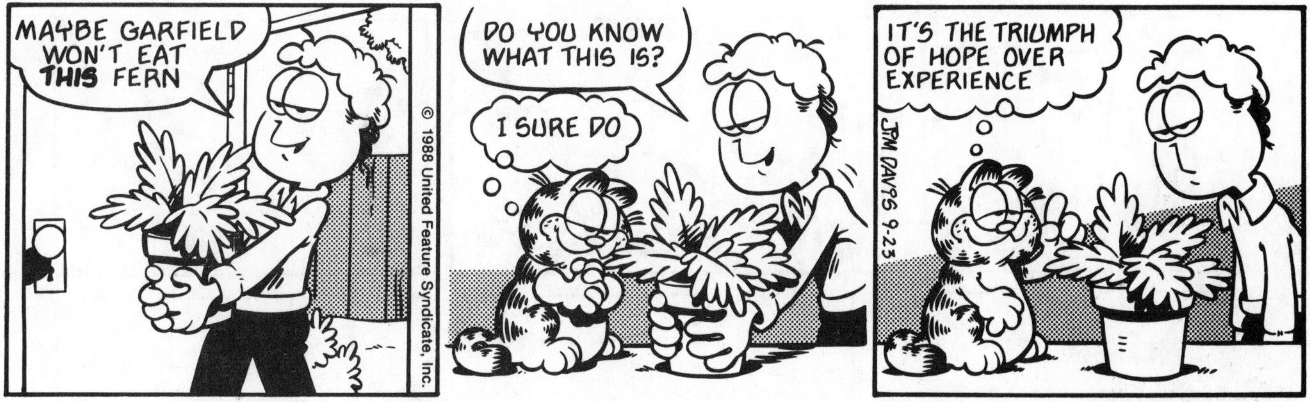
MAYBE GARFIELD WON'T EAT **THIS** FERN
© 1988 United Feature Syndicate, Inc.
DO YOU KNOW WHAT THIS IS?
I SURE DO
JIM DAVIS 9-23
IT'S THE TRIUMPH OF HOPE OVER EXPERIENCE

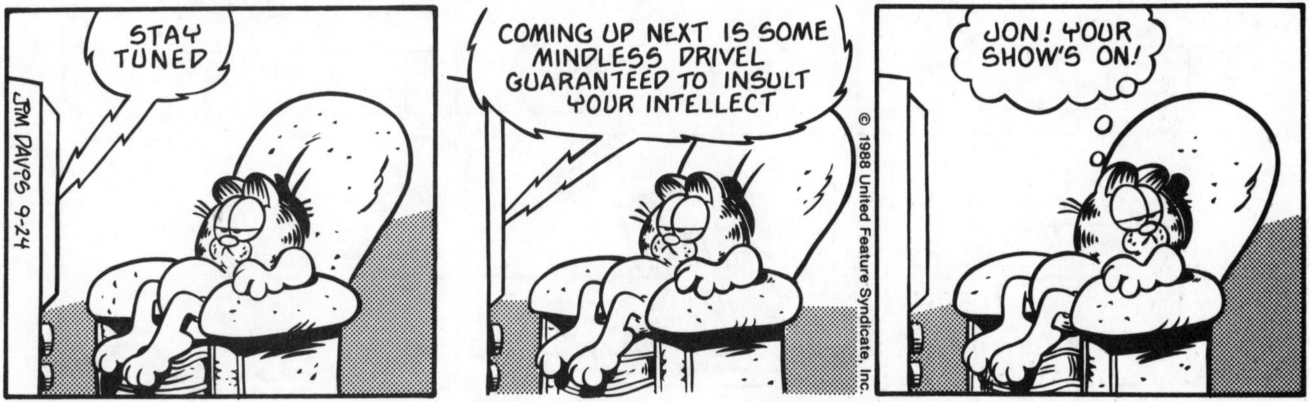
STAY TUNED
JIM DAVIS 9-24
COMING UP NEXT IS SOME MINDLESS DRIVEL GUARANTEED TO INSULT YOUR INTELLECT
© 1988 United Feature Syndicate, Inc.
JON! YOUR SHOW'S ON!

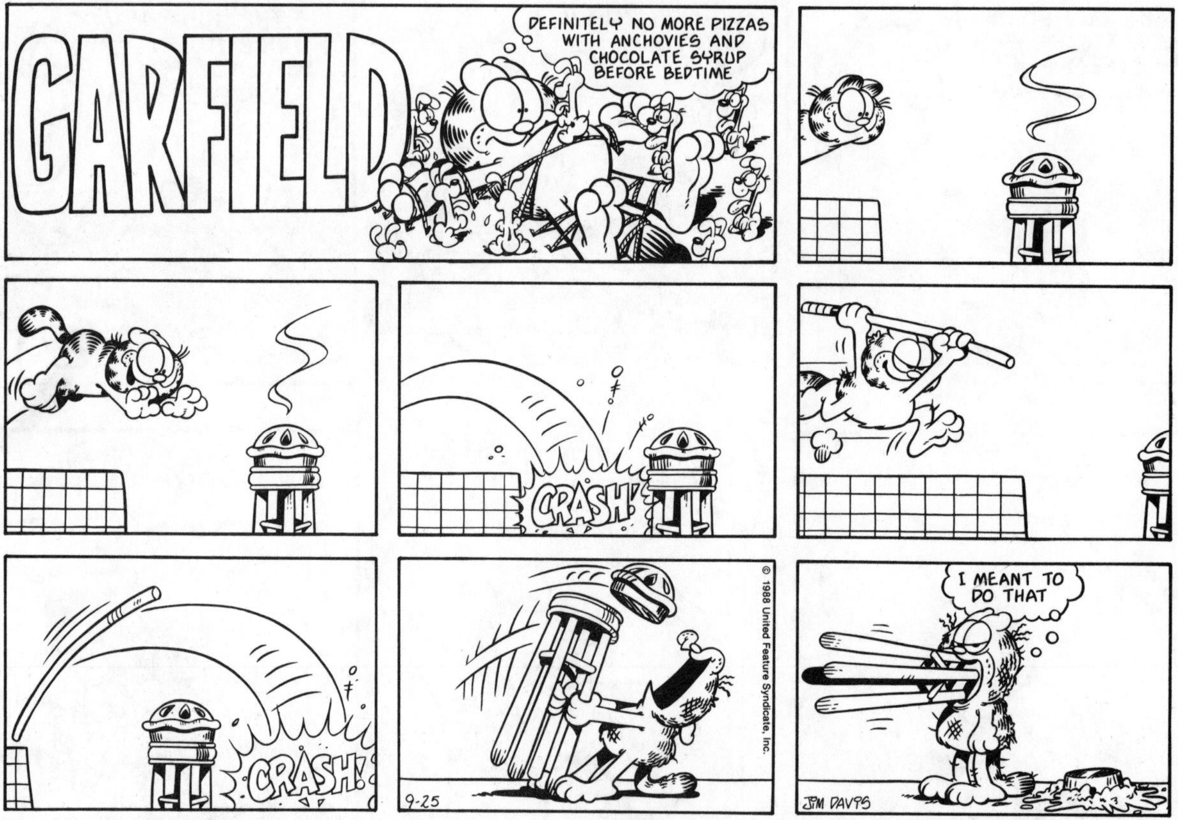
GARFIELD
DEFINITELY NO MORE PIZZAS WITH ANCHOVIES AND CHOCOLATE SYRUP BEFORE BEDTIME
CRASH!
CRASH!
9-25
© 1988 United Feature Syndicate, Inc.
I MEANT TO DO THAT
JIM DAVIS

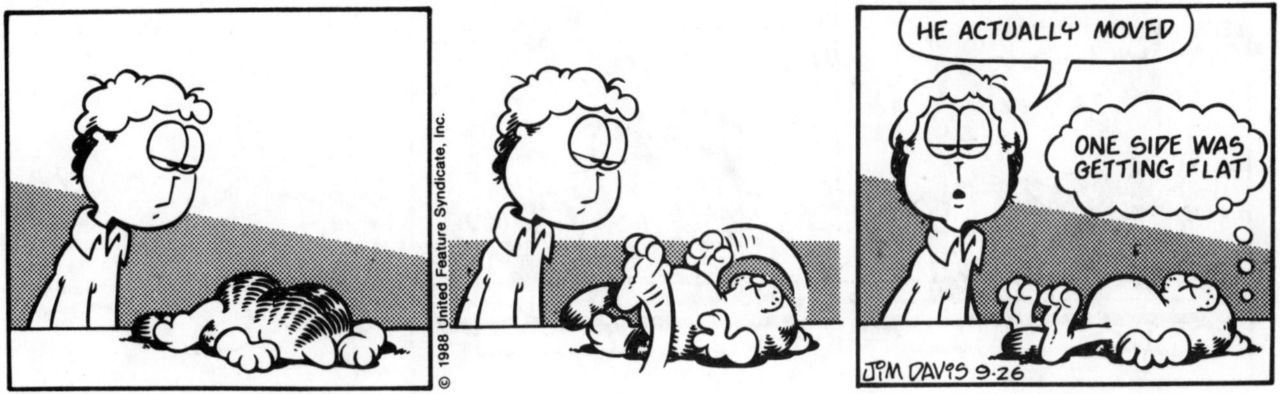
© 1988 United Feature Syndicate, Inc.
HE ACTUALLY MOVED
ONE SIDE WAS GETTING FLAT
JIM DAVIS 9-26

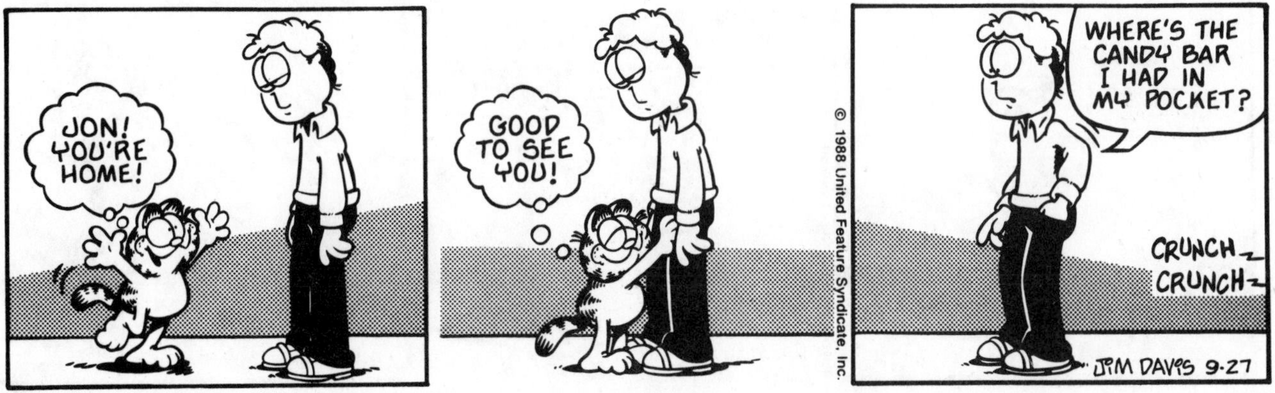
JON! YOU'RE HOME!
GOOD TO SEE YOU!
© 1988 United Feature Syndicate, Inc.
WHERE'S THE CANDY BAR I HAD IN MY POCKET?
CRUNCH
CRUNCH
JIM DAVIS 9-27

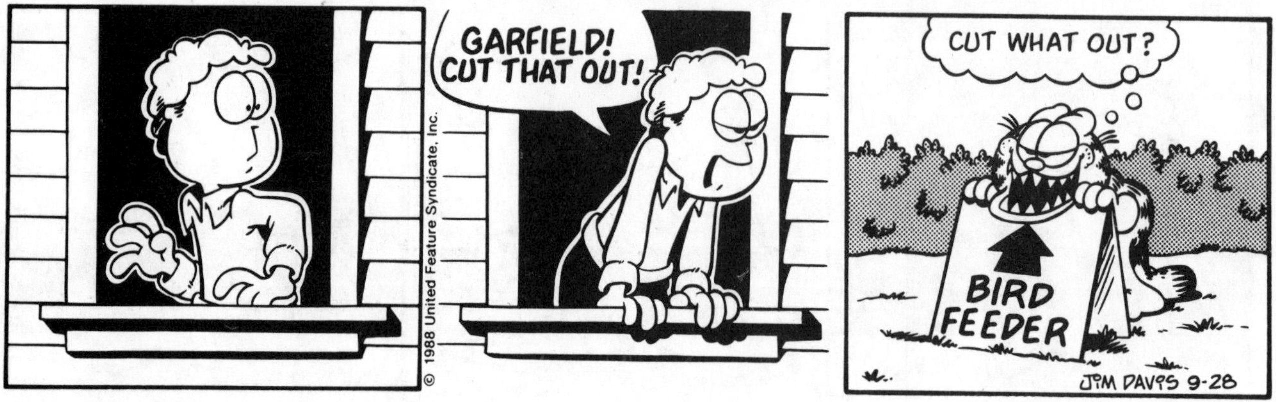
GARFIELD! CUT THAT OUT!
© 1988 United Feature Syndicate, Inc.
CUT WHAT OUT?
BIRD FEEDER
JIM DAVIS 9-28

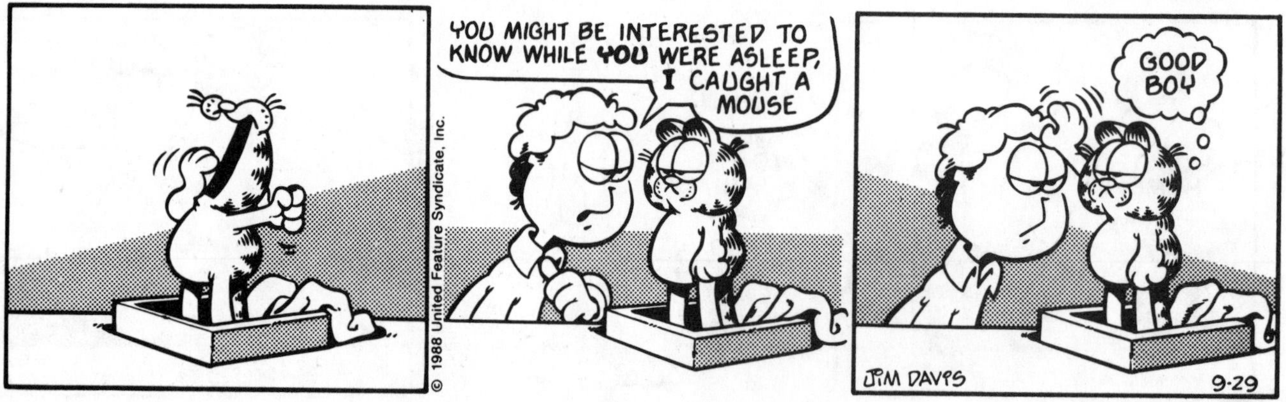
© 1988 United Feature Syndicate, Inc.
YOU MIGHT BE INTERESTED TO KNOW WHILE **YOU** WERE ASLEEP, **I** CAUGHT A MOUSE
GOOD BOY
JIM DAVIS
9-29

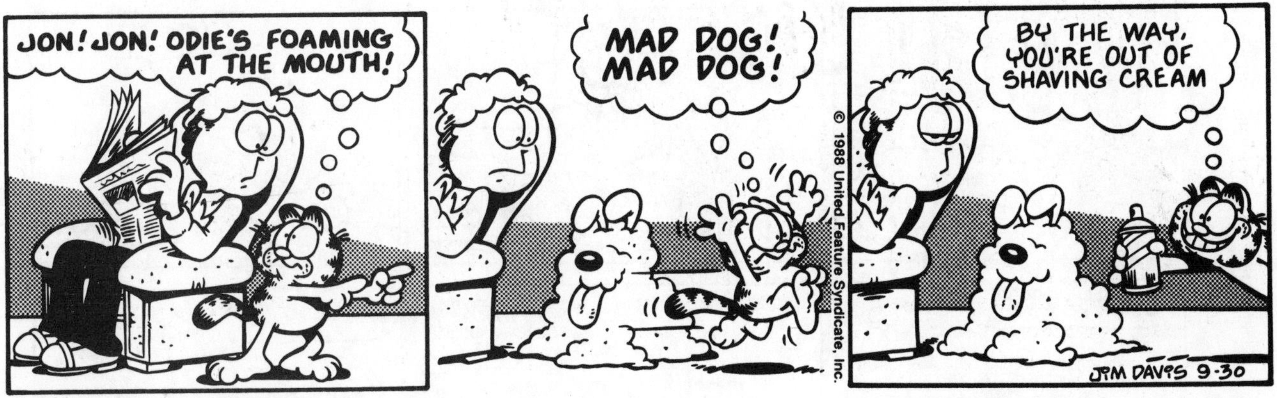

JON! JON! ODIE'S FOAMING AT THE MOUTH!
MAD DOG! MAD DOG!
BY THE WAY, YOU'RE OUT OF SHAVING CREAM
© 1988 United Feature Syndicate, Inc.
JIM DAVIS 9-30

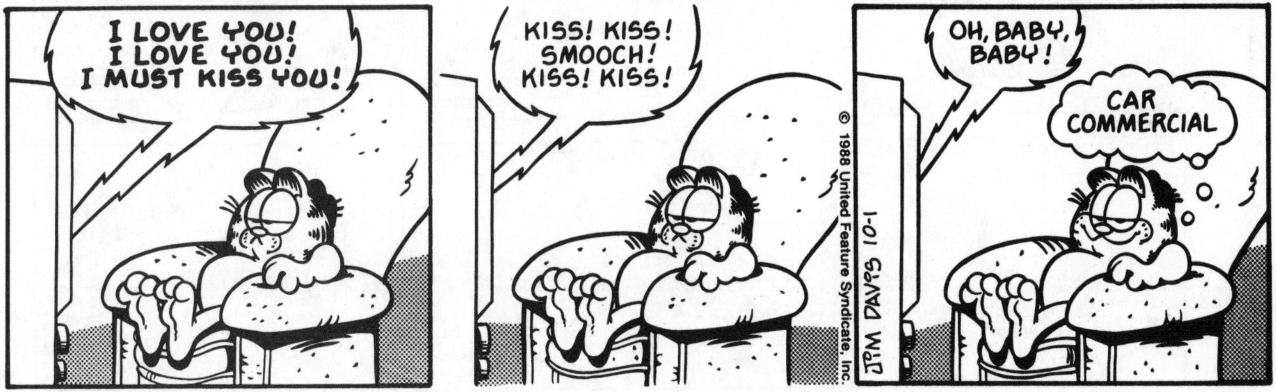

I LOVE YOU! I LOVE YOU! I MUST KISS YOU!
KISS! KISS! SMOOCH! KISS! KISS!
OH, BABY, BABY!
CAR COMMERCIAL
© 1988 United Feature Syndicate, Inc.
JIM DAVIS 10-1

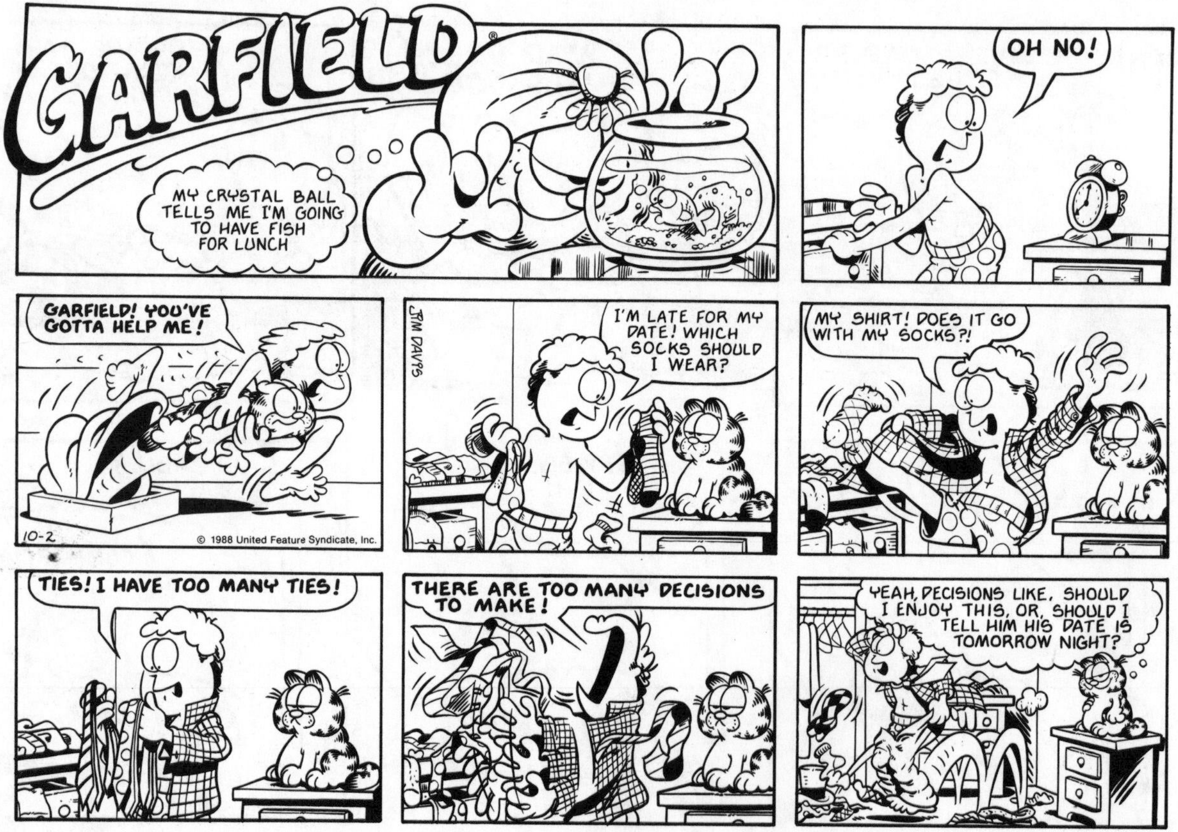
GARFIELD®
MY CRYSTAL BALL TELLS ME I'M GOING TO HAVE FISH FOR LUNCH
OH NO!
GARFIELD! YOU'VE GOTTA HELP ME!
10-2
© 1988 United Feature Syndicate, Inc.
JIM DAVIS
I'M LATE FOR MY DATE! WHICH SOCKS SHOULD I WEAR?
MY SHIRT! DOES IT GO WITH MY SOCKS?!
TIES! I HAVE TOO MANY TIES!
THERE ARE TOO MANY DECISIONS TO MAKE!
YEAH, DECISIONS LIKE, SHOULD I ENJOY THIS, OR, SHOULD I TELL HIM HIS DATE IS TOMORROW NIGHT?

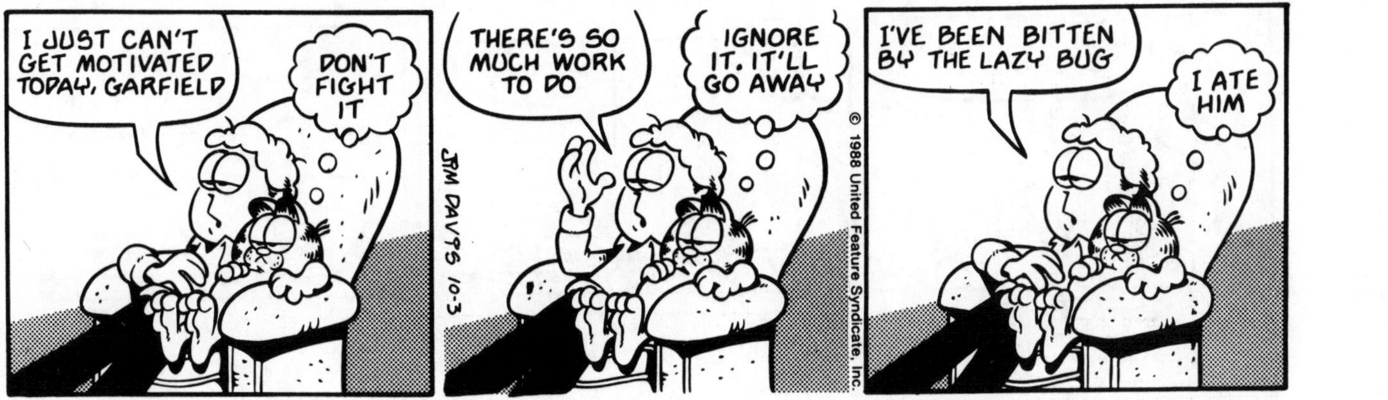
I JUST CAN'T GET MOTIVATED TODAY, GARFIELD
DON'T FIGHT IT
JIM DAVIS 10-3
THERE'S SO MUCH WORK TO DO
IGNORE IT. IT'LL GO AWAY
© 1988 United Feature Syndicate, Inc.
I'VE BEEN BITTEN BY THE LAZY BUG
I ATE HIM

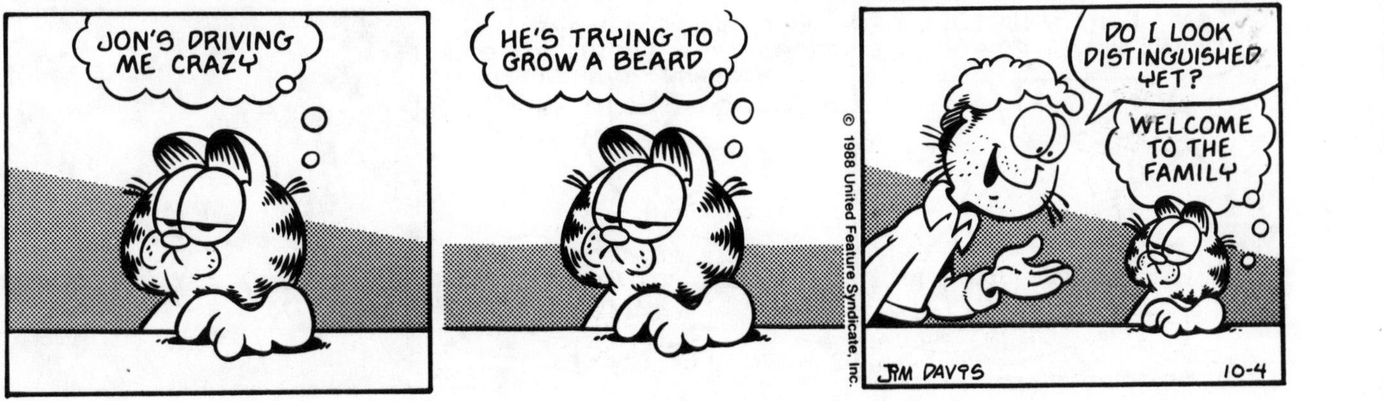
JON'S DRIVING ME CRAZY
HE'S TRYING TO GROW A BEARD
© 1988 United Feature Syndicate, Inc.
DO I LOOK DISTINGUISHED YET?
WELCOME TO THE FAMILY
JIM DAVIS
10-4

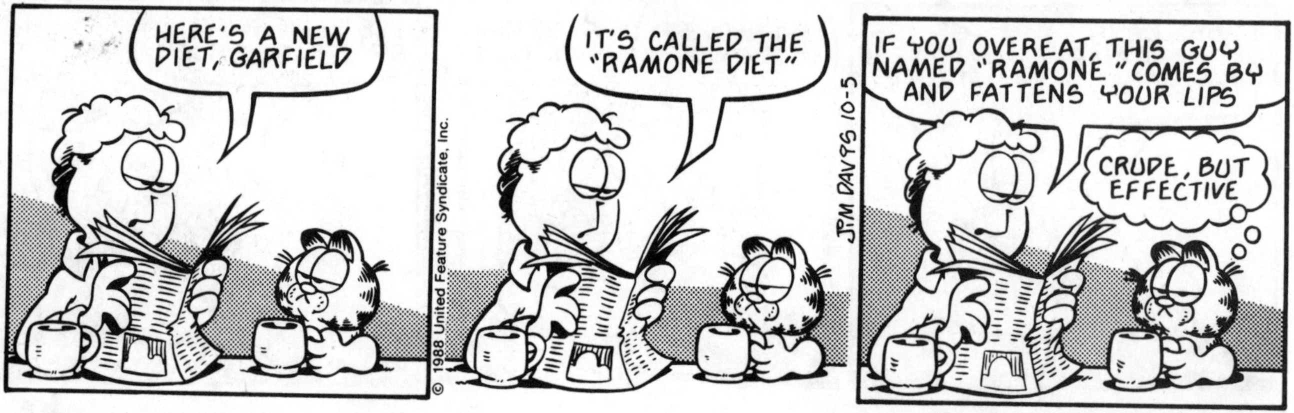
HERE'S A NEW DIET, GARFIELD
© 1988 United Feature Syndicate, Inc.
IT'S CALLED THE "RAMONE DIET"
JIM DAVIS 10-5
IF YOU OVEREAT, THIS GUY NAMED "RAMONE" COMES BY AND FATTENS YOUR LIPS
CRUDE, BUT EFFECTIVE

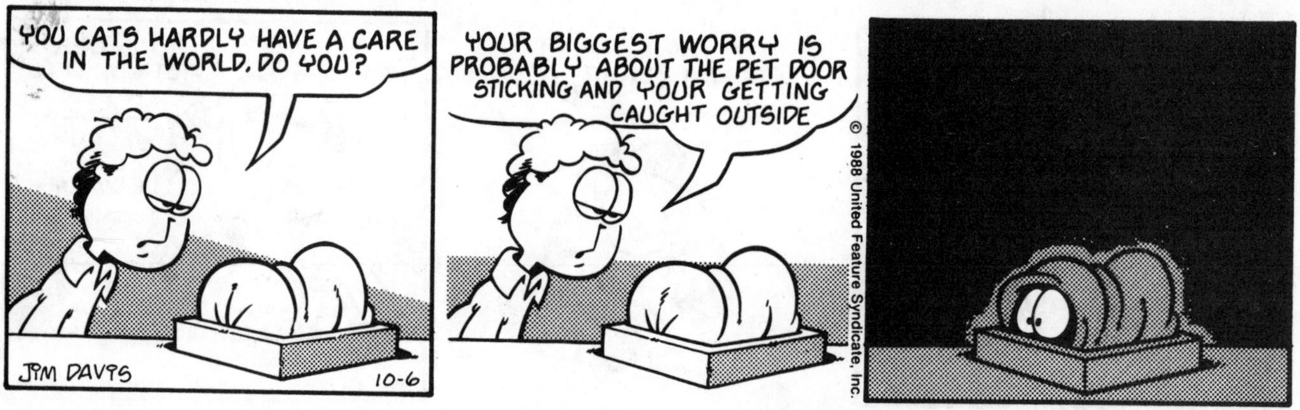
YOU CATS HARDLY HAVE A CARE IN THE WORLD, DO YOU?
JIM DAVIS
10-6
YOUR BIGGEST WORRY IS PROBABLY ABOUT THE PET DOOR STICKING AND YOUR GETTING CAUGHT OUTSIDE
© 1988 United Feature Syndicate, Inc.

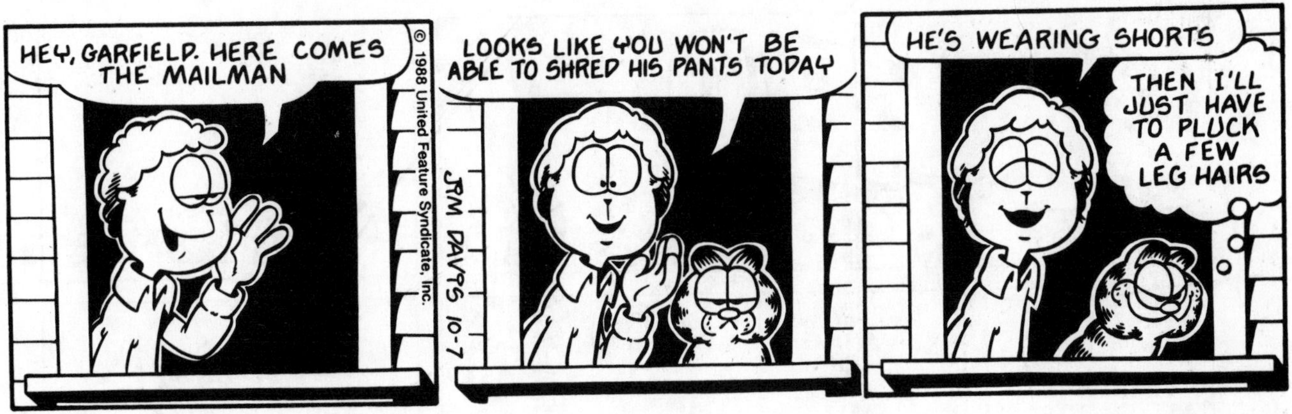

HEY, GARFIELD. HERE COMES THE MAILMAN
© 1988 United Feature Syndicate, Inc.
JIM DAVIS 10-7
LOOKS LIKE YOU WON'T BE ABLE TO SHRED HIS PANTS TODAY
HE'S WEARING SHORTS
THEN I'LL JUST HAVE TO PLUCK A FEW LEG HAIRS

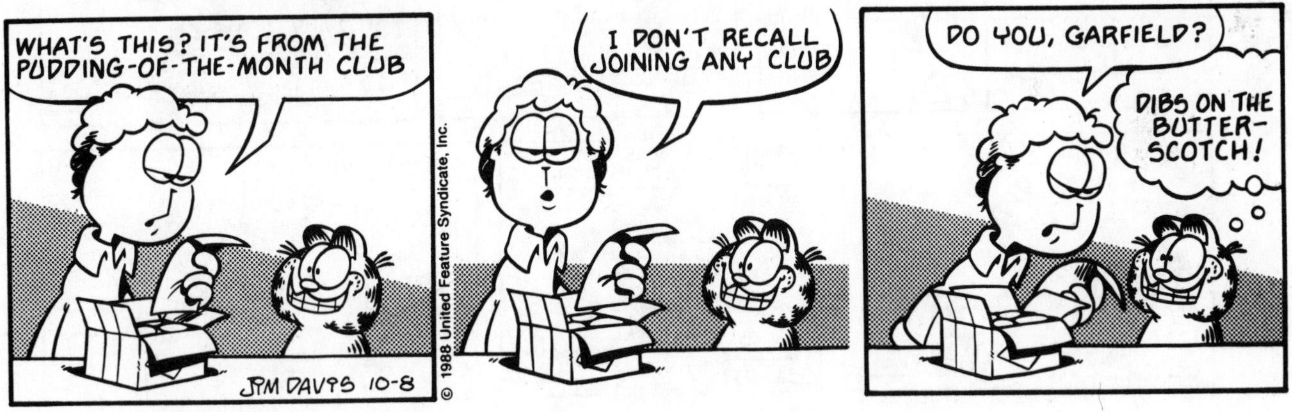

WHAT'S THIS? IT'S FROM THE PUDDING-OF-THE-MONTH CLUB
JIM DAVIS 10-8
© 1988 United Feature Syndicate, Inc.
I DON'T RECALL JOINING ANY CLUB
DO YOU, GARFIELD?
DIBS ON THE BUTTER-SCOTCH!

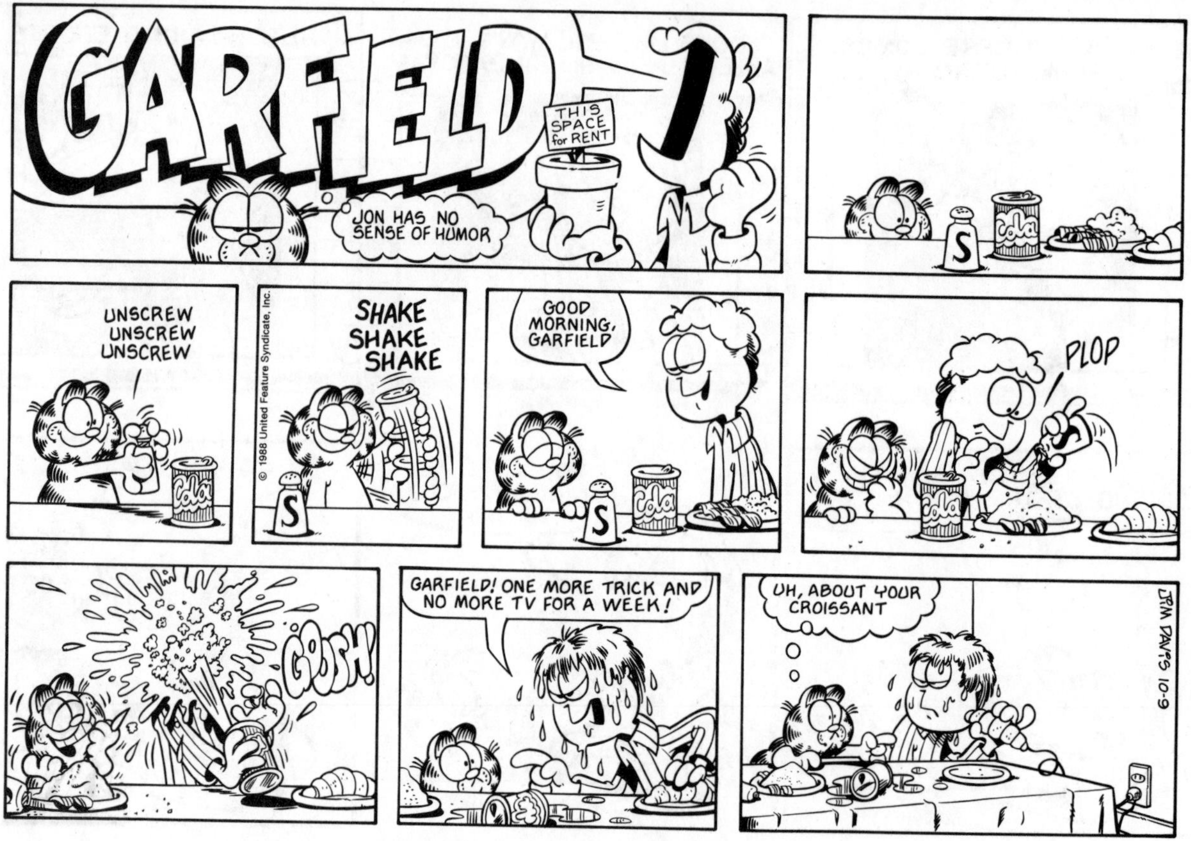
GARFIELD
THIS SPACE for RENT
JON HAS NO SENSE OF HUMOR
S
Cola
UNSCREW UNSCREW UNSCREW
© 1988 United Feature Syndicate, Inc.
SHAKE SHAKE SHAKE
GOOD MORNING, GARFIELD
PLOP
GOOSH!
GARFIELD! ONE MORE TRICK AND NO MORE TV FOR A WEEK!
UH, ABOUT YOUR CROISSANT
JPM DAVIS 10-9

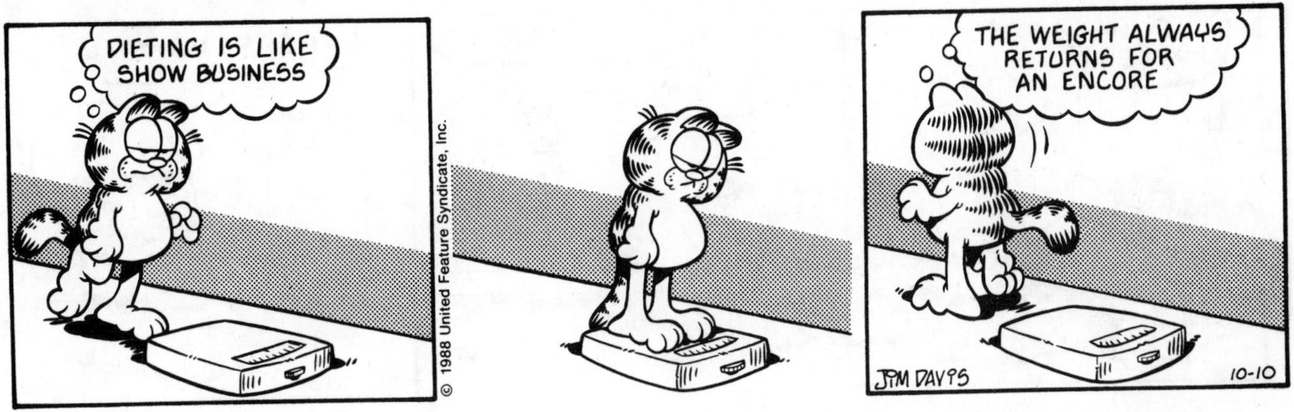
DIETING IS LIKE SHOW BUSINESS
© 1988 United Feature Syndicate, Inc.
THE WEIGHT ALWAYS RETURNS FOR AN ENCORE
JIM DAVIS
10-10

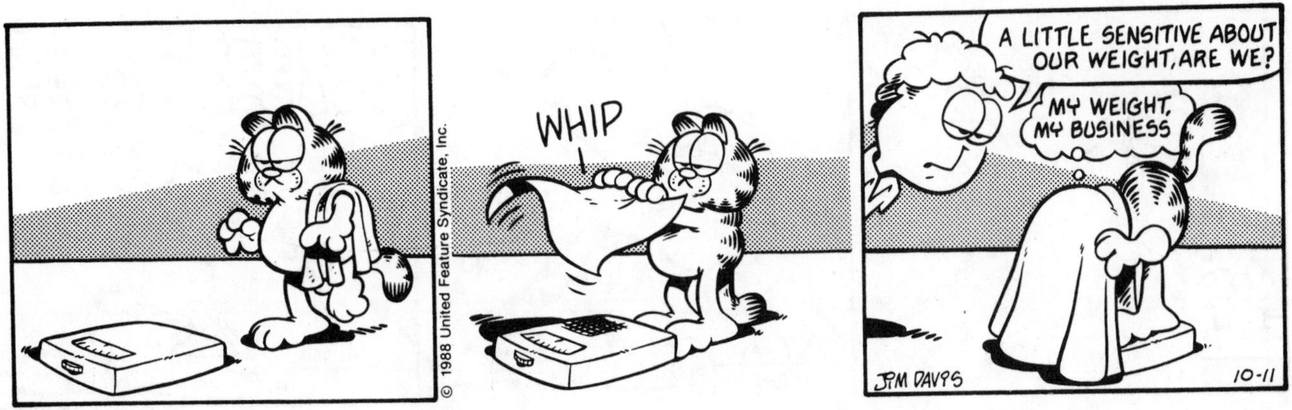
© 1988 United Feature Syndicate, Inc.
WHIP
A LITTLE SENSITIVE ABOUT OUR WEIGHT, ARE WE?
MY WEIGHT, MY BUSINESS
JIM DAVIS
10-11

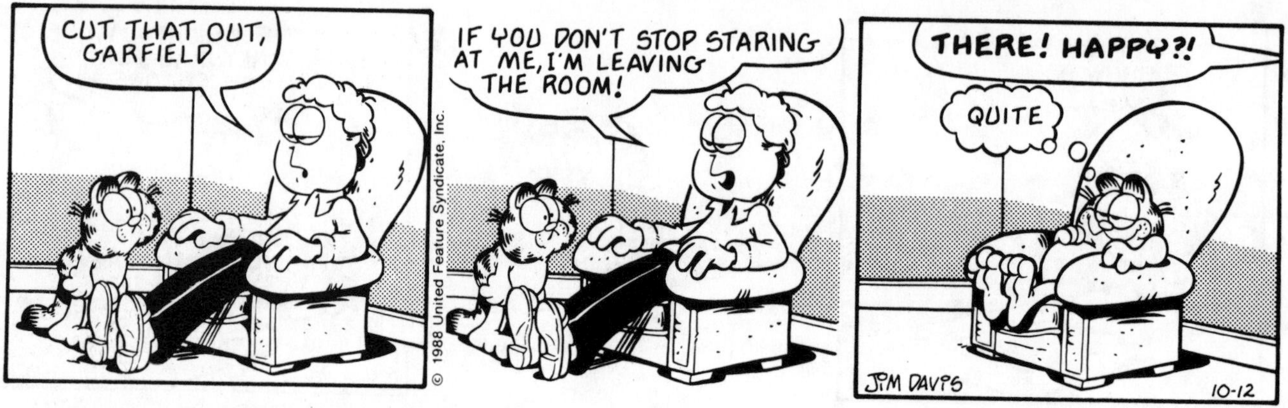
CUT THAT OUT, GARFIELD
IF YOU DON'T STOP STARING AT ME, I'M LEAVING THE ROOM!
THERE! HAPPY?!
QUITE
© 1988 United Feature Syndicate, Inc.
JIM DAVIS
10-12

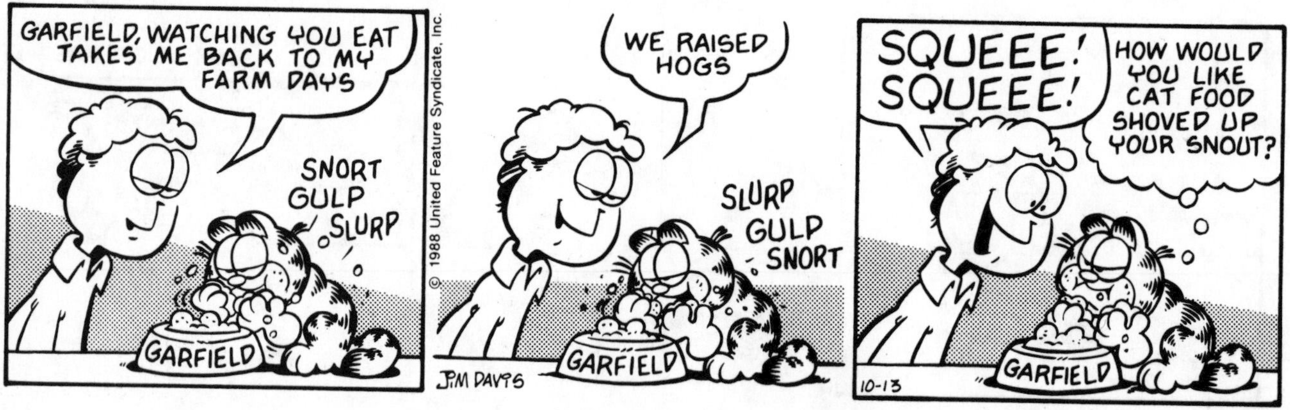
GARFIELD, WATCHING YOU EAT TAKES ME BACK TO MY FARM DAYS
SNORT GULP SLURP
GARFIELD
WE RAISED HOGS
SLURP GULP SNORT
GARFIELD
SQUEEE! SQUEEE!
HOW WOULD YOU LIKE CAT FOOD SHOVED UP YOUR SNOUT?
GARFIELD
© 1988 United Feature Syndicate, Inc.
JIM DAVIS
10-13

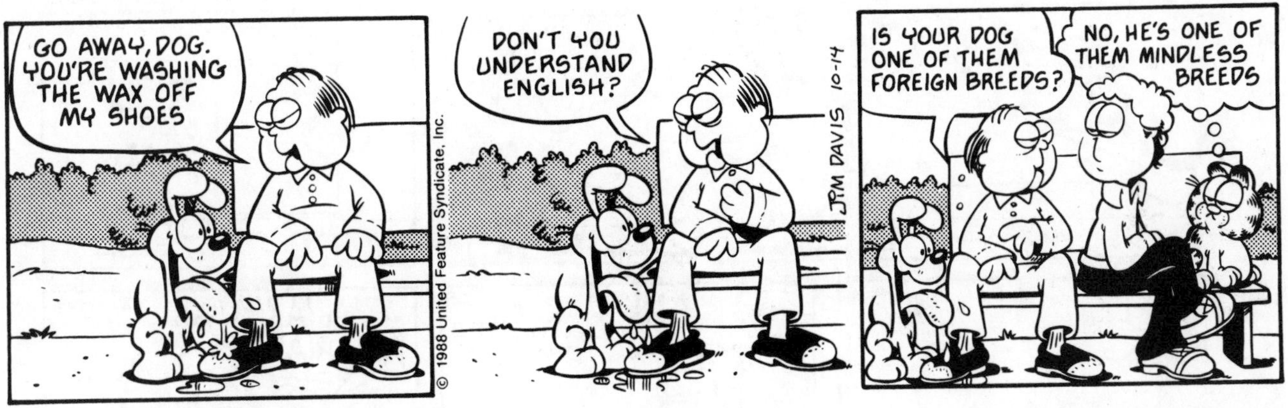
GO AWAY, DOG. YOU'RE WASHING THE WAX OFF MY SHOES
© 1988 United Feature Syndicate, Inc.
DON'T YOU UNDERSTAND ENGLISH?
JIM DAVIS 10-14
IS YOUR DOG ONE OF THEM FOREIGN BREEDS?
NO, HE'S ONE OF THEM MINDLESS BREEDS

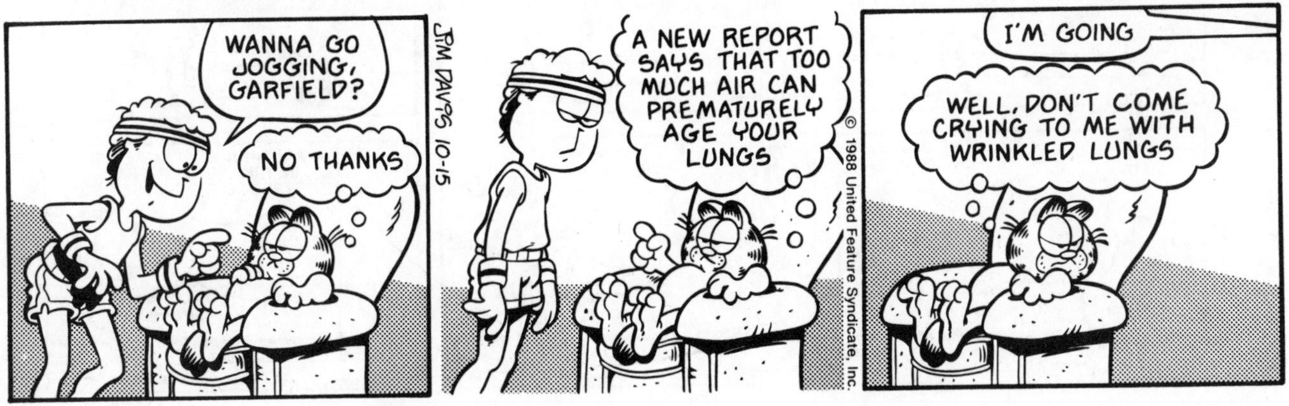
WANNA GO JOGGING, GARFIELD?
NO THANKS
JIM DAVIS 10-15
A NEW REPORT SAYS THAT TOO MUCH AIR CAN PREMATURELY AGE YOUR LUNGS
© 1988 United Feature Syndicate, Inc.
I'M GOING
WELL, DON'T COME CRYING TO ME WITH WRINKLED LUNGS

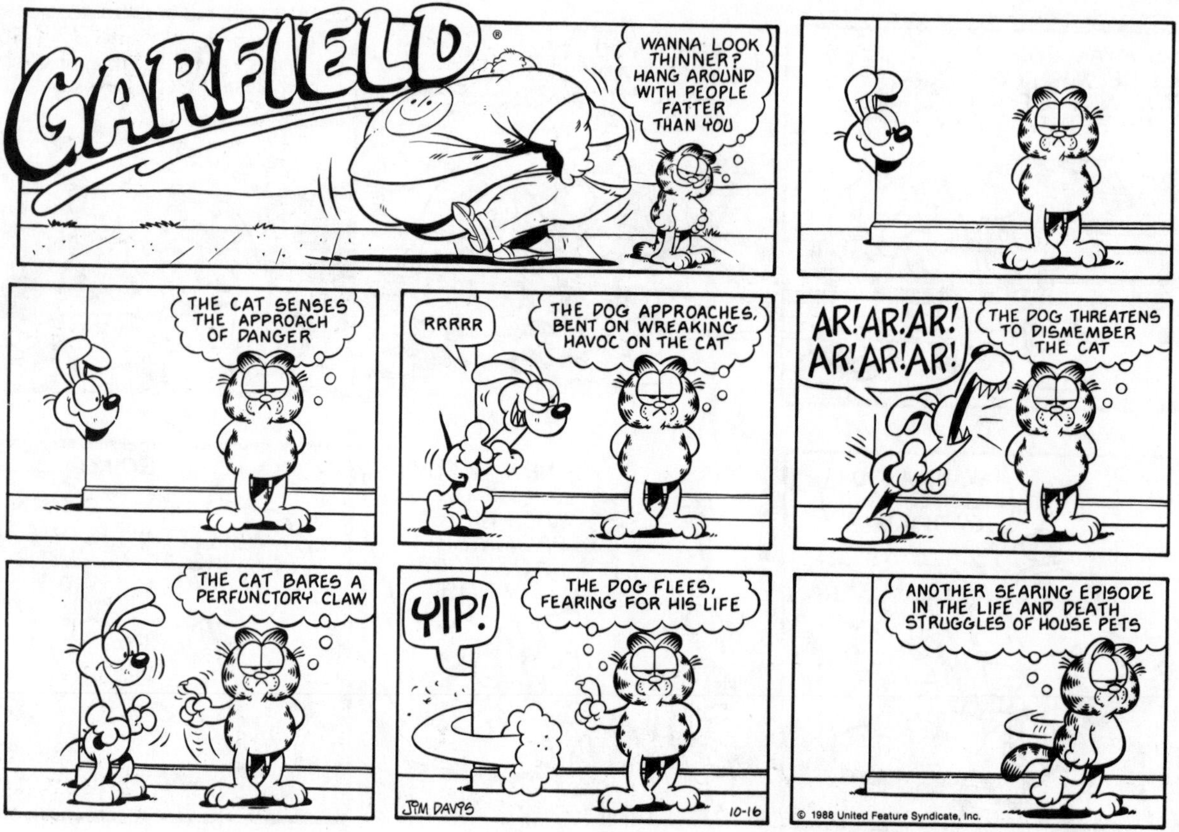
GARFIELD®
WANNA LOOK THINNER? HANG AROUND WITH PEOPLE FATTER THAN YOU
THE CAT SENSES THE APPROACH OF DANGER
RRRRR
THE DOG APPROACHES, BENT ON WREAKING HAVOC ON THE CAT
AR! AR! AR! AR! AR! AR!
THE DOG THREATENS TO DISMEMBER THE CAT
THE CAT BARES A PERFUNCTORY CLAW
YIP!
THE DOG FLEES, FEARING FOR HIS LIFE
JIM DAVIS
10-16
ANOTHER SEARING EPISODE IN THE LIFE AND DEATH STRUGGLES OF HOUSE PETS
© 1988 United Feature Syndicate, Inc.

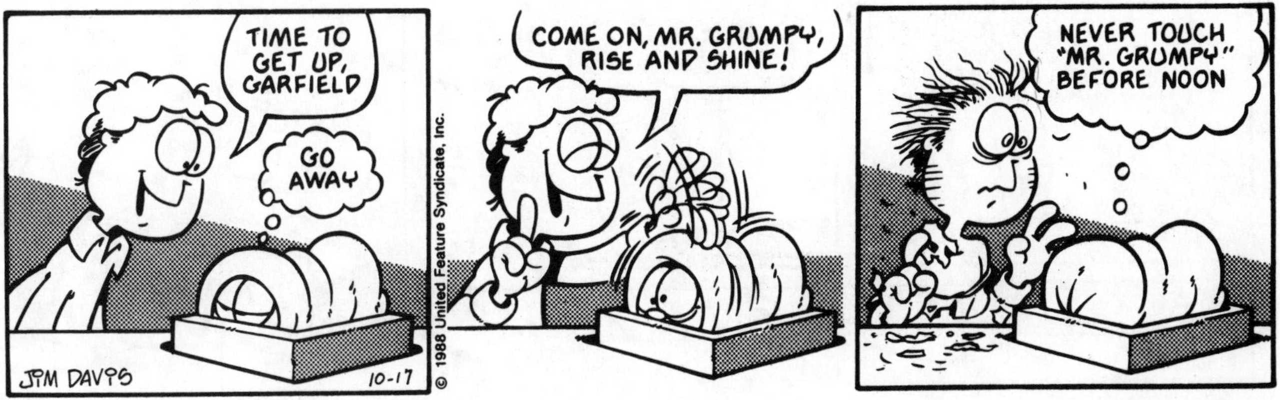
TIME TO GET UP, GARFIELD
GO AWAY
JIM DAVIS
10-17
© 1988 United Feature Syndicate, Inc.
COME ON, MR. GRUMPY, RISE AND SHINE!
NEVER TOUCH "MR. GRUMPY" BEFORE NOON

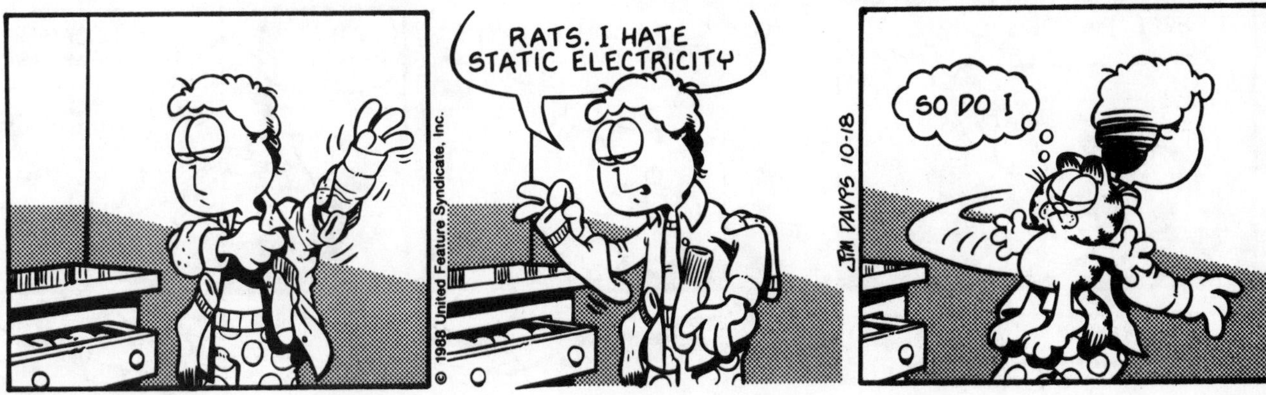
© 1988 United Feature Syndicate, Inc.
RATS. I HATE STATIC ELECTRICITY
JIM DAVIS 10-18
SO DO I

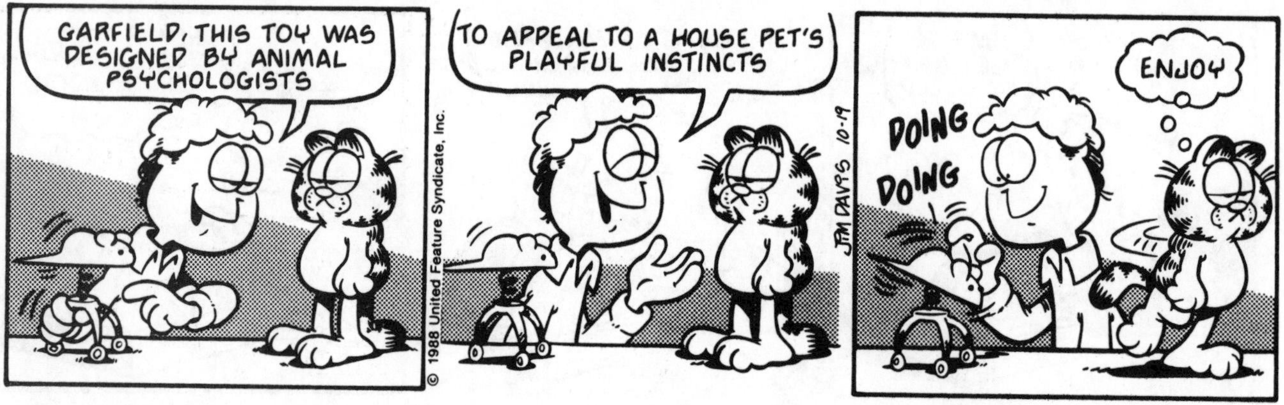
GARFIELD, THIS TOY WAS DESIGNED BY ANIMAL PSYCHOLOGISTS
© 1988 United Feature Syndicate, Inc.
TO APPEAL TO A HOUSE PET'S PLAYFUL INSTINCTS
JIM DAVIS 10-19
DOING
DOING
ENJOY

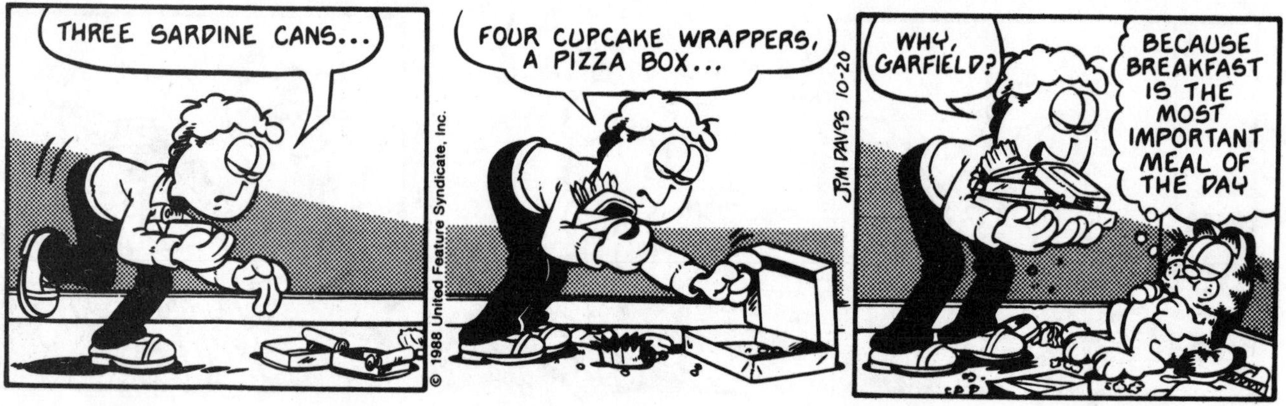
THREE SARDINE CANS...
© 1988 United Feature Syndicate, Inc.
FOUR CUPCAKE WRAPPERS, A PIZZA BOX...
JIM DAVIS 10-20
WHY, GARFIELD?
BECAUSE BREAKFAST IS THE MOST IMPORTANT MEAL OF THE DAY

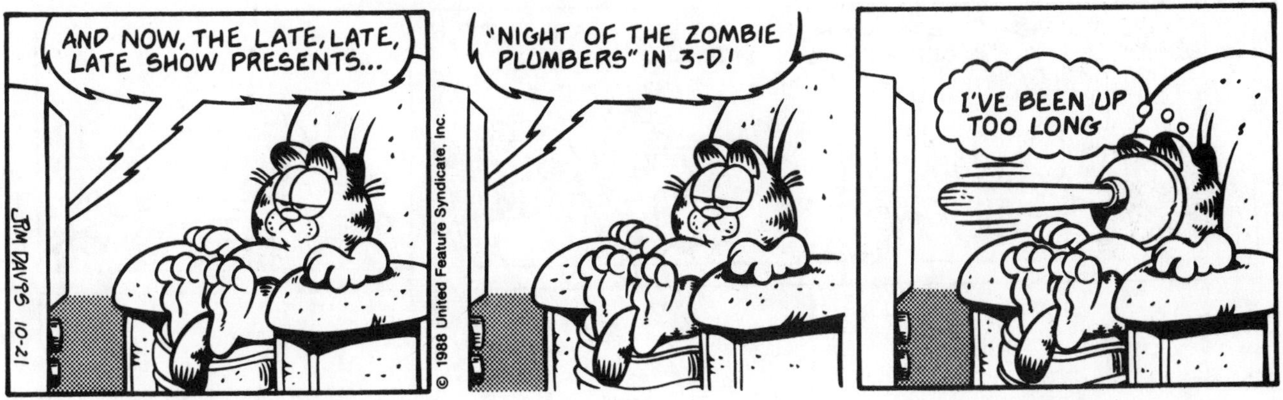
AND NOW, THE LATE, LATE, LATE SHOW PRESENTS...
"NIGHT OF THE ZOMBIE PLUMBERS" IN 3-D!
I'VE BEEN UP TOO LONG
JIM DAVIS 10-21
© 1988 United Feature Syndicate, Inc.

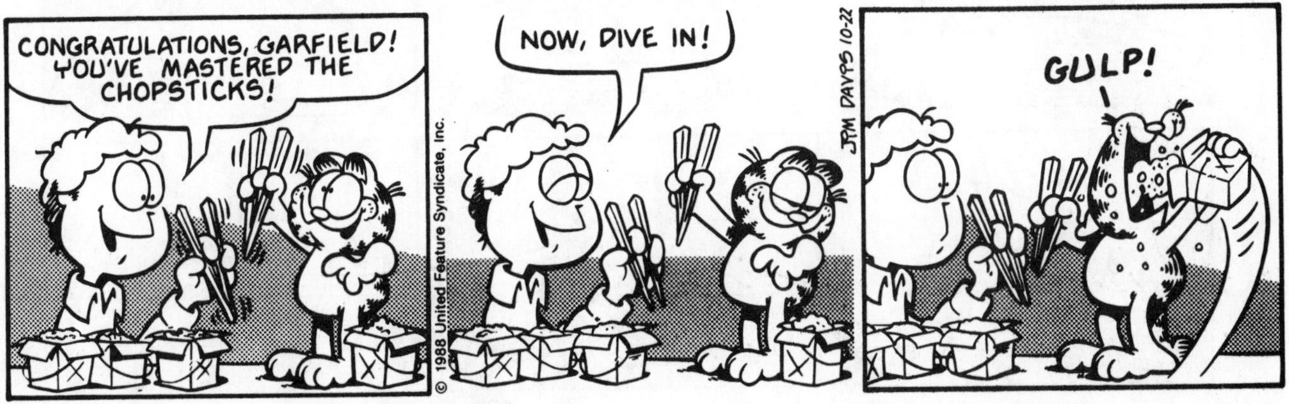
CONGRATULATIONS, GARFIELD! YOU'VE MASTERED THE CHOPSTICKS!
NOW, DIVE IN!
GULP!
JIM DAVIS 10-22
© 1988 United Feature Syndicate, Inc.

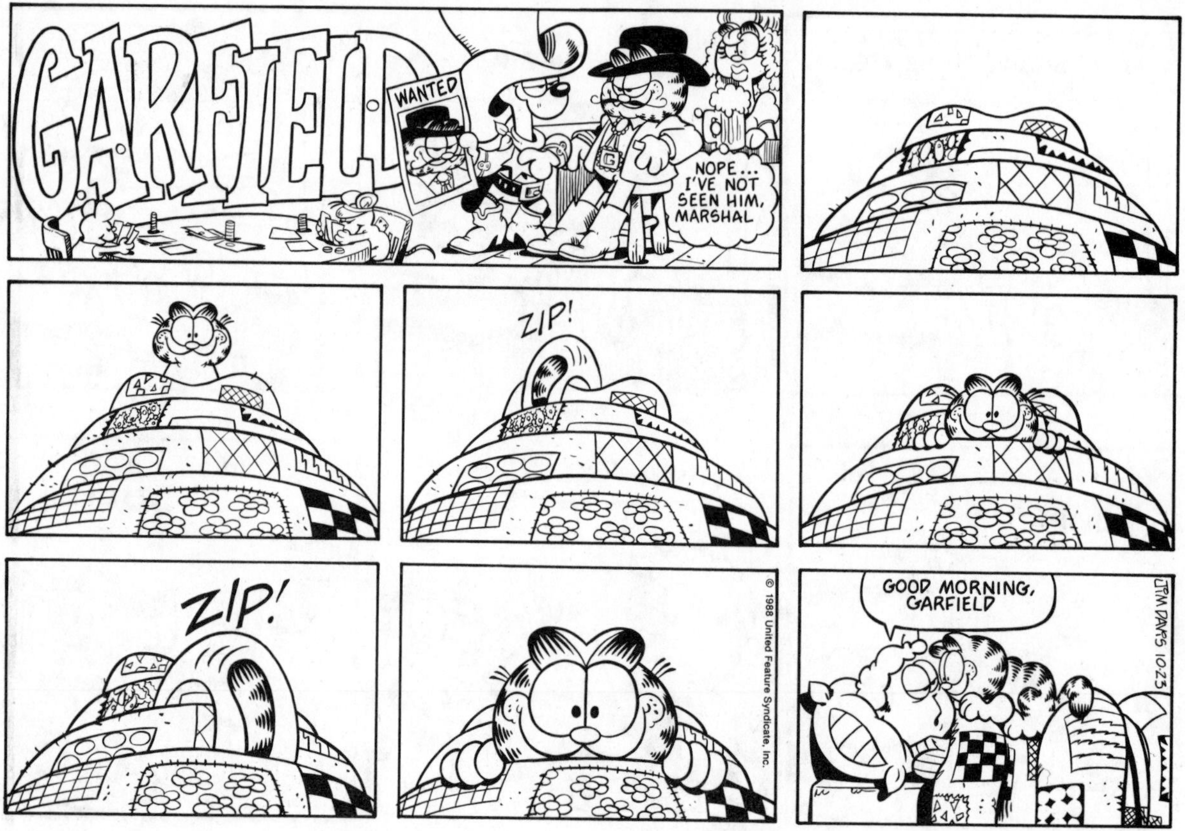

GARFIELD
WANTED
NOPE... I'VE NOT SEEN HIM, MARSHAL
ZIP!
ZIP!
© 1988 United Feature Syndicate, Inc.
GOOD MORNING, GARFIELD
JIM DAVIS 10-23

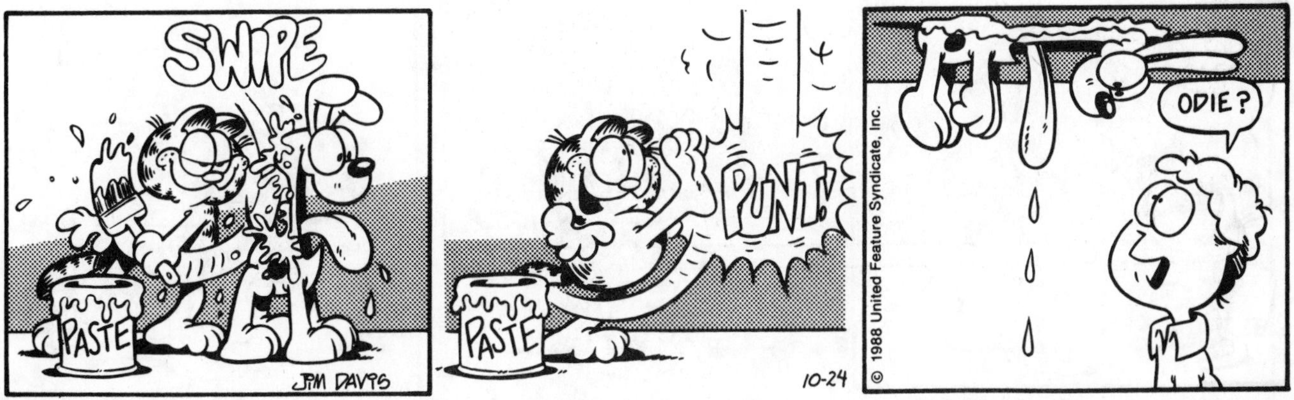
SWIPE
PASTE
JIM DAVIS
PUNT!
PASTE
10-24
© 1988 United Feature Syndicate, Inc.
ODIE?

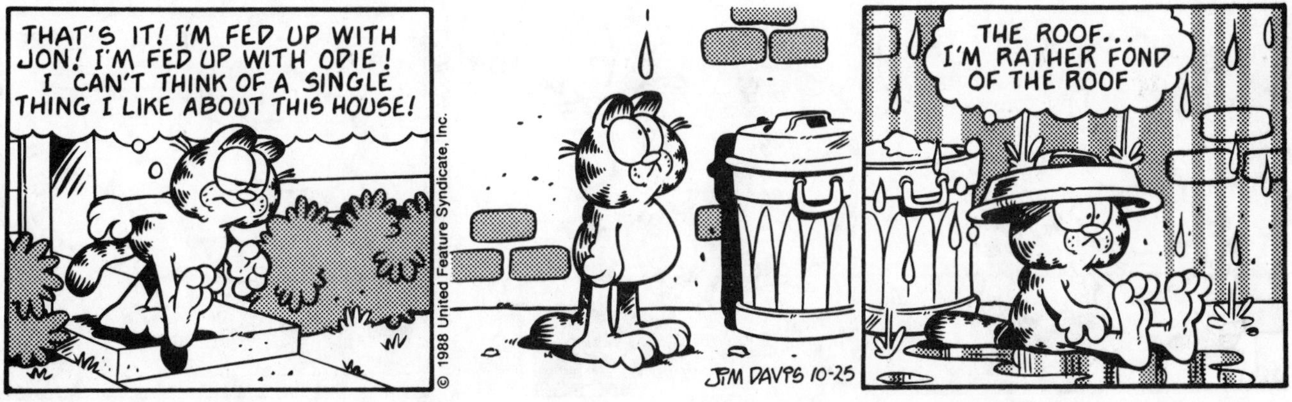
THAT'S IT! I'M FED UP WITH JON! I'M FED UP WITH ODIE! I CAN'T THINK OF A SINGLE THING I LIKE ABOUT THIS HOUSE!
© 1988 United Feature Syndicate, Inc.
JIM DAVIS 10-25
THE ROOF... I'M RATHER FOND OF THE ROOF

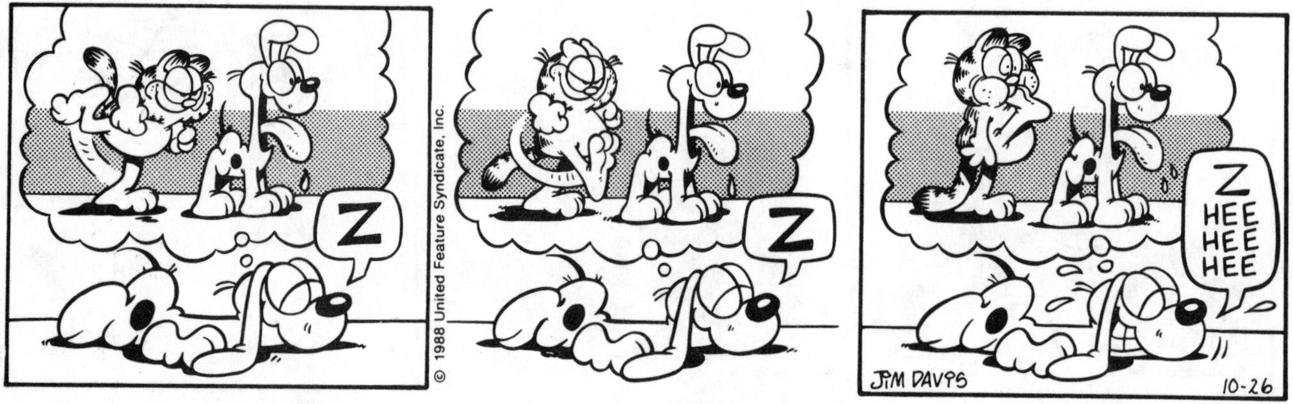
Z
© 1988 United Feature Syndicate, Inc.
Z
Z
HEE
HEE
HEE
JIM DAVIS
10-26

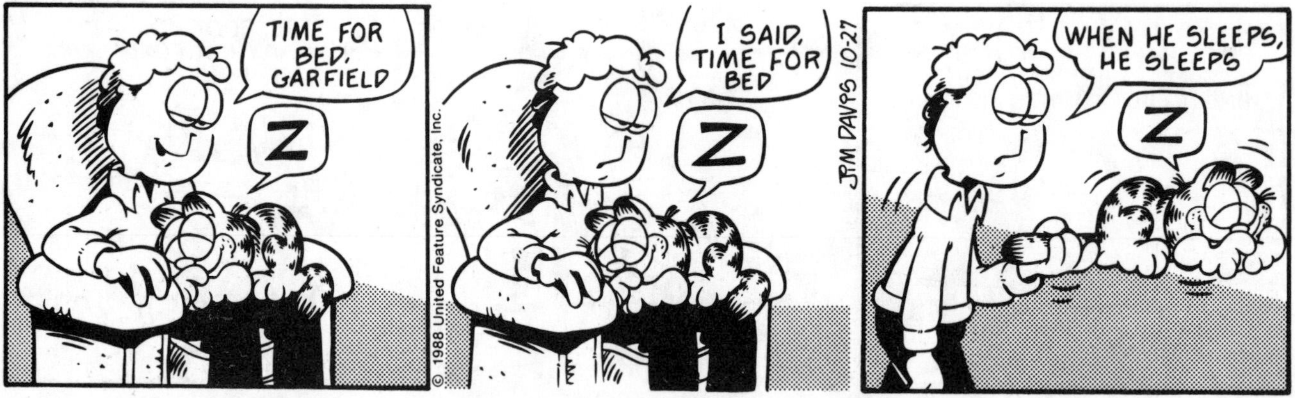
TIME FOR BED, GARFIELD
Z
© 1988 United Feature Syndicate, Inc.
I SAID, TIME FOR BED
Z
JIM DAVIS 10-27
WHEN HE SLEEPS, HE SLEEPS
Z

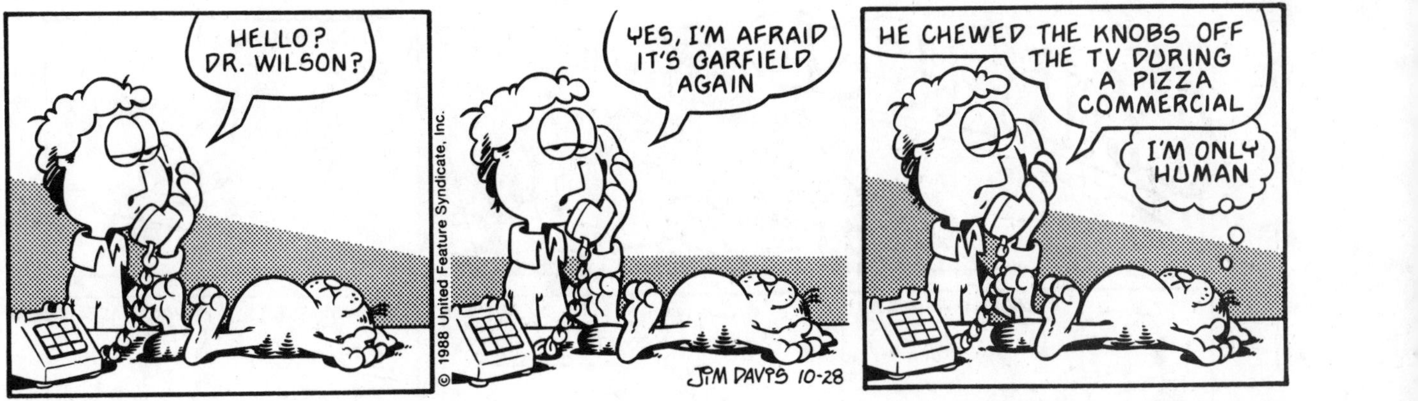
HELLO? DR. WILSON?
YES, I'M AFRAID IT'S GARFIELD AGAIN
HE CHEWED THE KNOBS OFF THE TV DURING A PIZZA COMMERCIAL
I'M ONLY HUMAN
© 1988 United Feature Syndicate, Inc.
JIM DAVIS 10-28

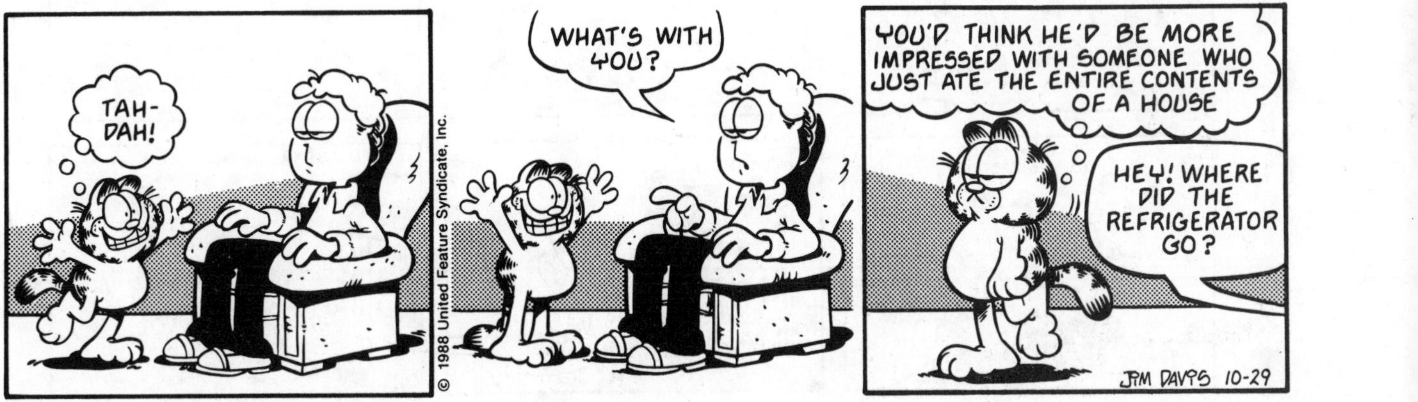
TAH-DAH!
WHAT'S WITH YOU?
YOU'D THINK HE'D BE MORE IMPRESSED WITH SOMEONE WHO JUST ATE THE ENTIRE CONTENTS OF A HOUSE
HEY! WHERE DID THE REFRIGERATOR GO?
© 1988 United Feature Syndicate, Inc.
JIM DAVIS 10-29

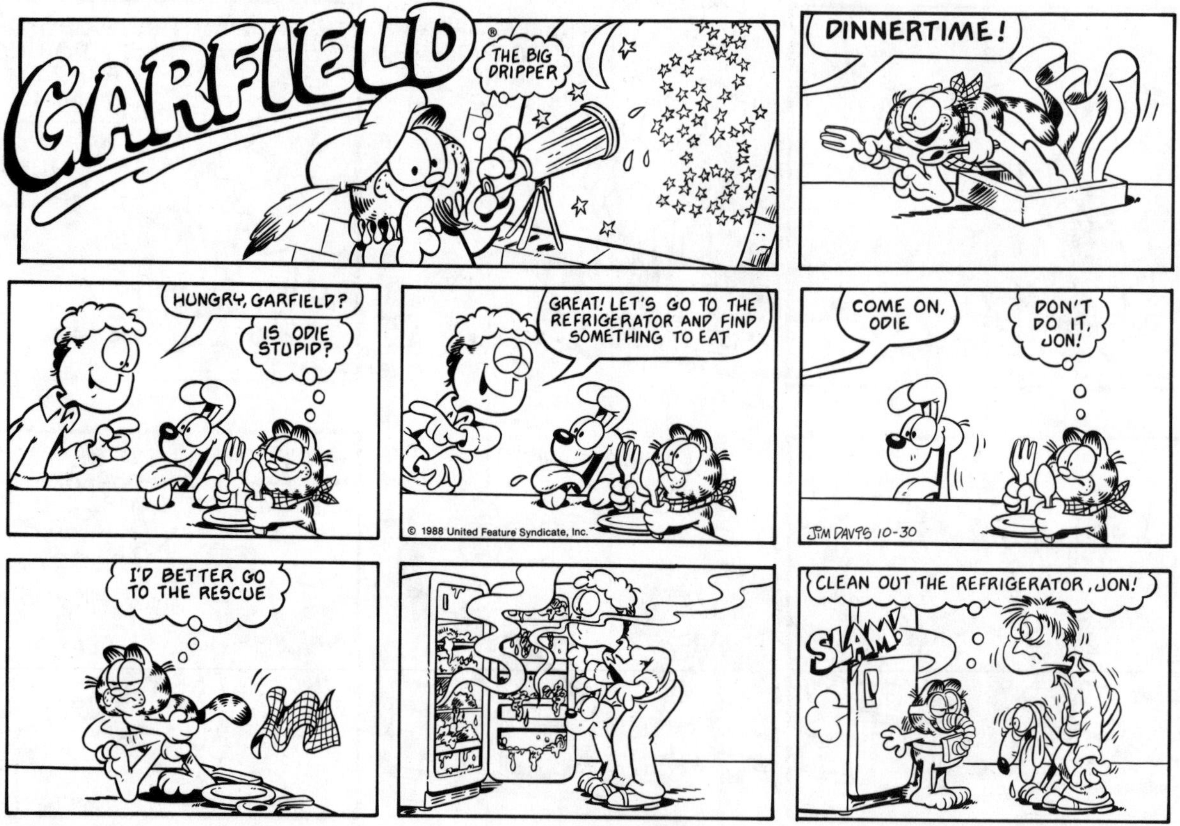

GARFIELD®
THE BIG DRIPPER
DINNERTIME!
HUNGRY, GARFIELD?
IS ODIE STUPID?
GREAT! LET'S GO TO THE REFRIGERATOR AND FIND SOMETHING TO EAT
© 1988 United Feature Syndicate, Inc.
COME ON, ODIE
DON'T DO IT, JON!
JIM DAVIS 10-30
I'D BETTER GO TO THE RESCUE
CLEAN OUT THE REFRIGERATOR, JON!
SLAM!

GOOD EVENING, LADIES AND GERMS!
TAPPITY TAPPITY
10-31
JIM DAVIS
© 1988 United Feature Syndicate, Inc.
SPLAT!
BOP!
WHAP!
I SEE SOME OF YOU STAYED FOR THE SECOND SHOW

I KNEW A DOG WHO WAS SO STUPID, HE CHASED BONES AND BURIED CARS!
11-1
JIM DAVIS
ROWF!
MEOW!
YIP
ZIP
BARK!
GRRR
ARF!
© 1988 United Feature Syndicate, Inc.
WHO BOOKED ME INTO THIS JOINT ANYWAY?
DOG POUND

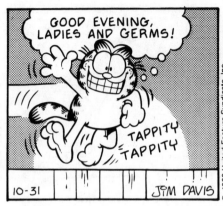

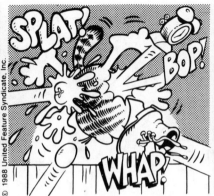

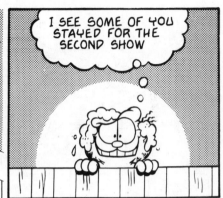

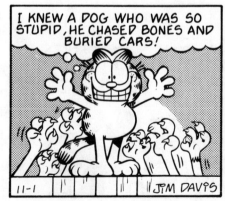

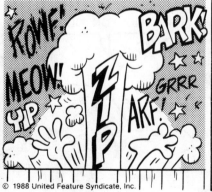

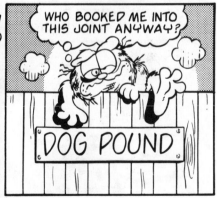

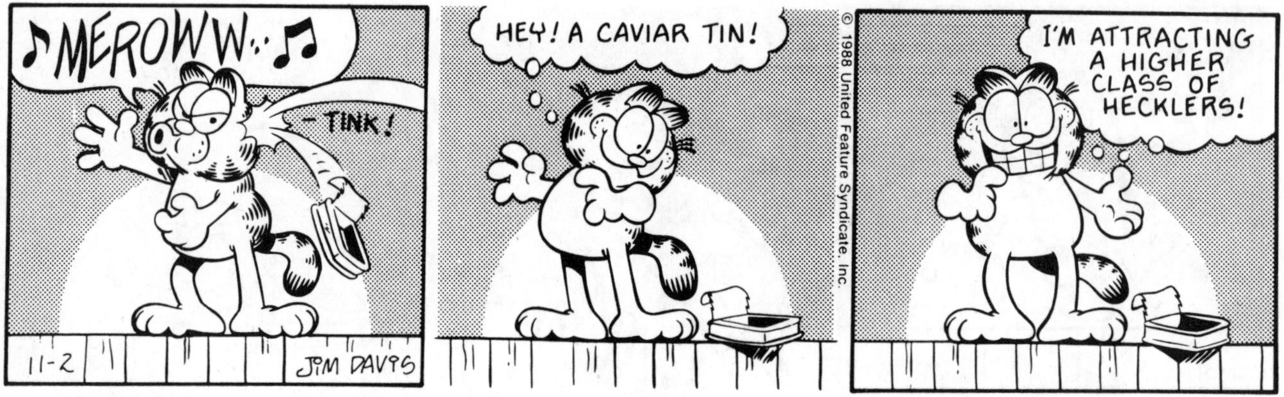
♪MEROWW..♫
-TINK!
11-2
JIM DAVIS
HEY! A CAVIAR TIN!
© 1988 United Feature Syndicate, Inc.
I'M ATTRACTING A HIGHER CLASS OF HECKLERS!

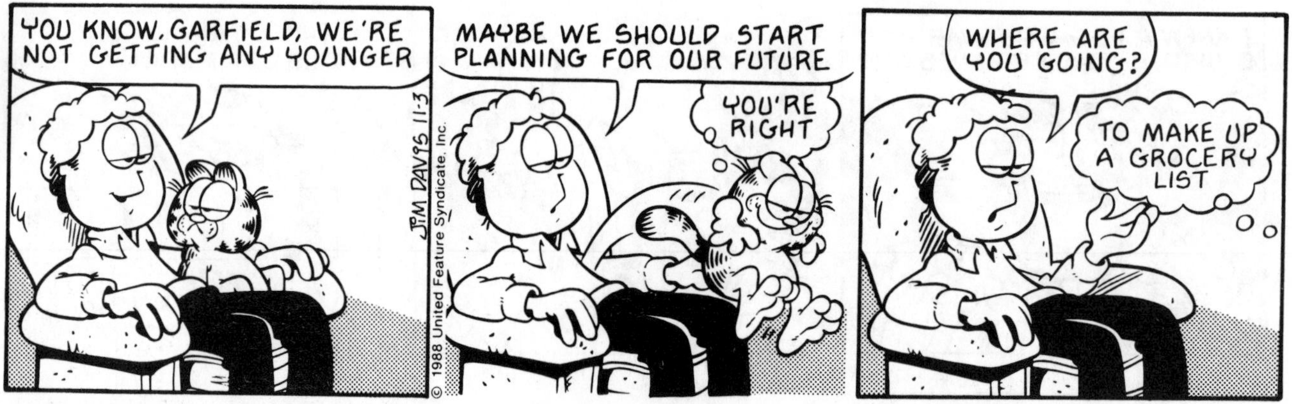
YOU KNOW, GARFIELD, WE'RE NOT GETTING ANY YOUNGER
JIM DAVIS 11-3
© 1988 United Feature Syndicate, Inc.
MAYBE WE SHOULD START PLANNING FOR OUR FUTURE
YOU'RE RIGHT
WHERE ARE YOU GOING?
TO MAKE UP A GROCERY LIST

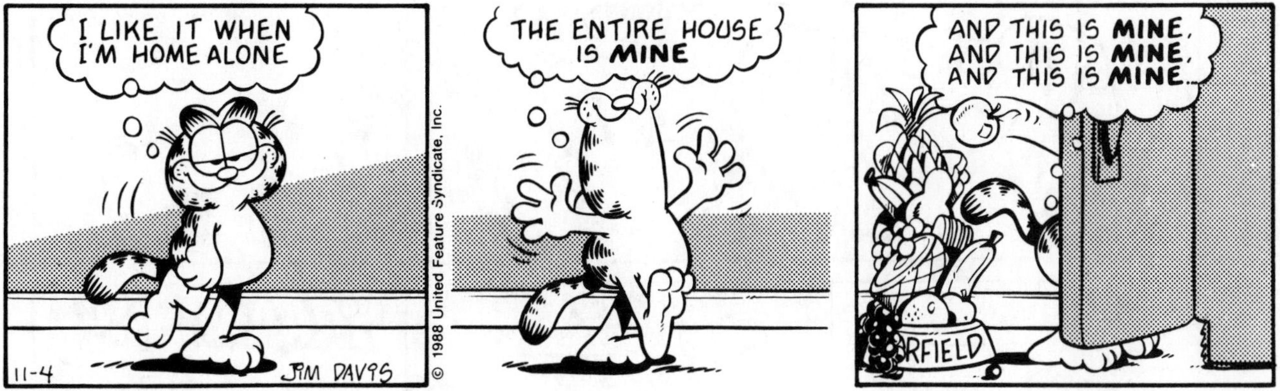
I LIKE IT WHEN I'M HOME ALONE
11-4
JIM DAVIS
© 1988 United Feature Syndicate, Inc.
THE ENTIRE HOUSE IS **MINE**
AND THIS IS **MINE**, AND THIS IS **MINE**, AND THIS IS **MINE**...
RFIELD

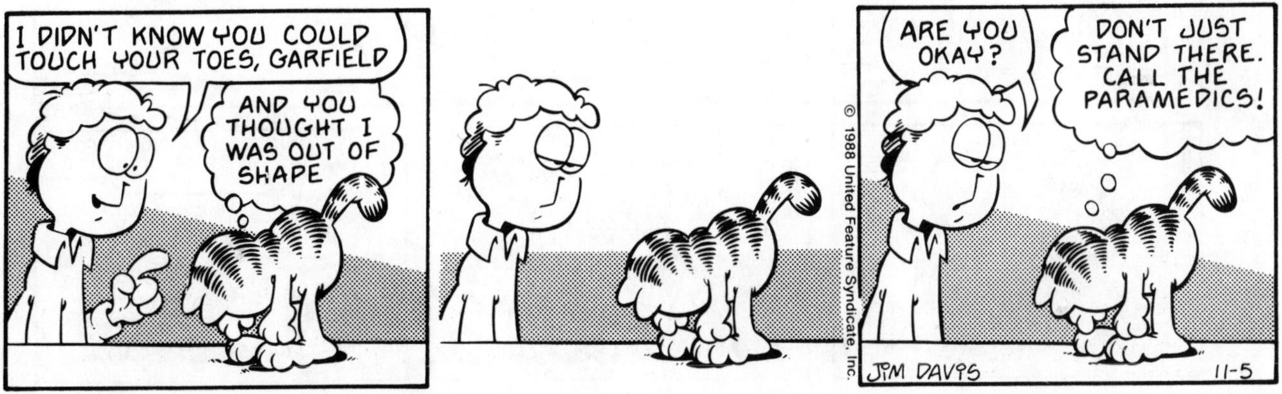
I DIDN'T KNOW YOU COULD TOUCH YOUR TOES, GARFIELD
AND YOU THOUGHT I WAS OUT OF SHAPE
© 1988 United Feature Syndicate, Inc.
ARE YOU OKAY?
DON'T JUST STAND THERE. CALL THE PARAMEDICS!
JIM DAVIS
11-5

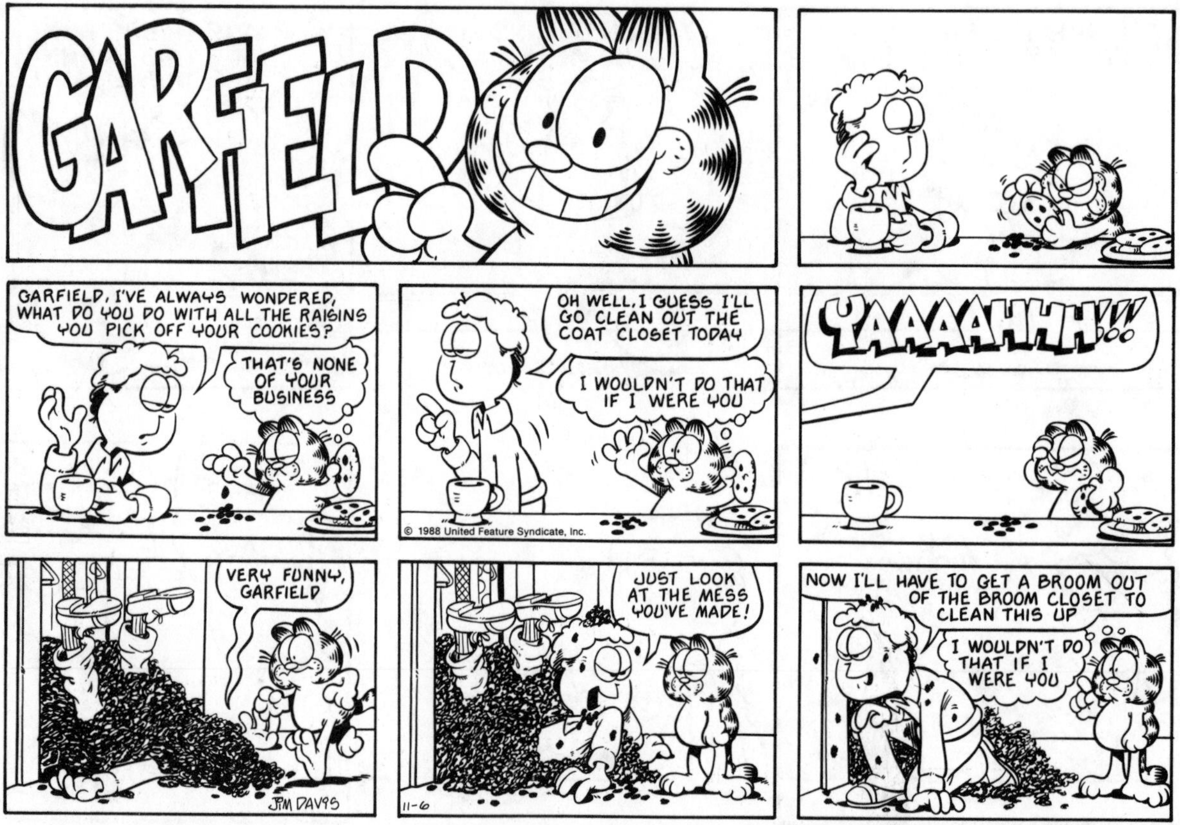
GARFIELD
GARFIELD, I'VE ALWAYS WONDERED, WHAT DO YOU DO WITH ALL THE RAISINS YOU PICK OFF YOUR COOKIES?
THAT'S NONE OF YOUR BUSINESS
OH WELL, I GUESS I'LL GO CLEAN OUT THE COAT CLOSET TODAY
I WOULDN'T DO THAT IF I WERE YOU
© 1988 United Feature Syndicate, Inc.
YAAAAHHH!!!
VERY FUNNY, GARFIELD
JIM DAVIS
JUST LOOK AT THE MESS YOU'VE MADE!
11-6
NOW I'LL HAVE TO GET A BROOM OUT OF THE BROOM CLOSET TO CLEAN THIS UP
I WOULDN'T DO THAT IF I WERE YOU

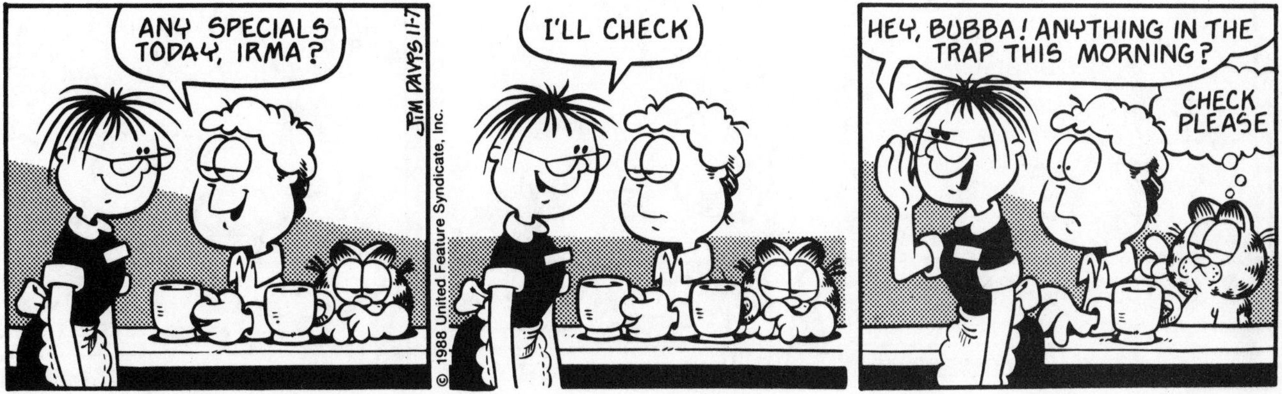
ANY SPECIALS TODAY, IRMA?
JIM DAVIS 11-7
© 1988 United Feature Syndicate, Inc.
I'LL CHECK
HEY, BUBBA! ANYTHING IN THE TRAP THIS MORNING?
CHECK PLEASE

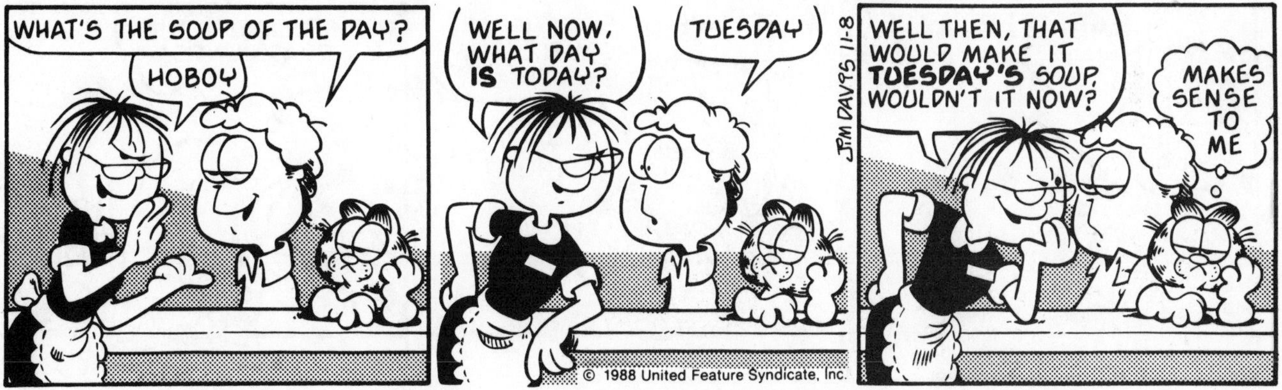
WHAT'S THE SOUP OF THE DAY?
HOBOY
WELL NOW, WHAT DAY **IS** TODAY?
TUESDAY
© 1988 United Feature Syndicate, Inc.
JIM DAVIS 11-8
WELL THEN, THAT WOULD MAKE IT **TUESDAY'S** SOUP, WOULDN'T IT NOW?
MAKES SENSE TO ME

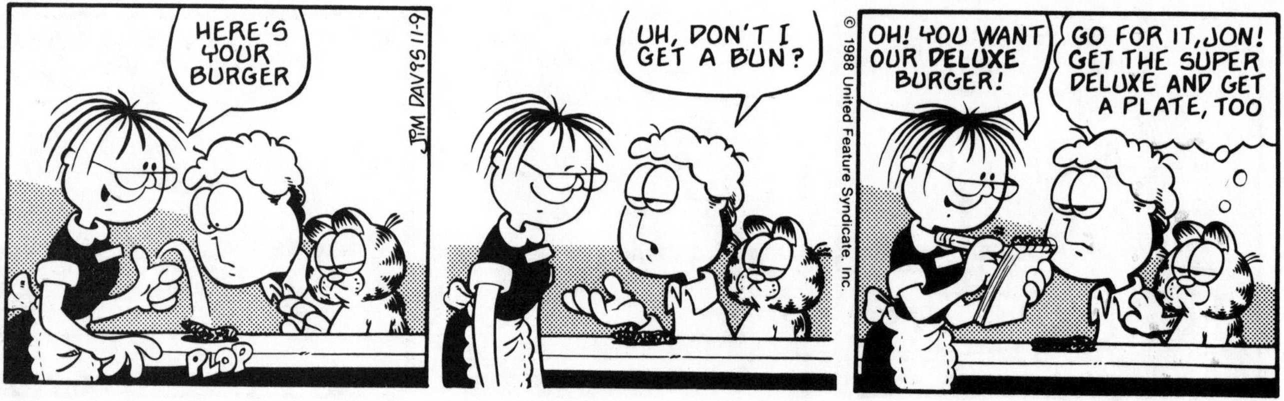
HERE'S YOUR BURGER
PLOP
JIM DAVIS 11-9
UH, DON'T I GET A BUN?
© 1988 United Feature Syndicate, Inc.
OH! YOU WANT OUR DELUXE BURGER!
GO FOR IT, JON! GET THE SUPER DELUXE AND GET A PLATE, TOO

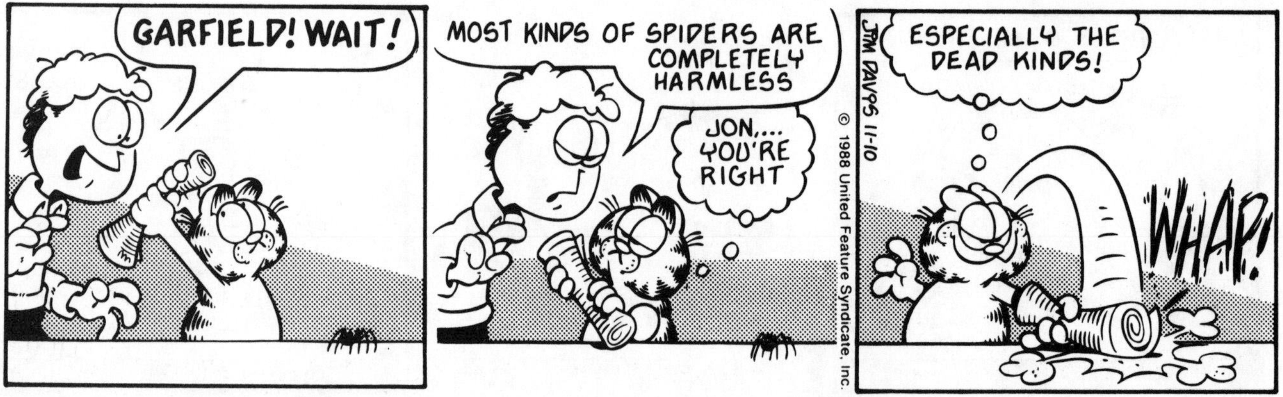
GARFIELD! WAIT!
MOST KINDS OF SPIDERS ARE COMPLETELY HARMLESS
JON,... YOU'RE RIGHT
© 1988 United Feature Syndicate, Inc.
JIM DAVIS 11-10
ESPECIALLY THE DEAD KINDS!
WHAP!

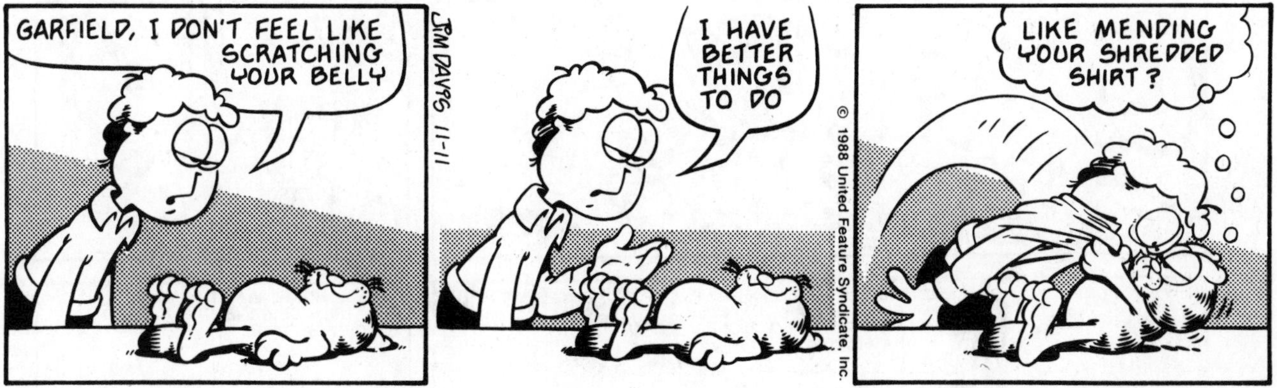
GARFIELD, I DON'T FEEL LIKE SCRATCHING YOUR BELLY
JIM DAVIS 11-11
I HAVE BETTER THINGS TO DO
© 1988 United Feature Syndicate, Inc.
LIKE MENDING YOUR SHREDDED SHIRT?

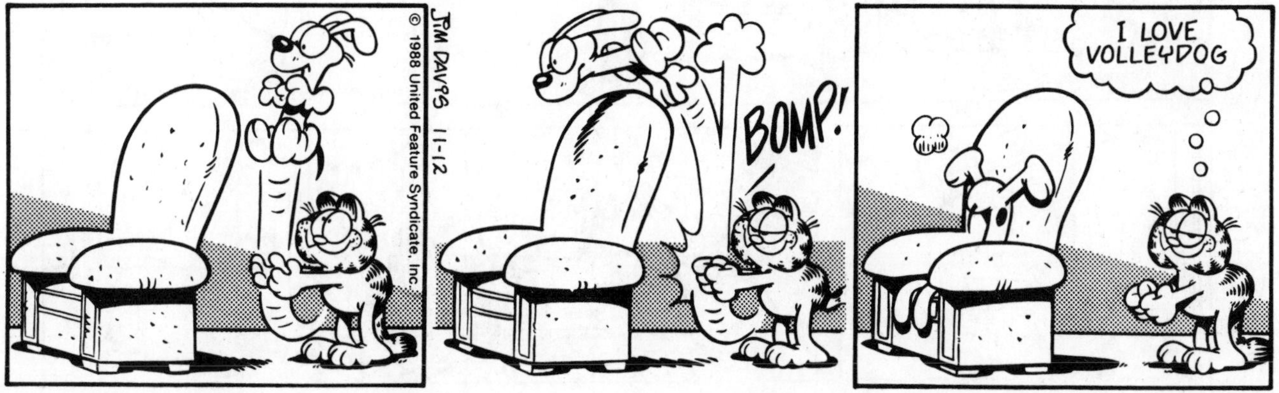
© 1988 United Feature Syndicate, Inc.
JIM DAVIS 11-12
BOMP!
I LOVE VOLLEYDOG

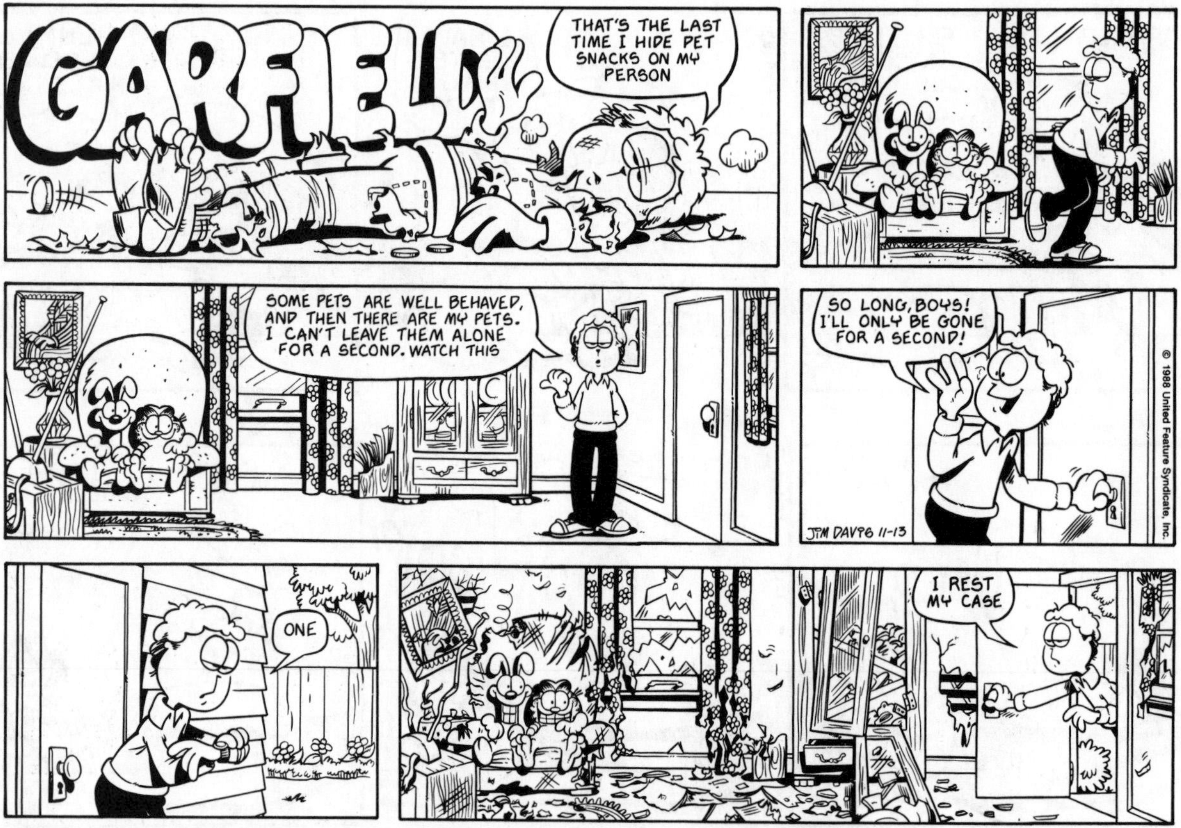
GARFIELD
THAT'S THE LAST TIME I HIDE PET SNACKS ON MY PERSON
SOME PETS ARE WELL BEHAVED, AND THEN THERE ARE MY PETS. I CAN'T LEAVE THEM ALONE FOR A SECOND. WATCH THIS
SO LONG, BOYS! I'LL ONLY BE GONE FOR A SECOND!
JIM DAVIS 11-13
© 1988 United Feature Syndicate, Inc.
ONE
I REST MY CASE

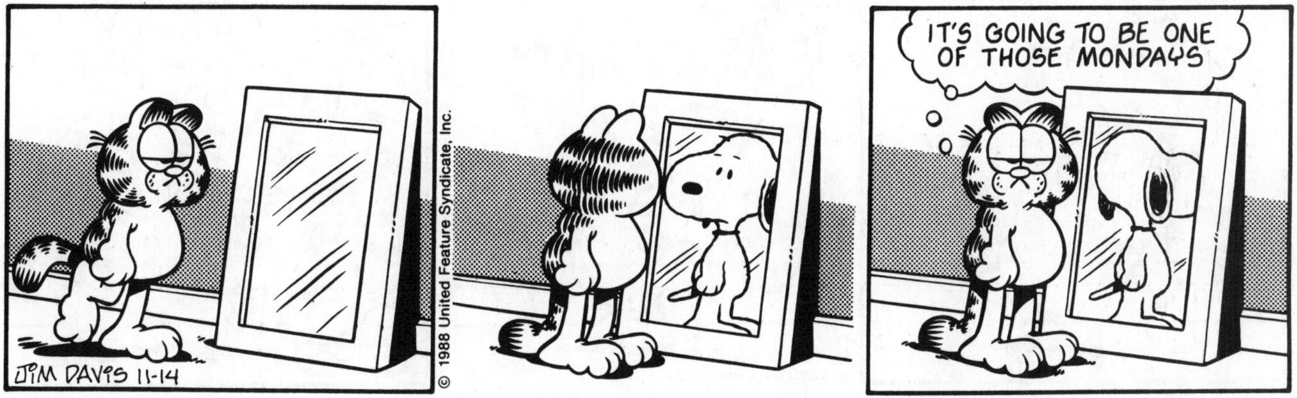
JIM DAVIS 11-14
© 1988 United Feature Syndicate, Inc.
IT'S GOING TO BE ONE OF THOSE MONDAYS

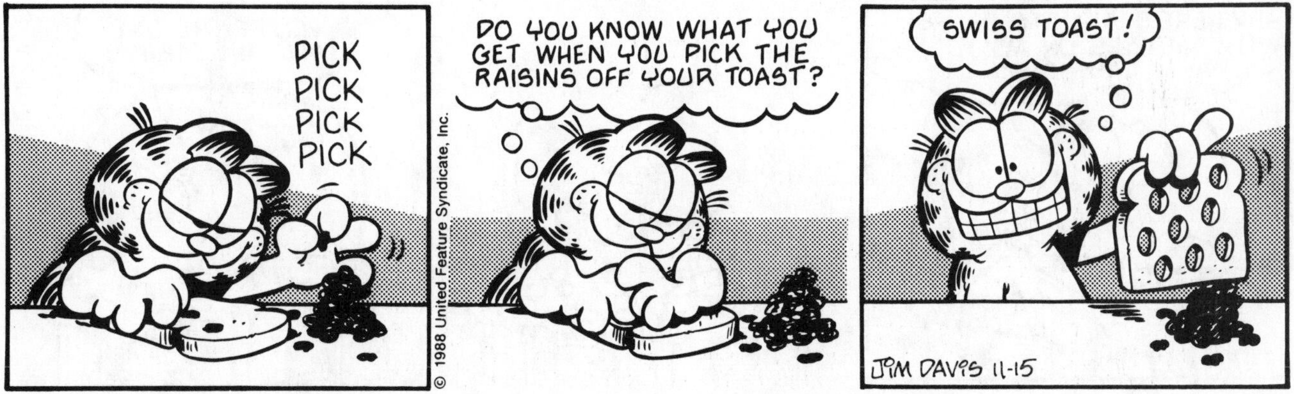
PICK PICK PICK PICK
© 1988 United Feature Syndicate, Inc.
DO YOU KNOW WHAT YOU GET WHEN YOU PICK THE RAISINS OFF YOUR TOAST?
SWISS TOAST!
JIM DAVIS 11-15

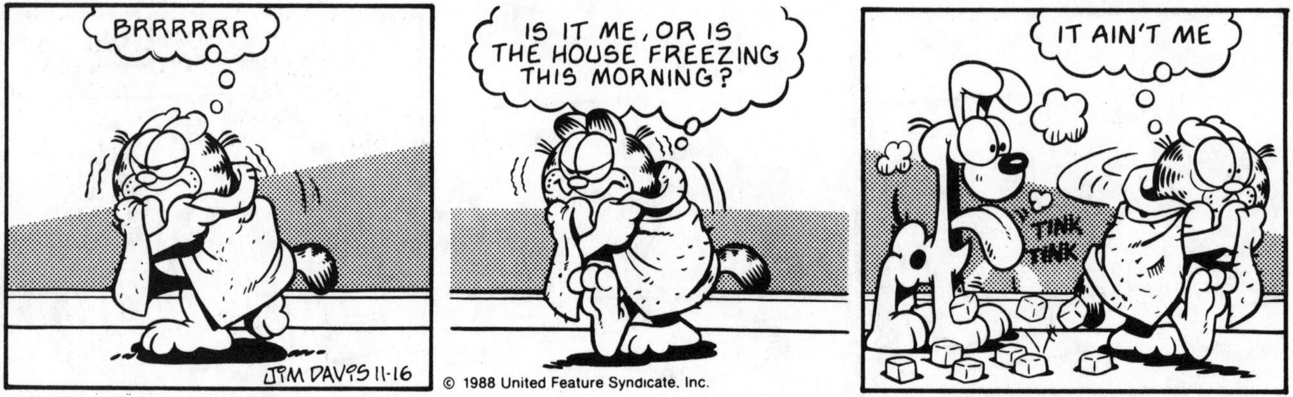
BRRRRRR
IS IT ME, OR IS THE HOUSE FREEZING THIS MORNING?
TINK TINK
IT AIN'T ME
JIM DAVIS 11-16
© 1988 United Feature Syndicate, Inc.

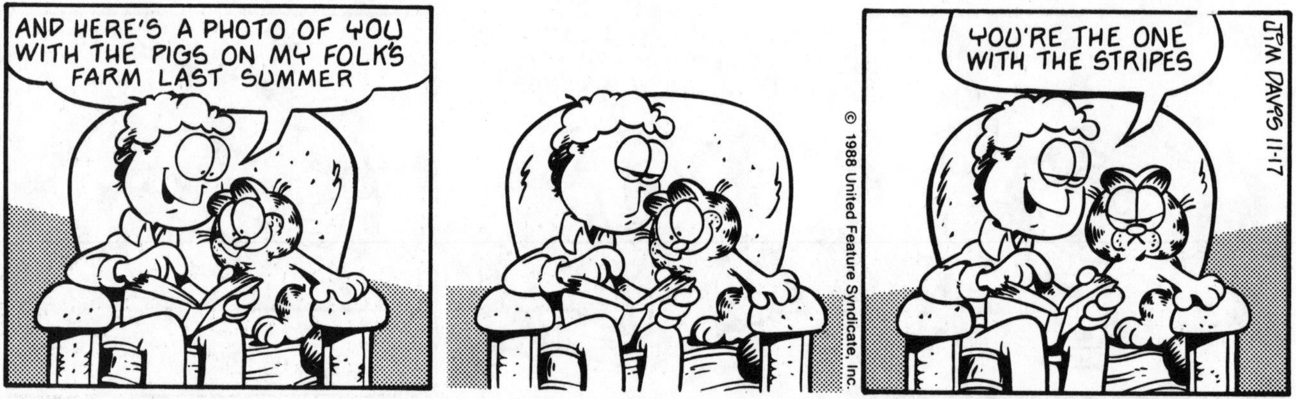
AND HERE'S A PHOTO OF YOU WITH THE PIGS ON MY FOLK'S FARM LAST SUMMER
YOU'RE THE ONE WITH THE STRIPES
JIM DAVIS 11-17
© 1988 United Feature Syndicate, Inc.

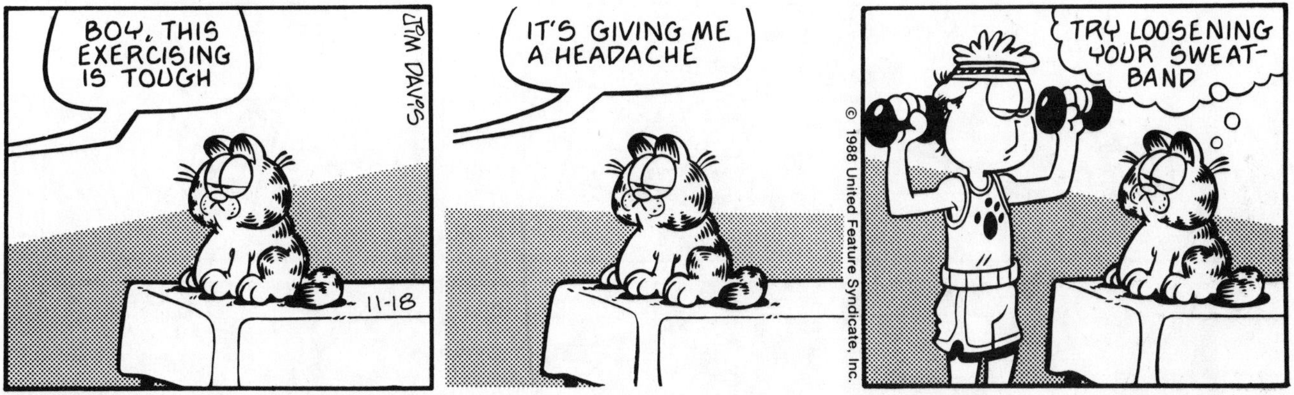
BOY, THIS EXERCISING IS TOUGH
JIM DAVIS
11-18
IT'S GIVING ME A HEADACHE
© 1988 United Feature Syndicate, Inc.
TRY LOOSENING YOUR SWEAT-BAND

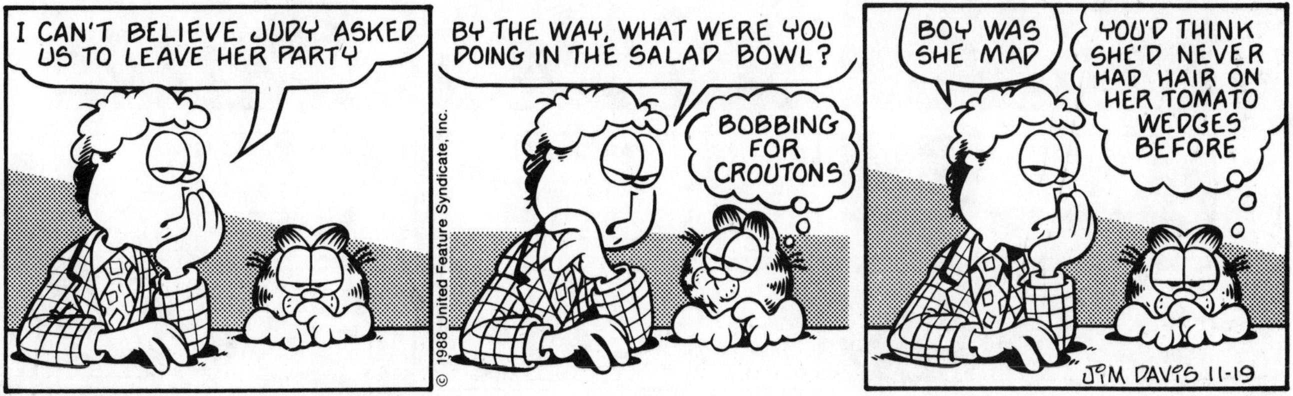
I CAN'T BELIEVE JUDY ASKED US TO LEAVE HER PARTY
© 1988 United Feature Syndicate, Inc.
BY THE WAY, WHAT WERE YOU DOING IN THE SALAD BOWL?
BOBBING FOR CROUTONS
BOY WAS SHE MAD
YOU'D THINK SHE'D NEVER HAD HAIR ON HER TOMATO WEDGES BEFORE
JIM DAVIS 11-19

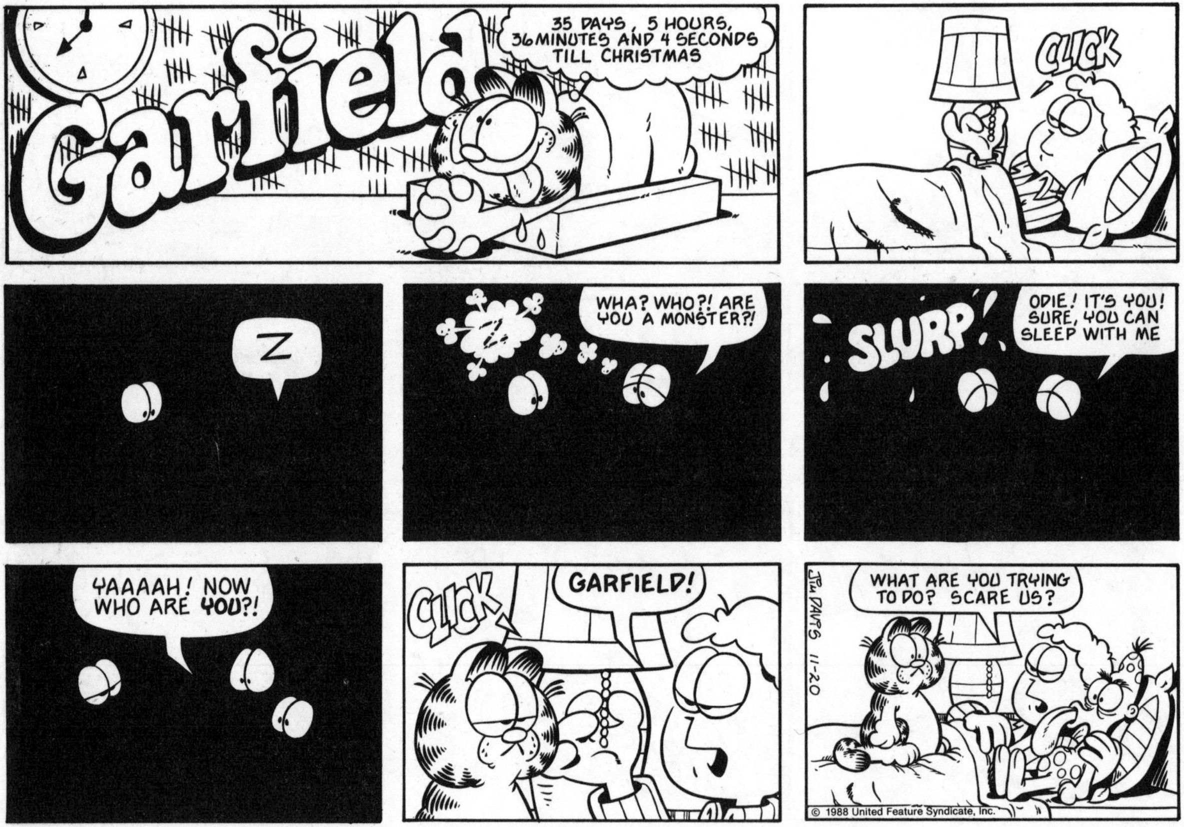
Garfield
35 DAYS, 5 HOURS, 36 MINUTES AND 4 SECONDS TILL CHRISTMAS
CLICK
Z
WHA? WHO?! ARE YOU A MONSTER?!
SLURP
ODIE! IT'S YOU! SURE, YOU CAN SLEEP WITH ME
YAAAAH! NOW WHO ARE YOU?!
CLICK
GARFIELD!
JIM DAVIS 11-20
WHAT ARE YOU TRYING TO DO? SCARE US?
© 1988 United Feature Syndicate, Inc.

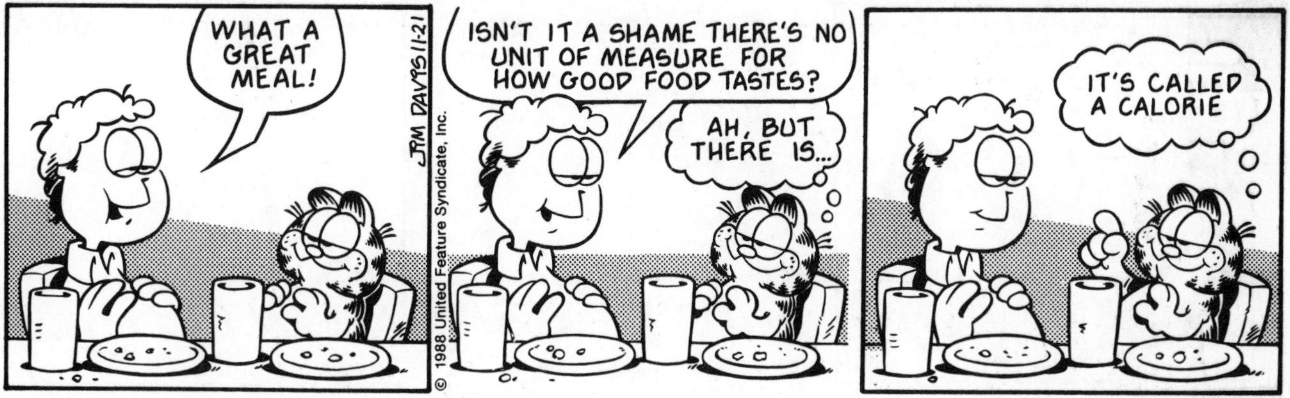
WHAT A GREAT MEAL!
JIM DAVIS 11-21
© 1988 United Feature Syndicate, Inc.
ISN'T IT A SHAME THERE'S NO UNIT OF MEASURE FOR HOW GOOD FOOD TASTES?
AH, BUT THERE IS...
IT'S CALLED A CALORIE

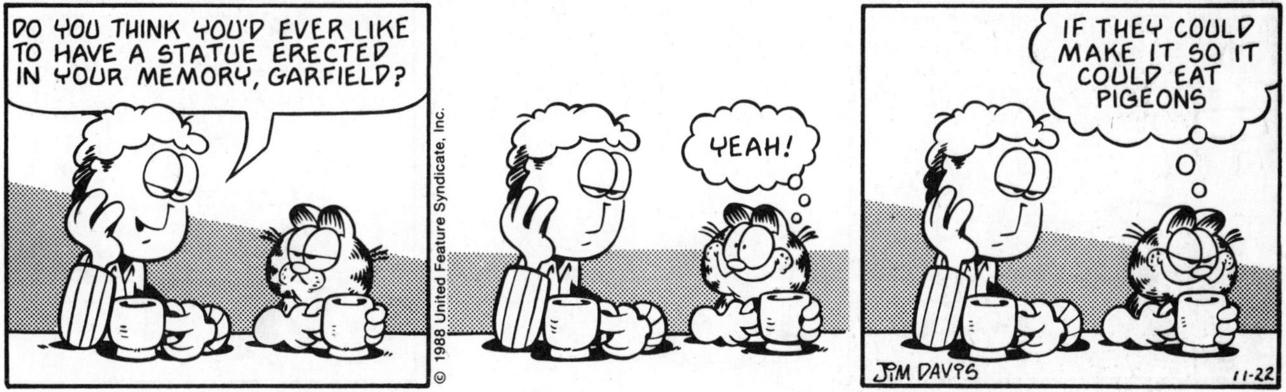
DO YOU THINK YOU'D EVER LIKE TO HAVE A STATUE ERECTED IN YOUR MEMORY, GARFIELD?
© 1988 United Feature Syndicate, Inc.
YEAH!
IF THEY COULD MAKE IT SO IT COULD EAT PIGEONS
JIM DAVIS
11-22

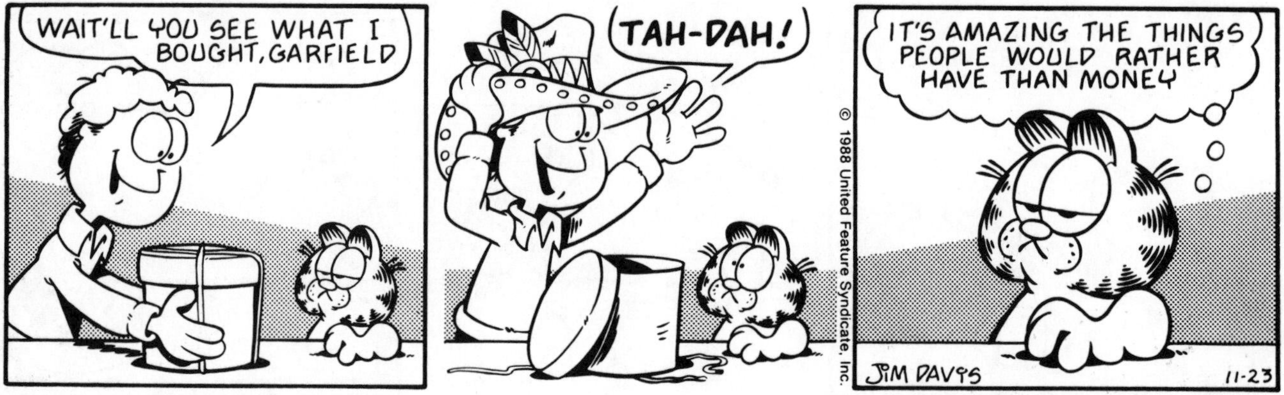
WAIT'LL YOU SEE WHAT I BOUGHT, GARFIELD
TAH-DAH!
IT'S AMAZING THE THINGS PEOPLE WOULD RATHER HAVE THAN MONEY
JIM DAVIS
11-23
© 1988 United Feature Syndicate, Inc.

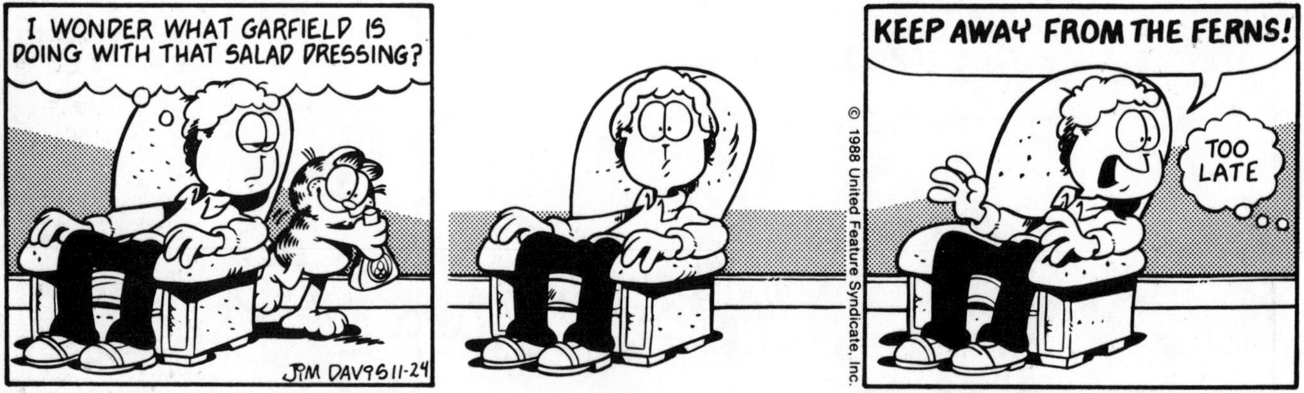
I WONDER WHAT GARFIELD IS DOING WITH THAT SALAD DRESSING?
JIM DAVIS 11-24
KEEP AWAY FROM THE FERNS!
TOO LATE
© 1988 United Feature Syndicate, Inc.

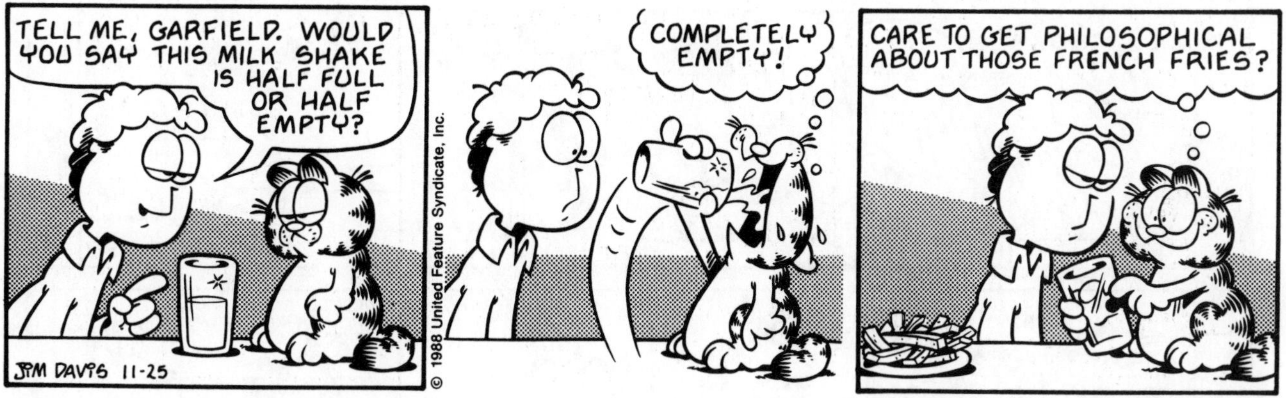
TELL ME, GARFIELD. WOULD YOU SAY THIS MILK SHAKE IS HALF FULL OR HALF EMPTY?
JIM DAVIS 11-25
© 1988 United Feature Syndicate, Inc.
COMPLETELY EMPTY!
CARE TO GET PHILOSOPHICAL ABOUT THOSE FRENCH FRIES?

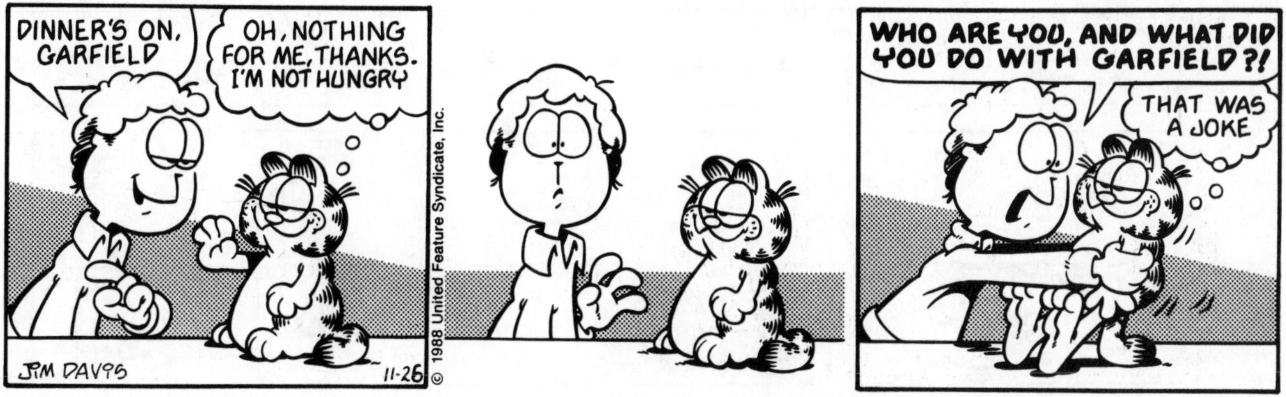
DINNER'S ON, GARFIELD
OH, NOTHING FOR ME, THANKS. I'M NOT HUNGRY
JIM DAVIS 11-26
© 1988 United Feature Syndicate, Inc.
WHO ARE YOU, AND WHAT DID YOU DO WITH GARFIELD?!
THAT WAS A JOKE

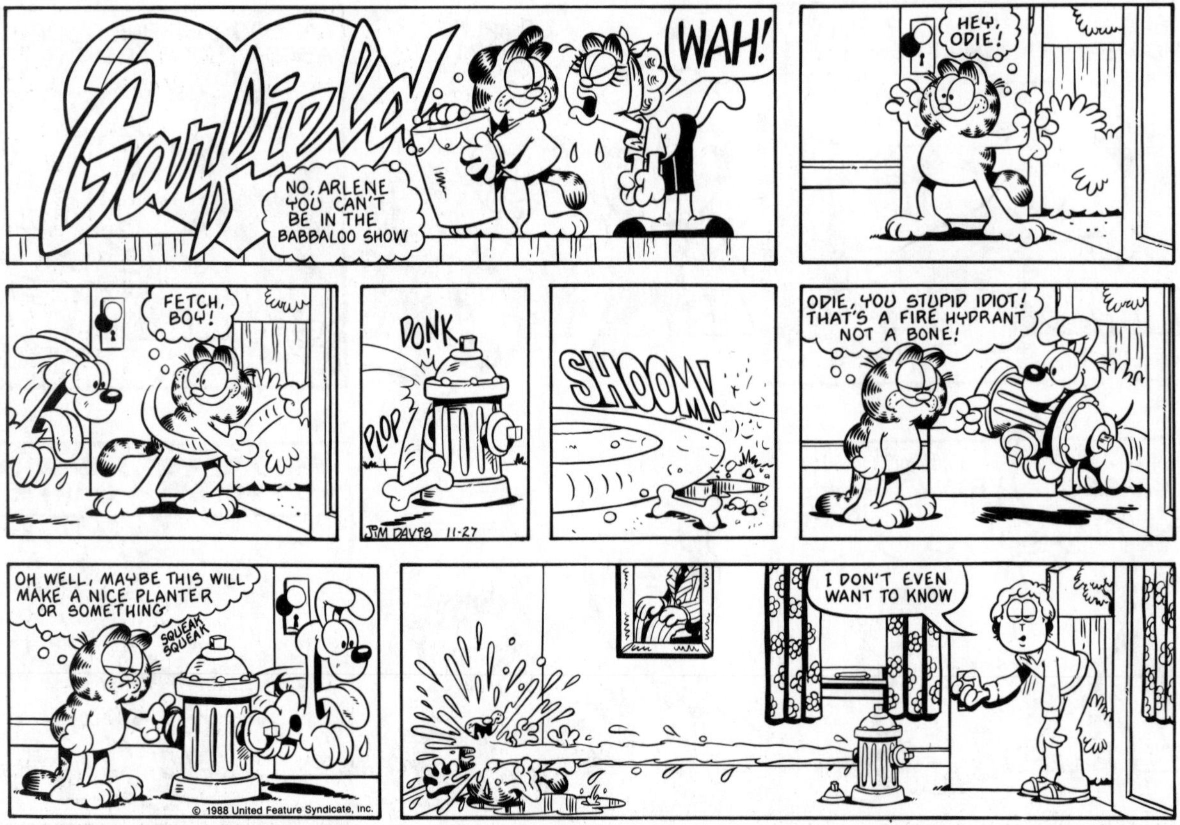
Garfield
NO, ARLENE YOU CAN'T BE IN THE BABBALOO SHOW
WAH!
HEY, ODIE!
FETCH, BOY!
DONK
PLOP
JIM DAVIS 11-27
SHOOM!
ODIE, YOU STUPID IDIOT! THAT'S A FIRE HYDRANT NOT A BONE!
OH WELL, MAYBE THIS WILL MAKE A NICE PLANTER OR SOMETHING
SQUEAK SQUEAK
© 1988 United Feature Syndicate, Inc.
I DON'T EVEN WANT TO KNOW

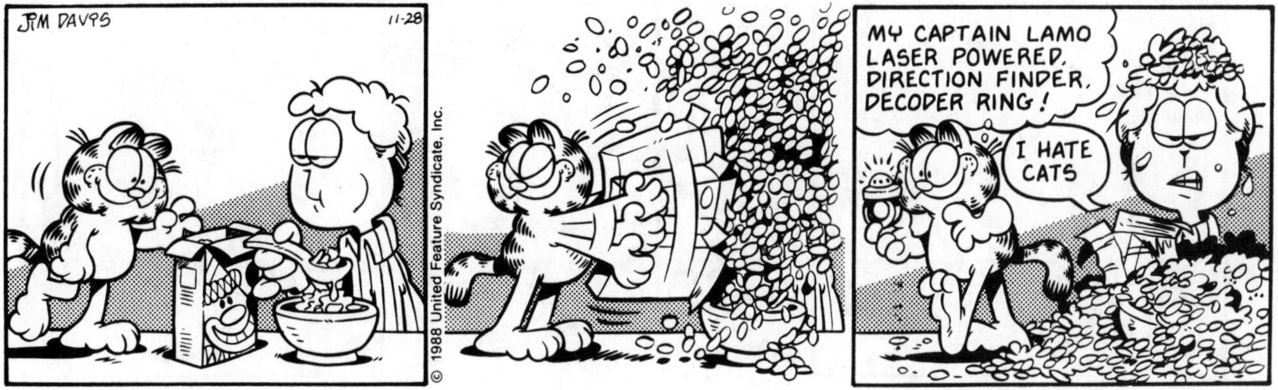
JIM DAVIS
11-28
© 1988 United Feature Syndicate, Inc.
MY CAPTAIN LAMO LASER POWERED, DIRECTION FINDER, DECODER RING!
I HATE CATS

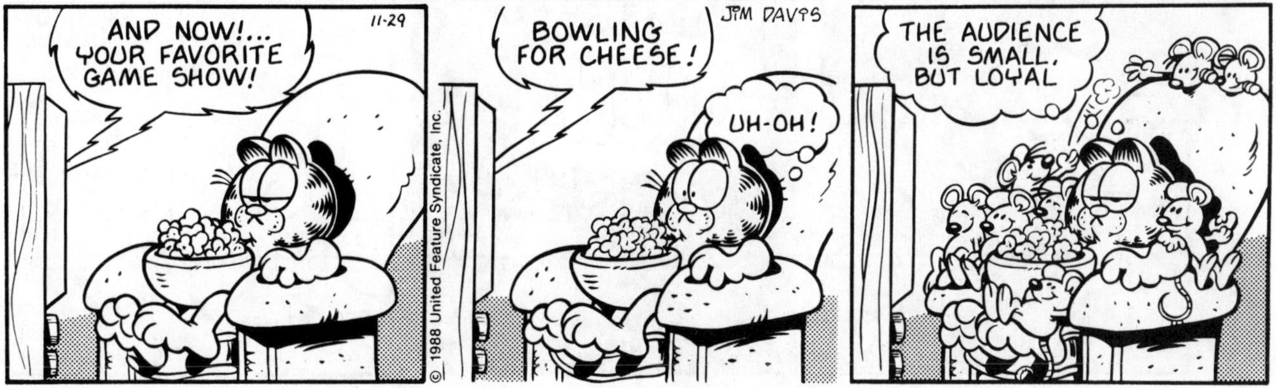
11-29
AND NOW!... YOUR FAVORITE GAME SHOW!
© 1988 United Feature Syndicate, Inc.
JIM DAVIS
BOWLING FOR CHEESE!
UH-OH!
THE AUDIENCE IS SMALL, BUT LOYAL

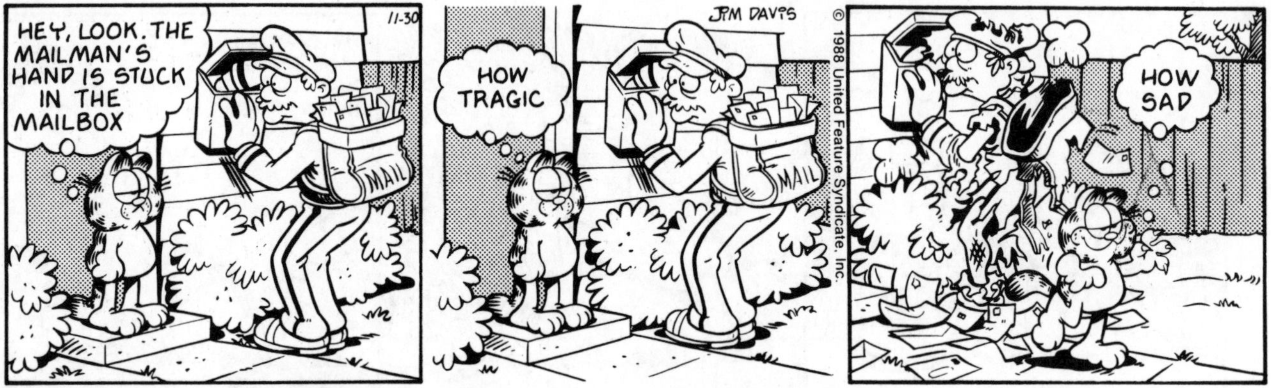
11-30
HEY, LOOK. THE MAILMAN'S HAND IS STUCK IN THE MAILBOX
HOW TRAGIC
JIM DAVIS
© 1988 United Feature Syndicate, Inc.
MAIL
HOW SAD

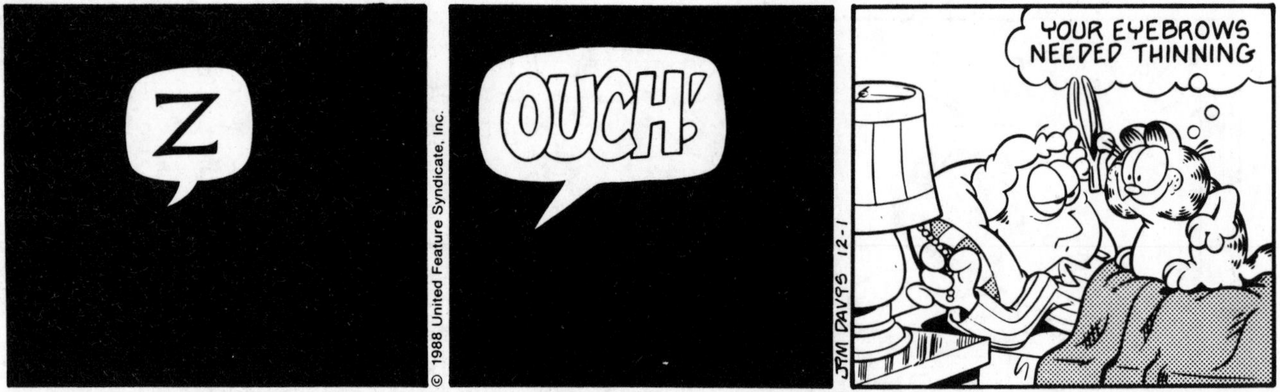
Z
© 1988 United Feature Syndicate, Inc.
OUCH!
JIM DAVIS 12-1
YOUR EYEBROWS NEEDED THINNING

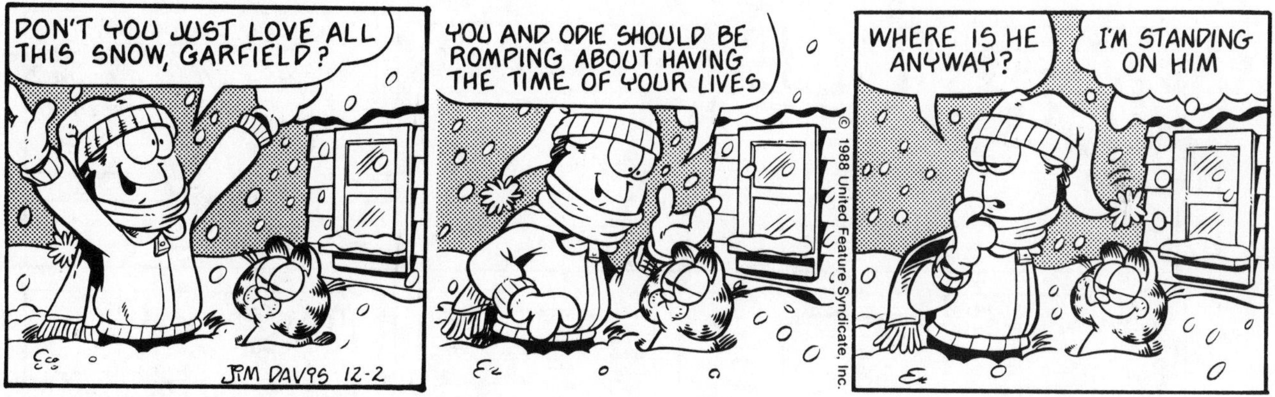
DON'T YOU JUST LOVE ALL THIS SNOW, GARFIELD?
JIM DAVIS 12-2
YOU AND ODIE SHOULD BE ROMPING ABOUT HAVING THE TIME OF YOUR LIVES
© 1988 United Feature Syndicate, Inc.
WHERE IS HE ANYWAY?
I'M STANDING ON HIM

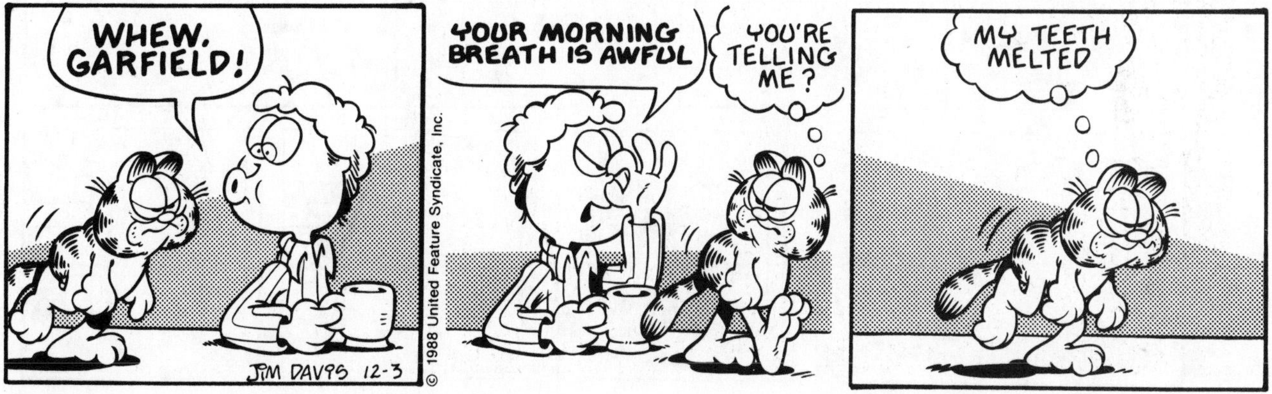
WHEW. GARFIELD!
JIM DAVIS 12-3
© 1988 United Feature Syndicate, Inc.
YOUR MORNING BREATH IS AWFUL
YOU'RE TELLING ME?
MY TEETH MELTED

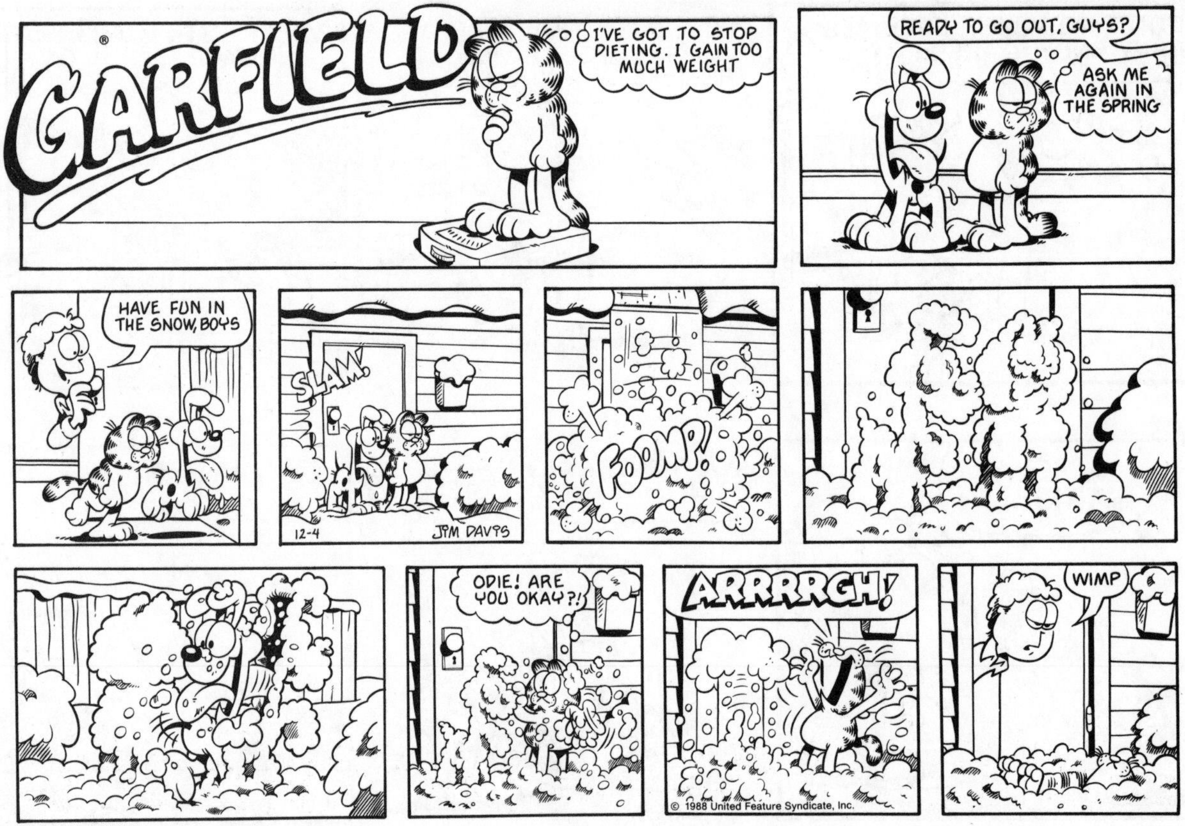
GARFIELD®
I'VE GOT TO STOP DIETING. I GAIN TOO MUCH WEIGHT
READY TO GO OUT, GUYS?
ASK ME AGAIN IN THE SPRING
HAVE FUN IN THE SNOW, BOYS
SLAM!
12-4
JIM DAVIS
FOOMP!
ODIE! ARE YOU OKAY?!
ARRRRGH!
© 1988 United Feature Syndicate, Inc.
WIMP

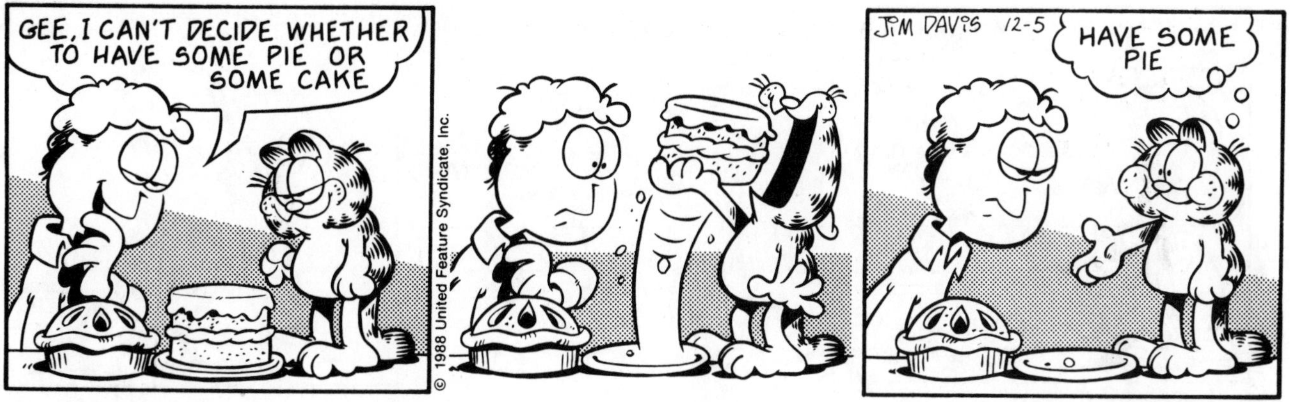
GEE, I CAN'T DECIDE WHETHER TO HAVE SOME PIE OR SOME CAKE
© 1988 United Feature Syndicate, Inc.
JIM DAVIS 12-5
HAVE SOME PIE

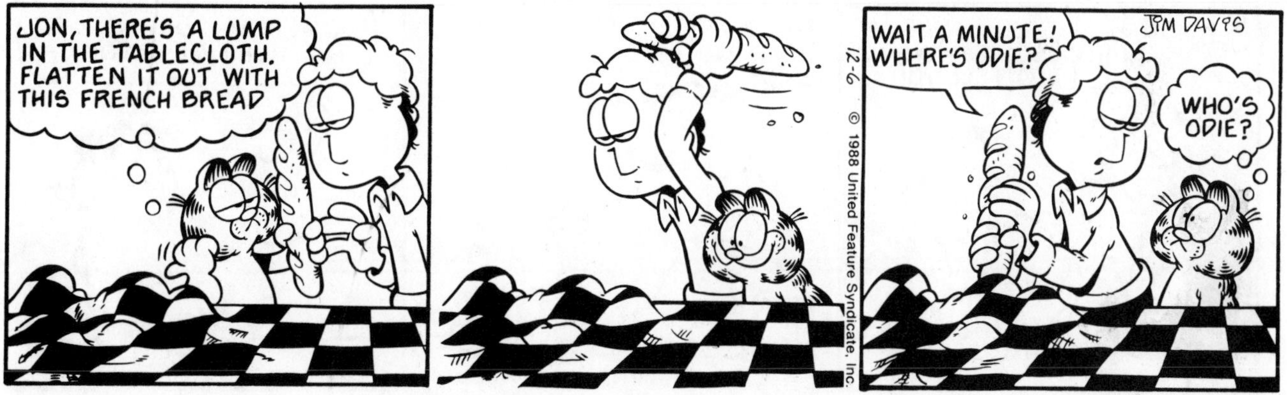
JON, THERE'S A LUMP IN THE TABLECLOTH. FLATTEN IT OUT WITH THIS FRENCH BREAD
12-6 © 1988 United Feature Syndicate, Inc.
WAIT A MINUTE! WHERE'S ODIE?
JIM DAVIS
WHO'S ODIE?

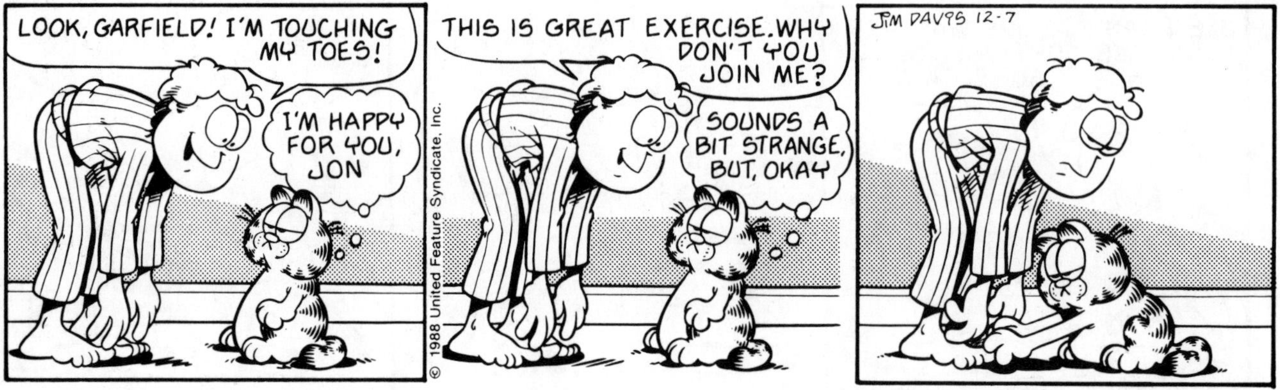
LOOK, GARFIELD! I'M TOUCHING MY TOES!
I'M HAPPY FOR YOU, JON
© 1988 United Feature Syndicate, Inc.
THIS IS GREAT EXERCISE. WHY DON'T YOU JOIN ME?
SOUNDS A BIT STRANGE, BUT, OKAY
JIM DAVIS 12-7

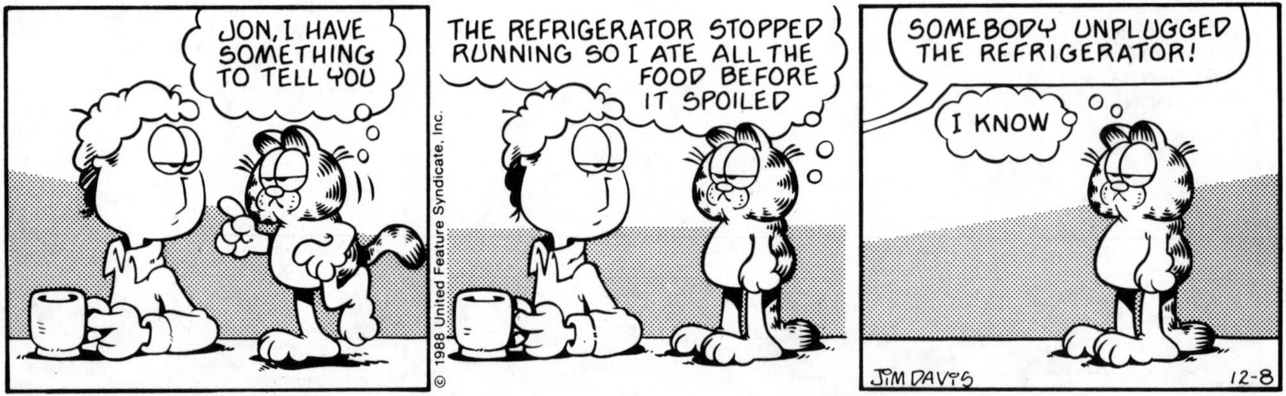
JON, I HAVE SOMETHING TO TELL YOU
© 1988 United Feature Syndicate, Inc.
THE REFRIGERATOR STOPPED RUNNING SO I ATE ALL THE FOOD BEFORE IT SPOILED
SOMEBODY UNPLUGGED THE REFRIGERATOR!
I KNOW
JIM DAVIS
12-8

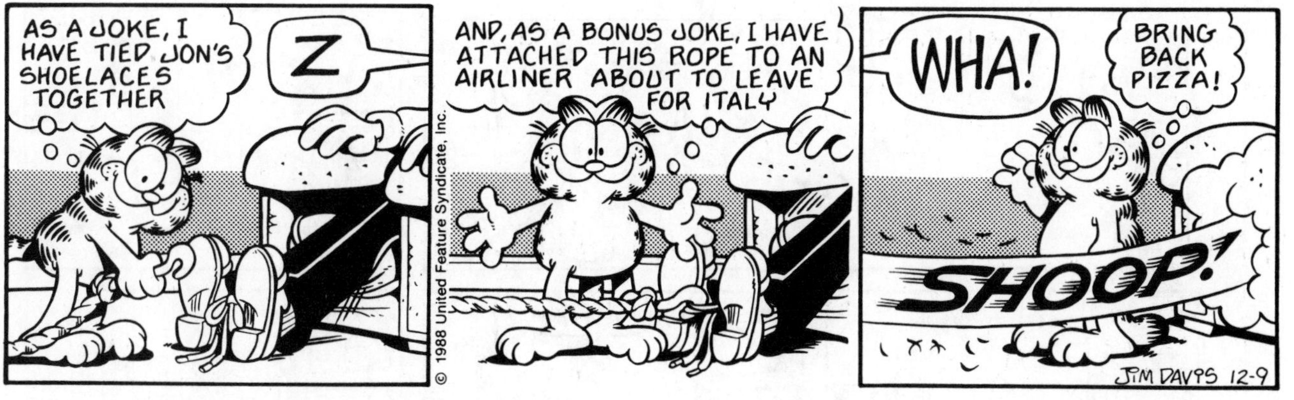
AS A JOKE, I HAVE TIED JON'S SHOELACES TOGETHER
Z
© 1988 United Feature Syndicate, Inc.
AND, AS A BONUS JOKE, I HAVE ATTACHED THIS ROPE TO AN AIRLINER ABOUT TO LEAVE FOR ITALY
WHA!
BRING BACK PIZZA!
SHOOP!
JIM DAVIS 12-9

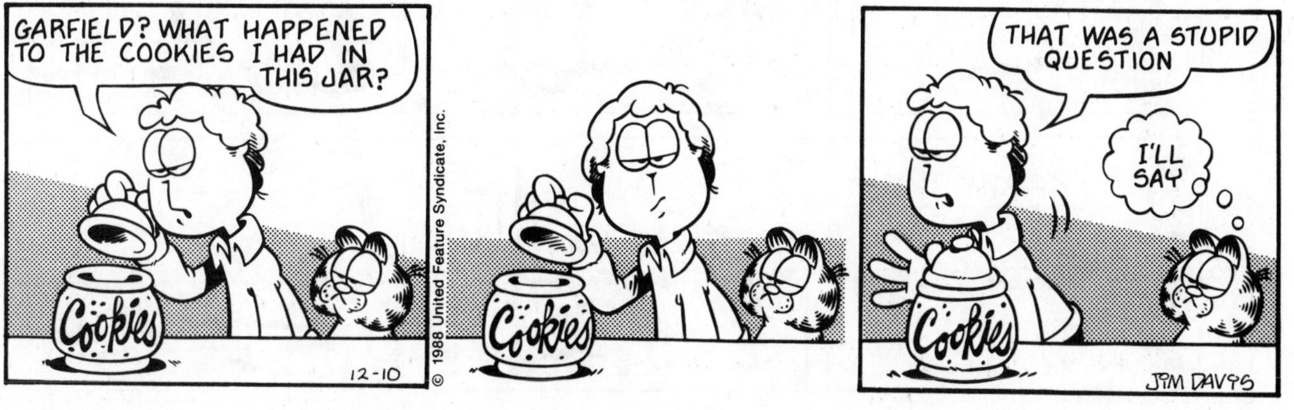
GARFIELD? WHAT HAPPENED TO THE COOKIES I HAD IN THIS JAR?
Cookies
12-10
© 1988 United Feature Syndicate, Inc.
Cookies
THAT WAS A STUPID QUESTION
I'LL SAY
Cookies
JIM DAVIS

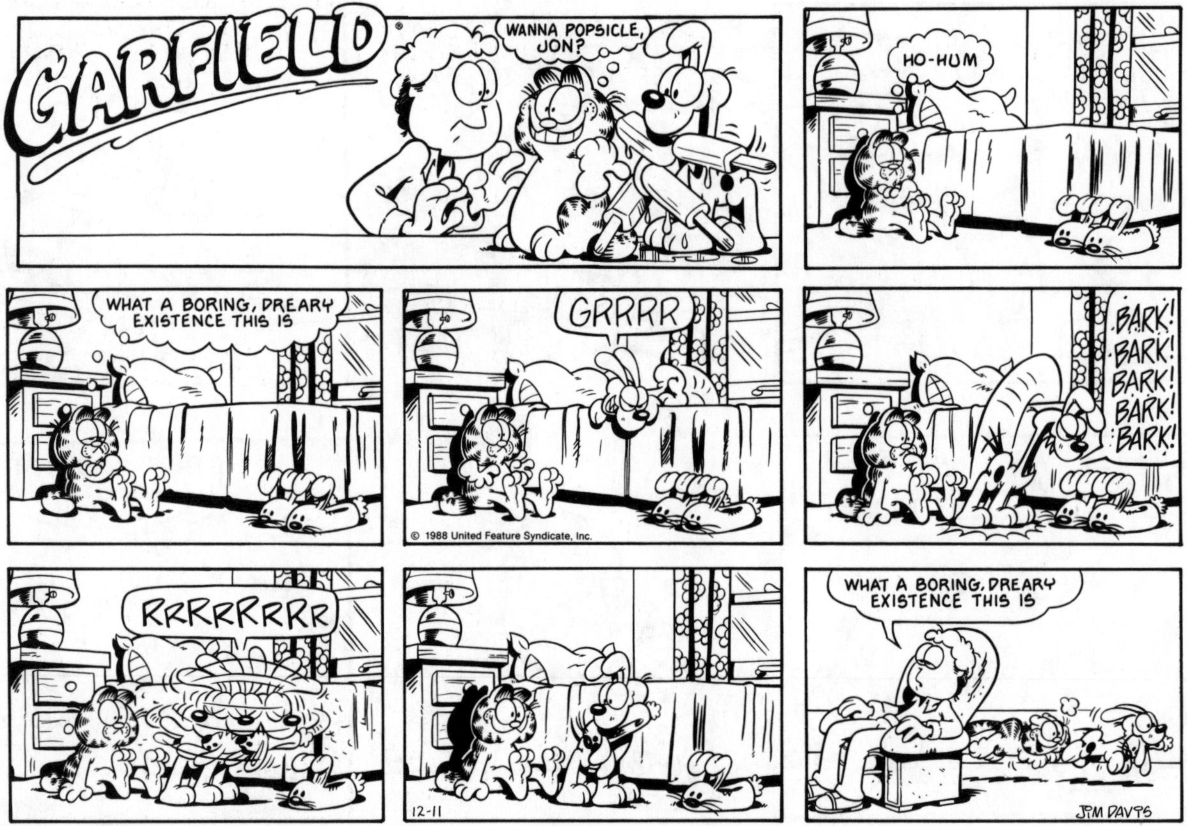
GARFIELD
WANNA POPSICLE, JON?
HO-HUM
WHAT A BORING, DREARY EXISTENCE THIS IS
GRRRR
BARK! BARK! BARK! BARK! BARK!
RRRRRRRR
12-11
WHAT A BORING, DREARY EXISTENCE THIS IS
JIM DAVIS

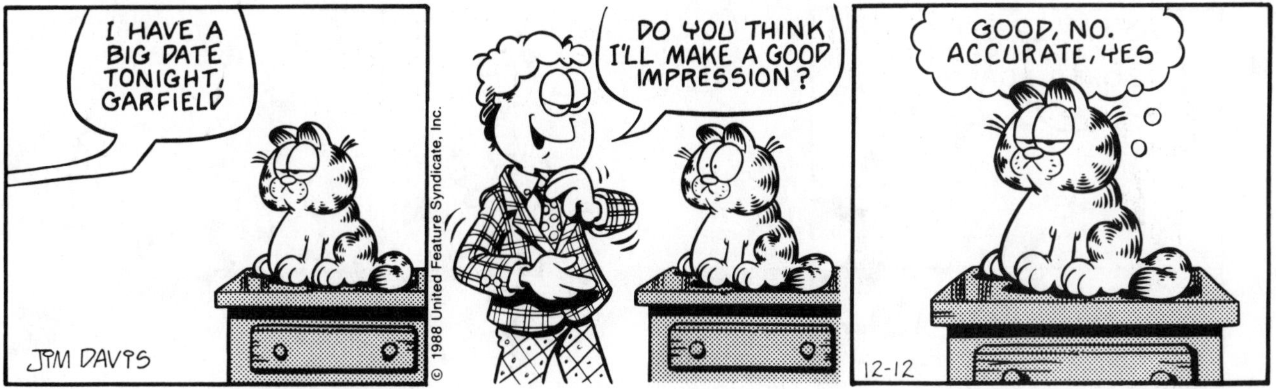
I HAVE A BIG DATE TONIGHT, GARFIELD
JIM DAVIS
© 1988 United Feature Syndicate, Inc.
DO YOU THINK I'LL MAKE A GOOD IMPRESSION?
GOOD, NO. ACCURATE, YES
12-12

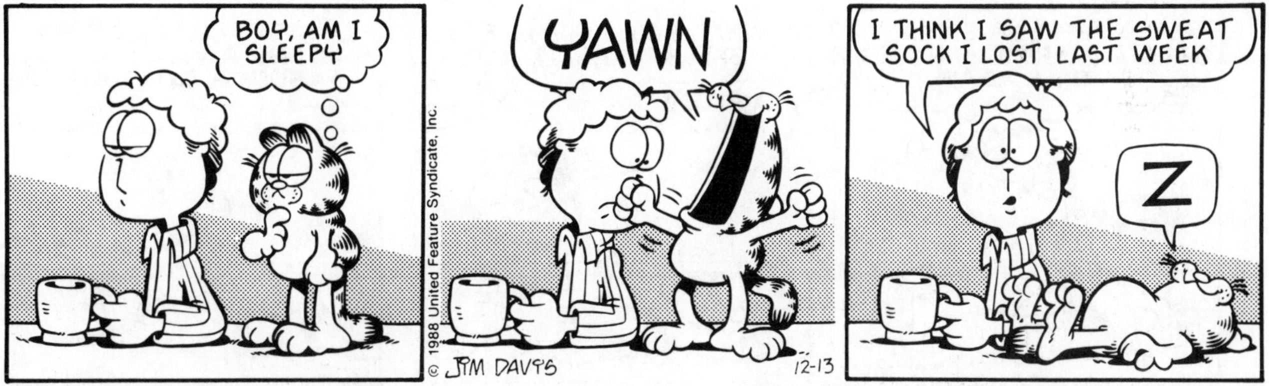
BOY, AM I SLEEPY
© 1988 United Feature Syndicate, Inc.
YAWN
JIM DAVIS
12-13
I THINK I SAW THE SWEAT SOCK I LOST LAST WEEK
Z

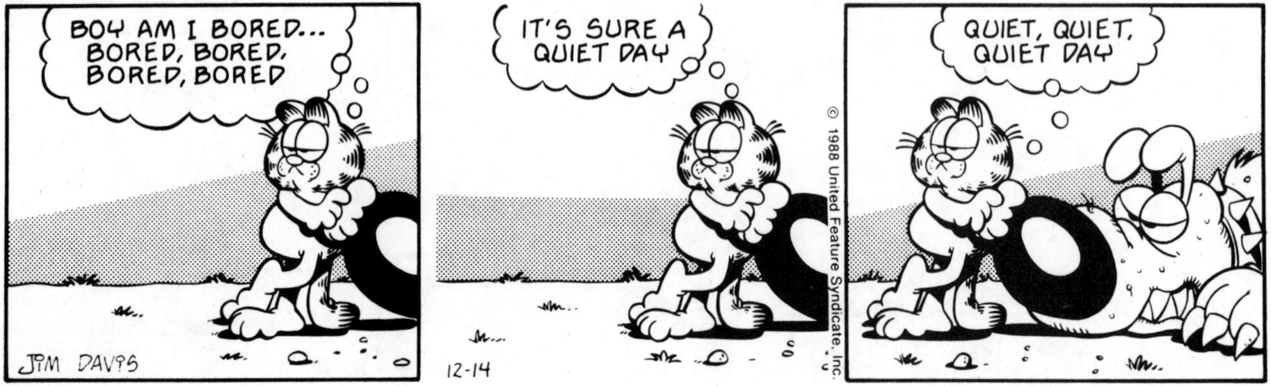
BOY AM I BORED...
BORED, BORED,
BORED, BORED
IT'S SURE A QUIET DAY
QUIET, QUIET, QUIET DAY
JIM DAVIS
12-14
© 1988 United Feature Syndicate, Inc.

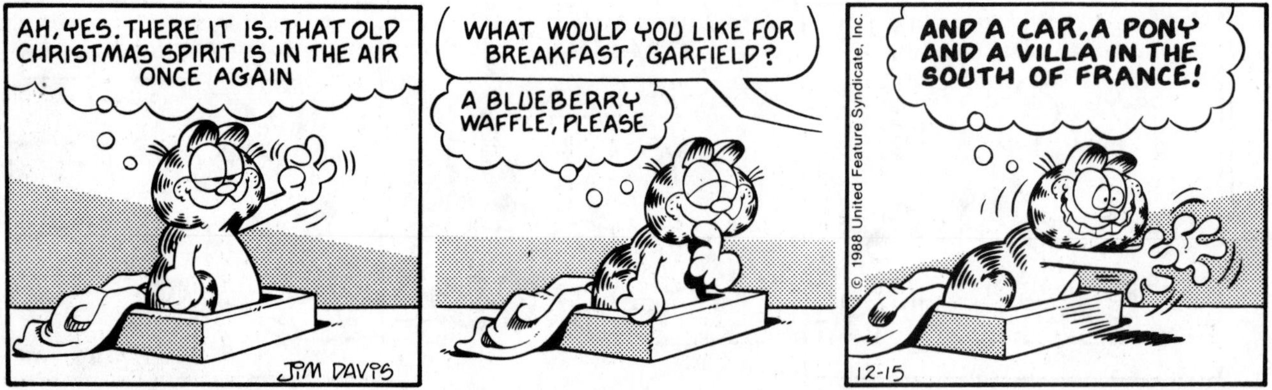
AH, YES. THERE IT IS. THAT OLD CHRISTMAS SPIRIT IS IN THE AIR ONCE AGAIN
JIM DAVIS
WHAT WOULD YOU LIKE FOR BREAKFAST, GARFIELD?
A BLUEBERRY WAFFLE, PLEASE
AND A CAR, A PONY AND A VILLA IN THE SOUTH OF FRANCE!
© 1988 United Feature Syndicate, Inc.
12-15

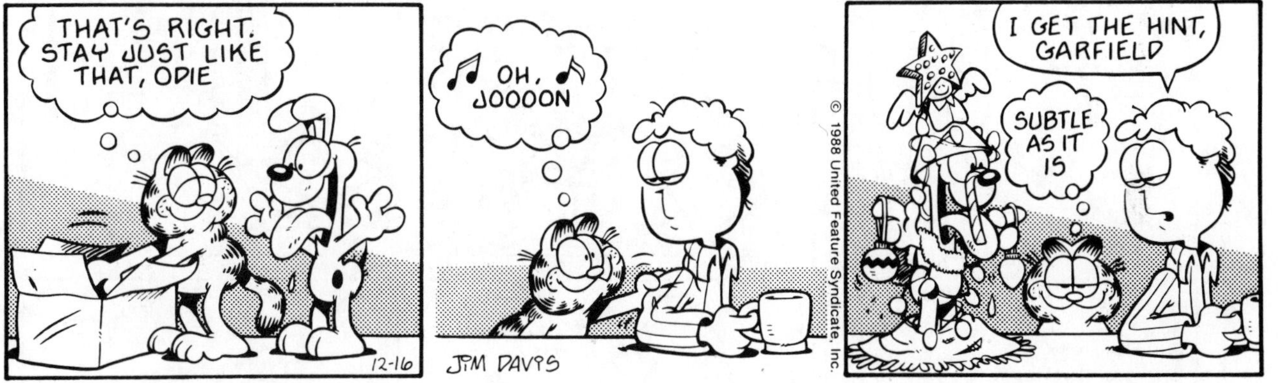
THAT'S RIGHT. STAY JUST LIKE THAT, ODIE
12-16
OH, JOOOON
JIM DAVIS
SUBTLE AS IT IS
I GET THE HINT, GARFIELD
© 1988 United Feature Syndicate, Inc.

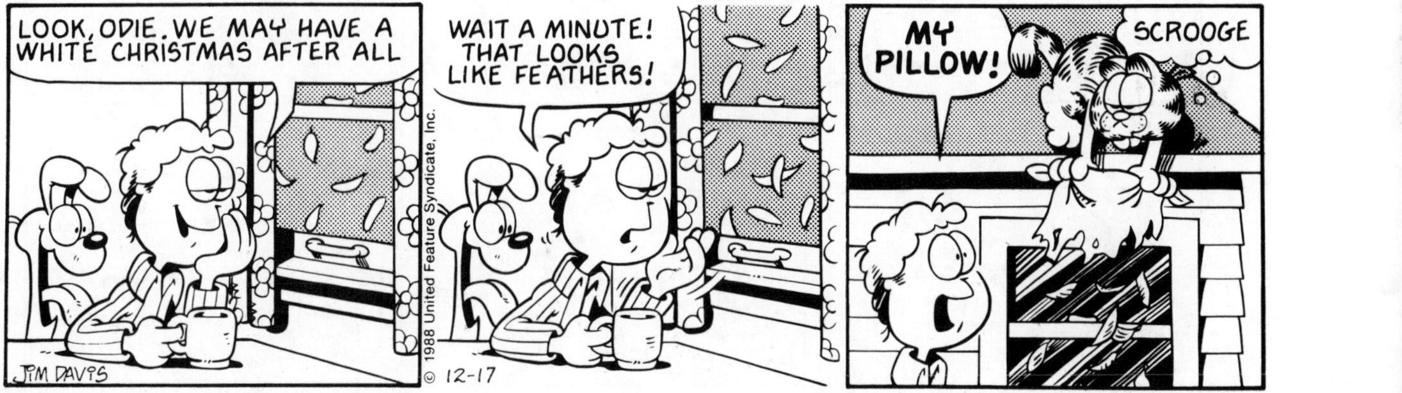
LOOK, ODIE. WE MAY HAVE A WHITE CHRISTMAS AFTER ALL
JIM DAVIS
© 1988 United Feature Syndicate, Inc.
WAIT A MINUTE! THAT LOOKS LIKE FEATHERS!
12-17
MY PILLOW!
SCROOGE

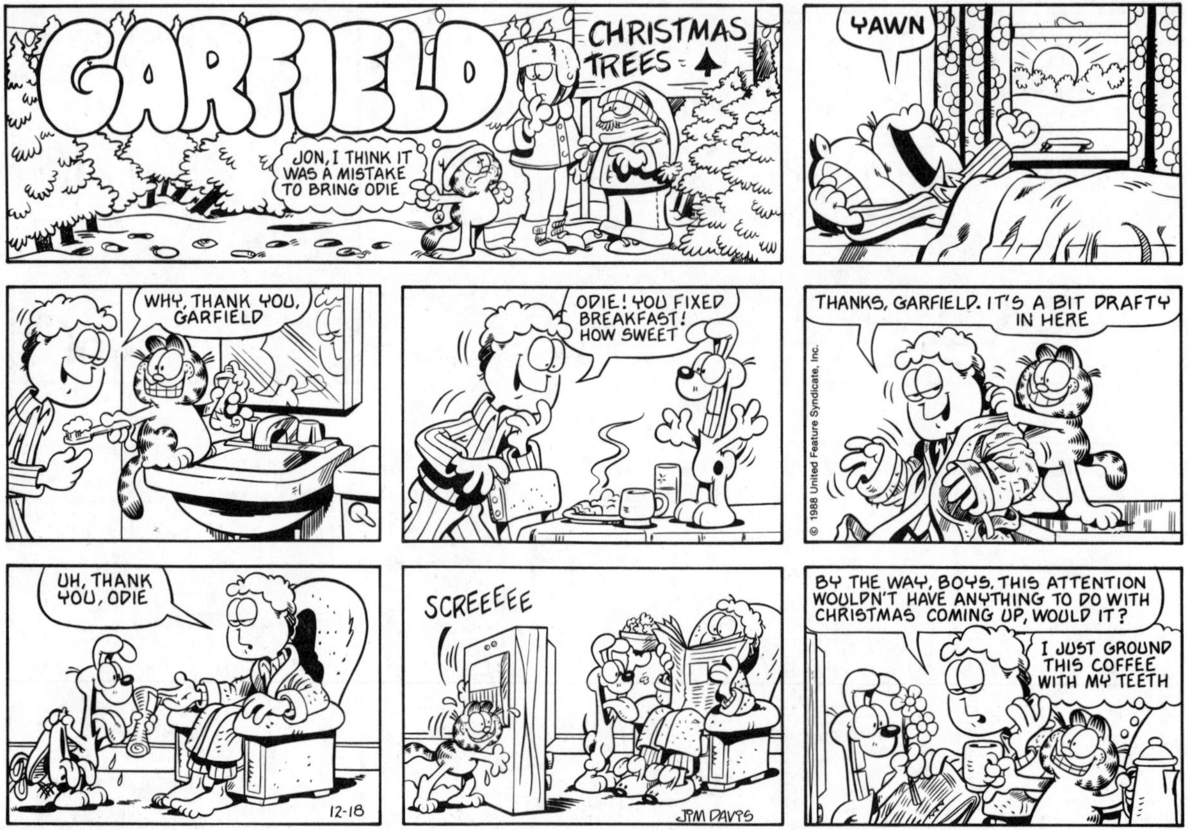
GARFIELD
CHRISTMAS TREES
JON, I THINK IT WAS A MISTAKE TO BRING ODIE
YAWN
WHY, THANK YOU, GARFIELD
ODIE! YOU FIXED BREAKFAST! HOW SWEET
THANKS, GARFIELD. IT'S A BIT DRAFTY IN HERE
© 1988 United Feature Syndicate, Inc.
UH, THANK YOU, ODIE
12-18
SCREEEEEE
JIM DAVIS
BY THE WAY, BOYS, THIS ATTENTION WOULDN'T HAVE ANYTHING TO DO WITH CHRISTMAS COMING UP, WOULD IT?
I JUST GROUND THIS COFFEE WITH MY TEETH

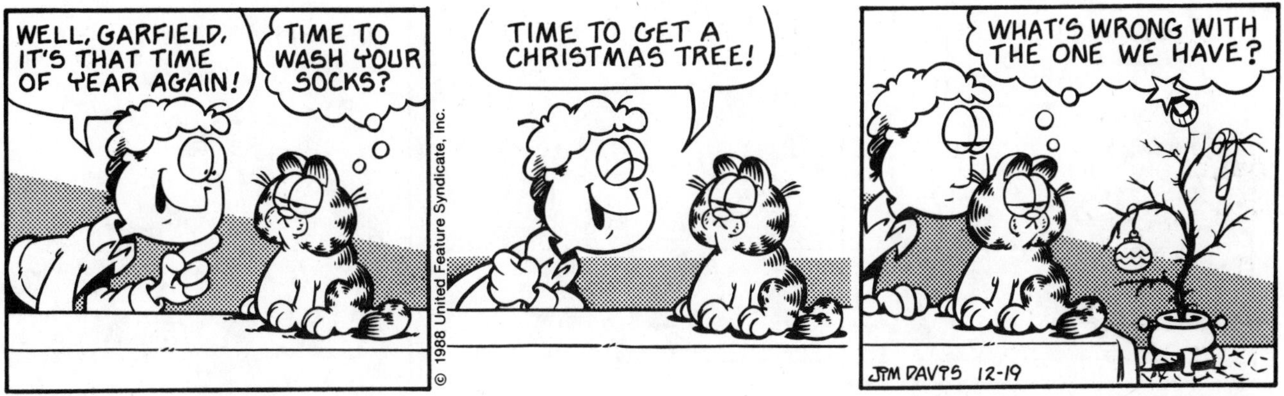
WELL, GARFIELD, IT'S THAT TIME OF YEAR AGAIN!
TIME TO WASH YOUR SOCKS?
TIME TO GET A CHRISTMAS TREE!
WHAT'S WRONG WITH THE ONE WE HAVE?
JIM DAVIS 12-19
© 1988 United Feature Syndicate, Inc.

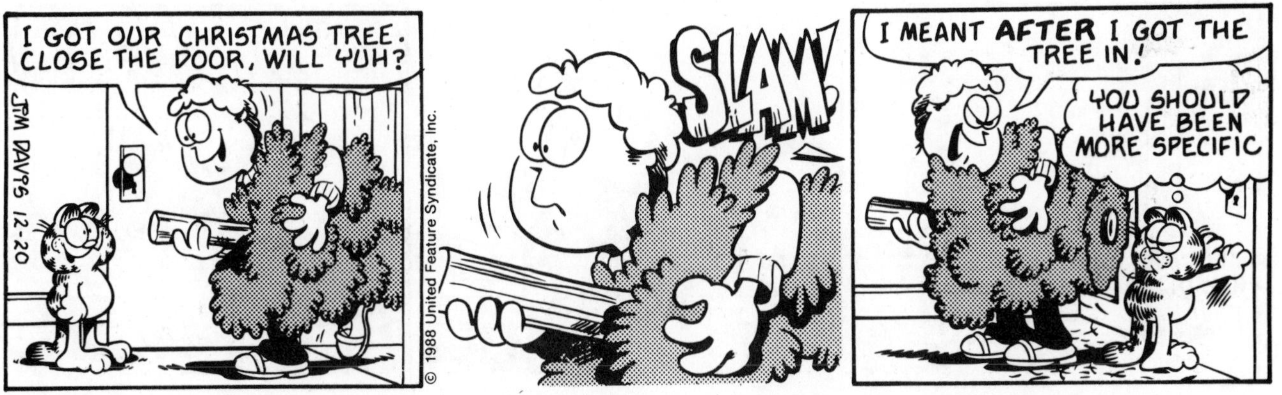
I GOT OUR CHRISTMAS TREE. CLOSE THE DOOR, WILL YUH?
JIM DAVIS 12-20
© 1988 United Feature Syndicate, Inc.
SLAM!
I MEANT **AFTER** I GOT THE TREE IN!
YOU SHOULD HAVE BEEN MORE SPECIFIC

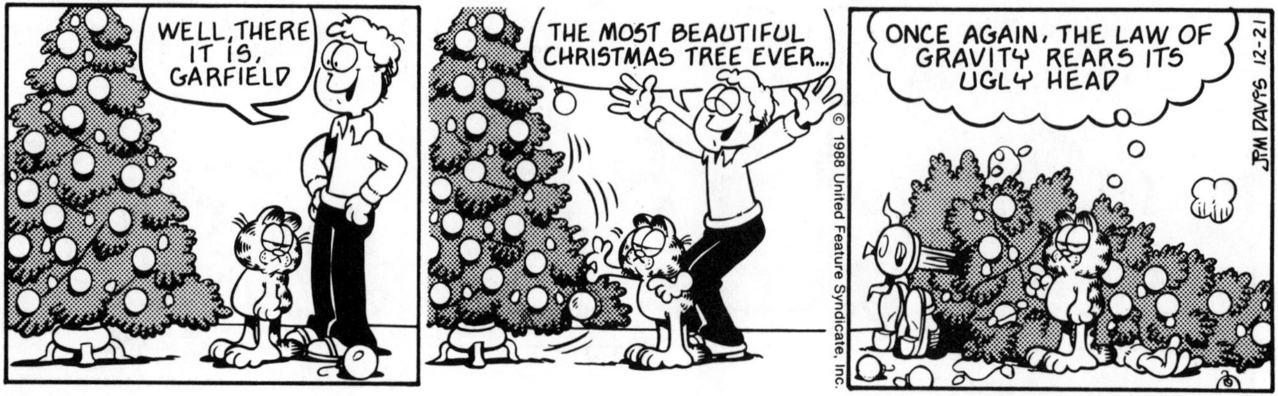
WELL, THERE IT IS, GARFIELD
THE MOST BEAUTIFUL CHRISTMAS TREE EVER...
© 1988 United Feature Syndicate, Inc.
ONCE AGAIN, THE LAW OF GRAVITY REARS ITS UGLY HEAD
JIM DAVIS 12-21

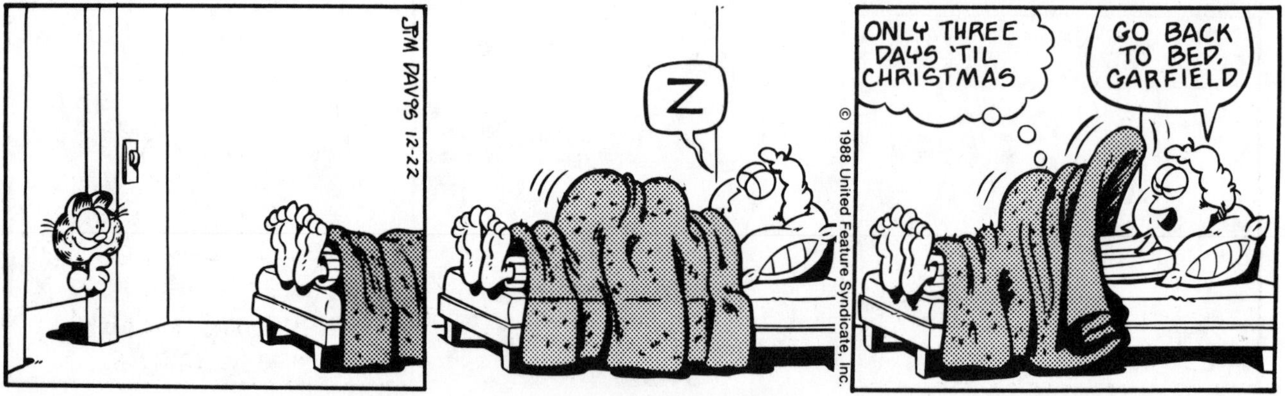
JIM DAVIS 12-22
Z
© 1988 United Feature Syndicate, Inc.
ONLY THREE DAYS 'TIL CHRISTMAS
GO BACK TO BED, GARFIELD

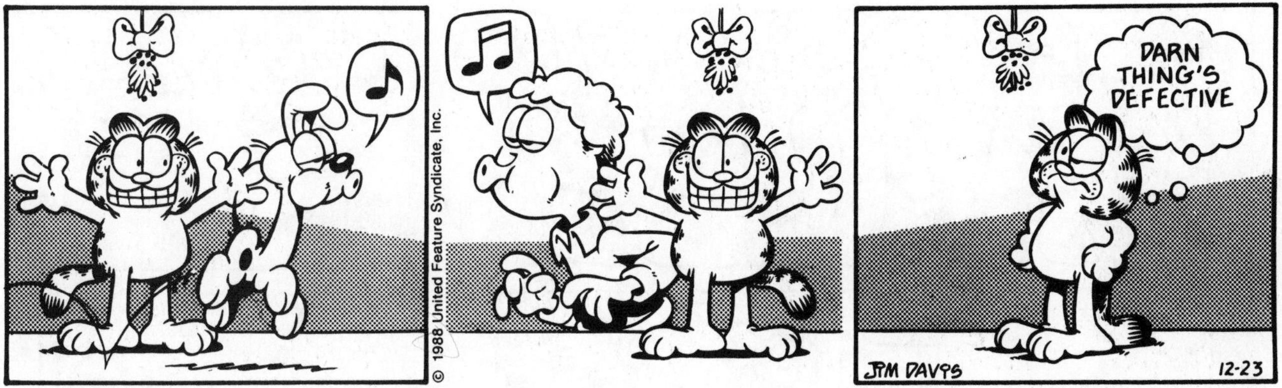
DARN THING'S DEFECTIVE
© 1988 United Feature Syndicate, Inc.
JIM DAVIS
12-23

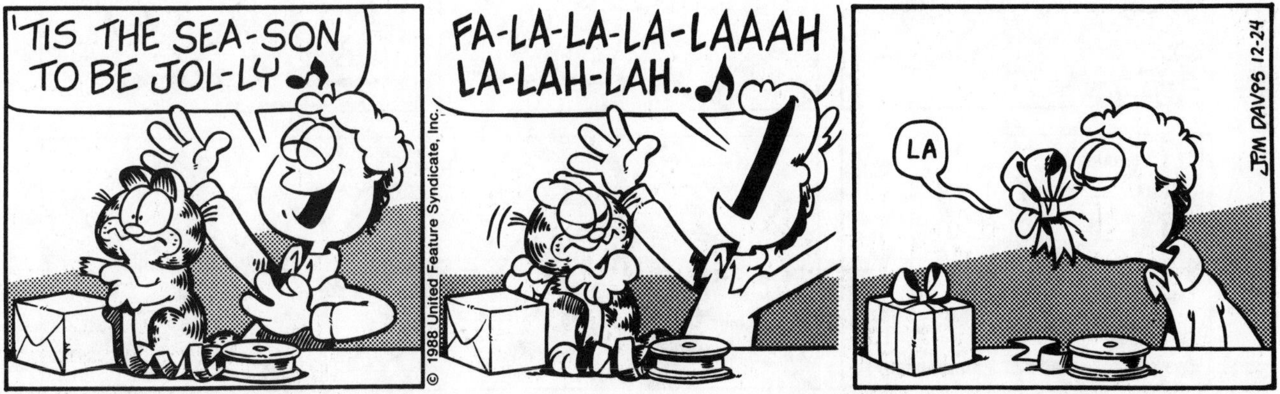
'TIS THE SEA-SON TO BE JOL-LY
FA-LA-LA-LA-LAAAH LA-LAH-LAH...
LA
© 1988 United Feature Syndicate, Inc.
JIM DAVIS 12-24

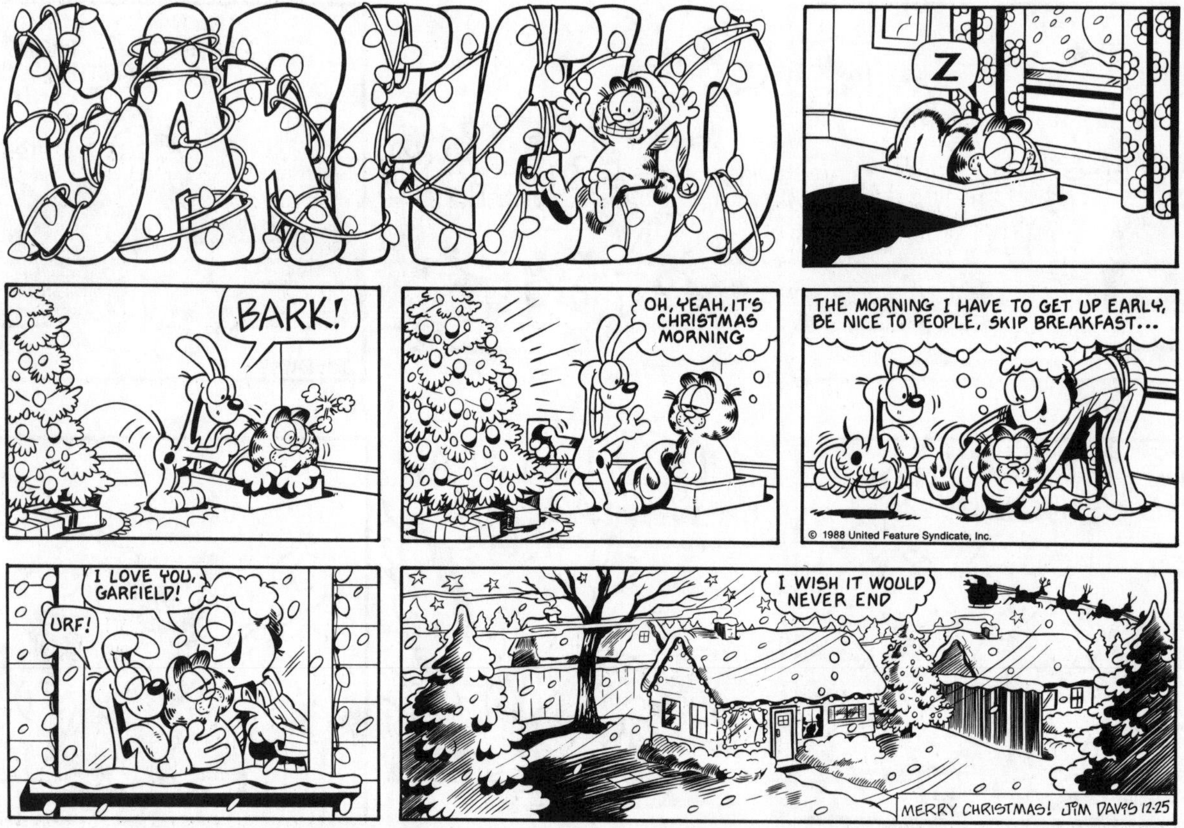

GARFIELD
Z
BARK!
OH, YEAH, IT'S CHRISTMAS MORNING
THE MORNING I HAVE TO GET UP EARLY, BE NICE TO PEOPLE, SKIP BREAKFAST...
© 1988 United Feature Syndicate, Inc.
I LOVE YOU, GARFIELD!
URF!
I WISH IT WOULD NEVER END
MERRY CHRISTMAS! JIM DAVIS 12-25

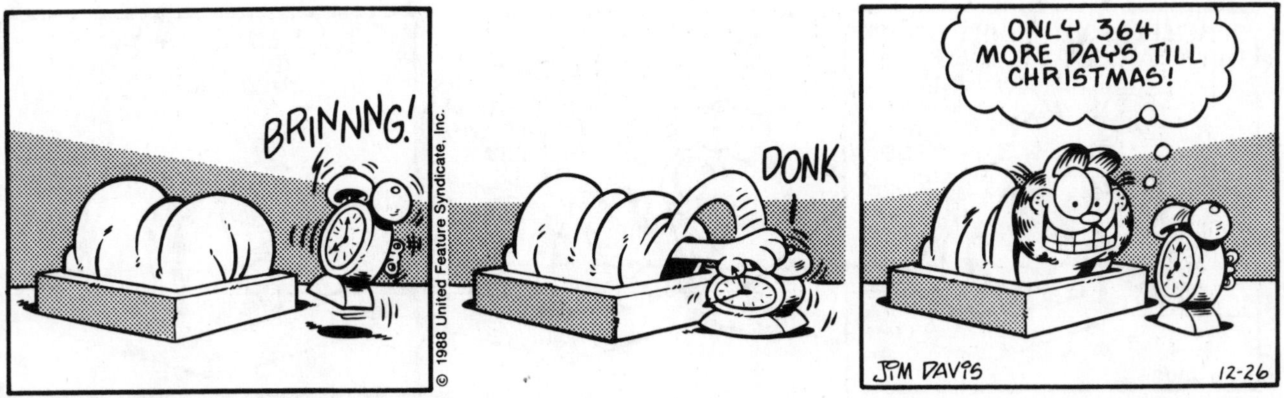
BRINNNG!
© 1988 United Feature Syndicate, Inc.
DONK
ONLY 364 MORE DAYS TILL CHRISTMAS!
JIM DAVIS
12-26

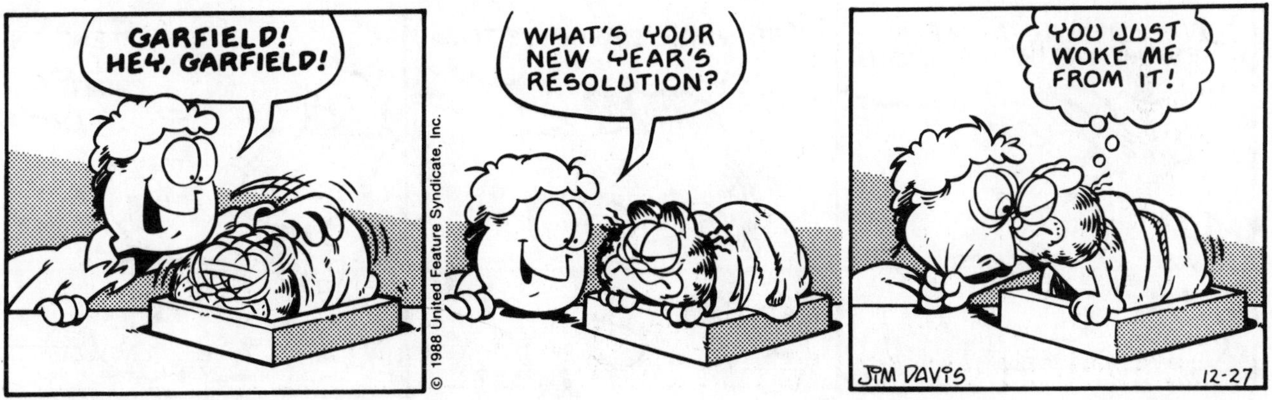
GARFIELD! HEY, GARFIELD!
© 1988 United Feature Syndicate, Inc.
WHAT'S YOUR NEW YEAR'S RESOLUTION?
YOU JUST WOKE ME FROM IT!
JIM DAVIS
12-27

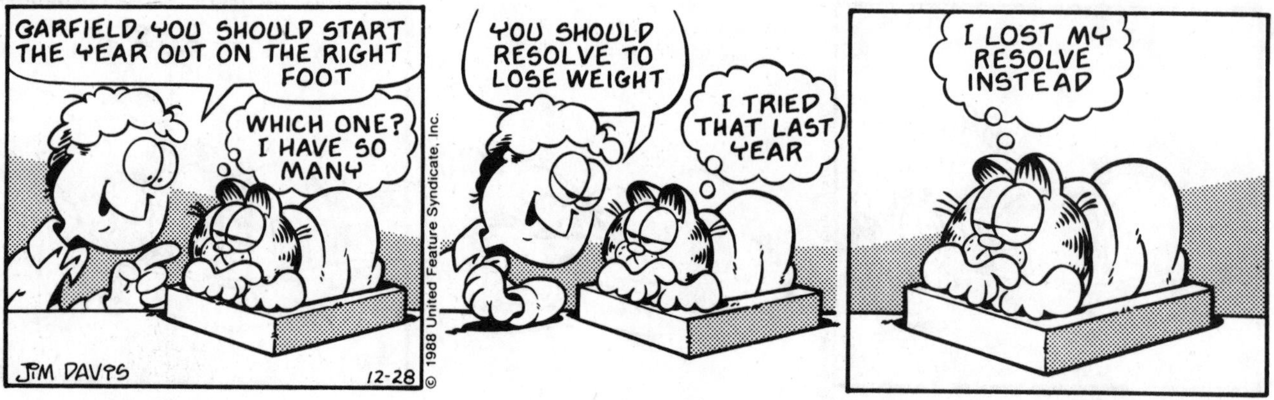
GARFIELD, YOU SHOULD START THE YEAR OUT ON THE RIGHT FOOT
WHICH ONE? I HAVE SO MANY
JIM DAVIS
12-28
© 1988 United Feature Syndicate, Inc.
YOU SHOULD RESOLVE TO LOSE WEIGHT
I TRIED THAT LAST YEAR
I LOST MY RESOLVE INSTEAD

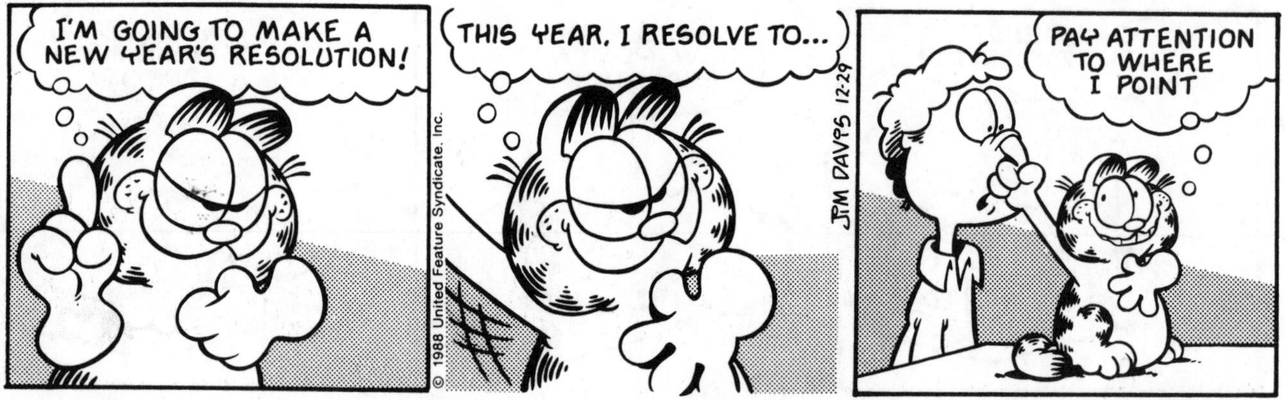
I'M GOING TO MAKE A NEW YEAR'S RESOLUTION!
© 1988 United Feature Syndicate, Inc.
THIS YEAR, I RESOLVE TO...
JIM DAVIS 12-29
PAY ATTENTION TO WHERE I POINT

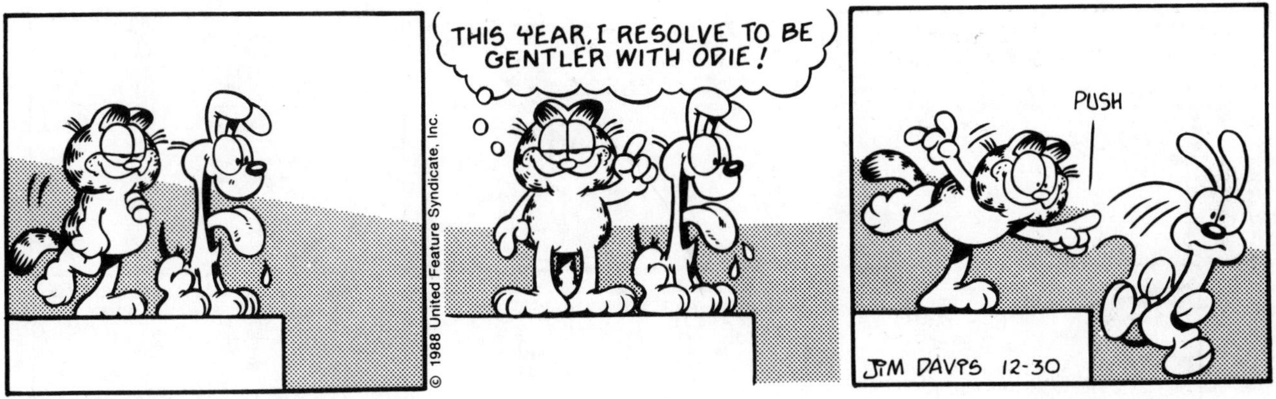
THIS YEAR, I RESOLVE TO BE GENTLER WITH ODIE!
PUSH
© 1988 United Feature Syndicate, Inc.
JIM DAVIS 12-30

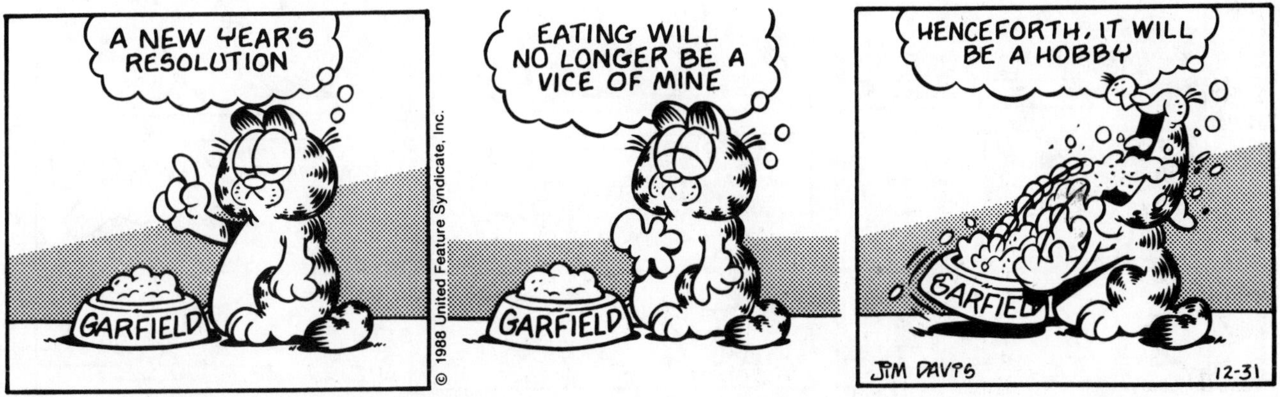
A NEW YEAR'S RESOLUTION
GARFIELD
EATING WILL NO LONGER BE A VICE OF MINE
GARFIELD
HENCEFORTH, IT WILL BE A HOBBY
GARFIELD
© 1988 United Feature Syndicate, Inc.
JIM DAVIS
12-31

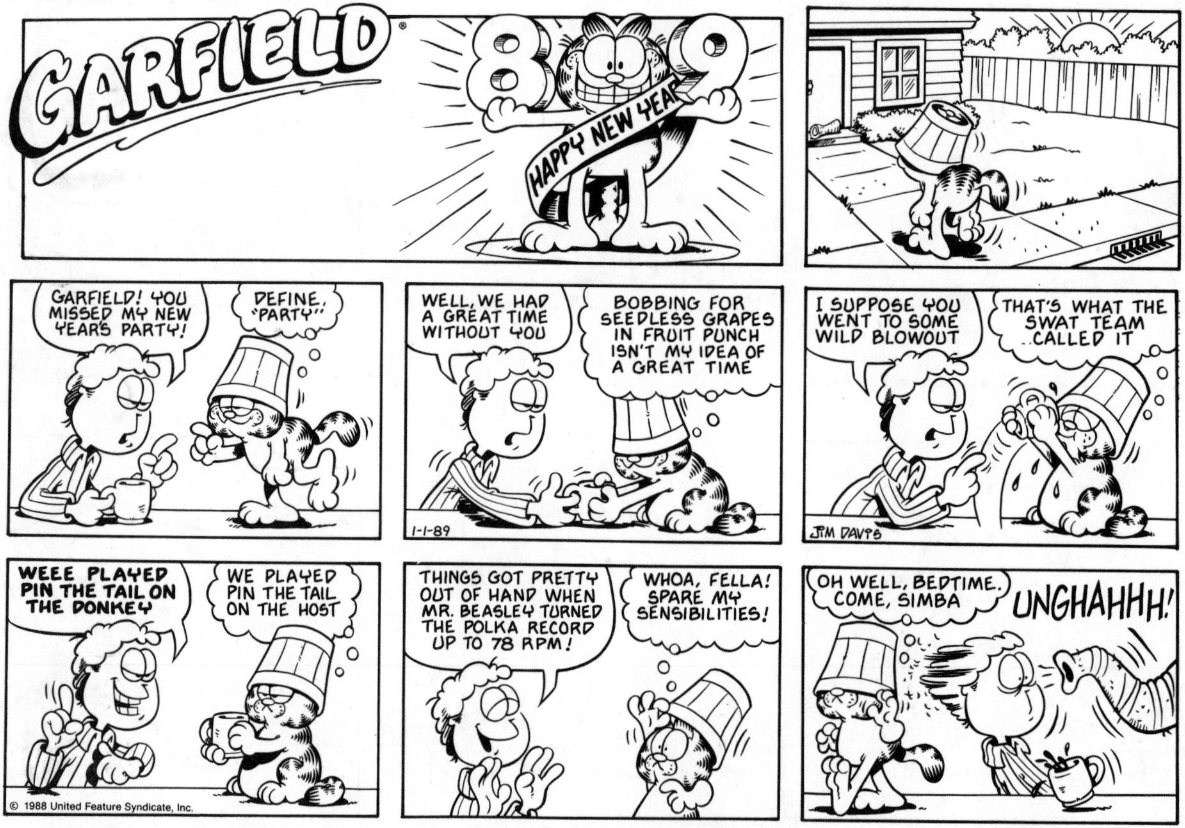
GARFIELD®
89
HAPPY NEW YEAR
GARFIELD! YOU MISSED MY NEW YEAR'S PARTY!
DEFINE "PARTY"
WELL, WE HAD A GREAT TIME WITHOUT YOU
BOBBING FOR SEEDLESS GRAPES IN FRUIT PUNCH ISN'T MY IDEA OF A GREAT TIME
1-1-89
I SUPPOSE YOU WENT TO SOME WILD BLOWOUT
THAT'S WHAT THE SWAT TEAM ..CALLED IT
JIM DAVIS
WEEE PLAYED PIN THE TAIL ON THE DONKEY
WE PLAYED PIN THE TAIL ON THE HOST
THINGS GOT PRETTY OUT OF HAND WHEN MR. BEASLEY TURNED THE POLKA RECORD UP TO 78 RPM!
WHOA, FELLA! SPARE MY SENSIBILITIES!
OH WELL, BEDTIME. COME, SIMBA
UNGHAHHH!

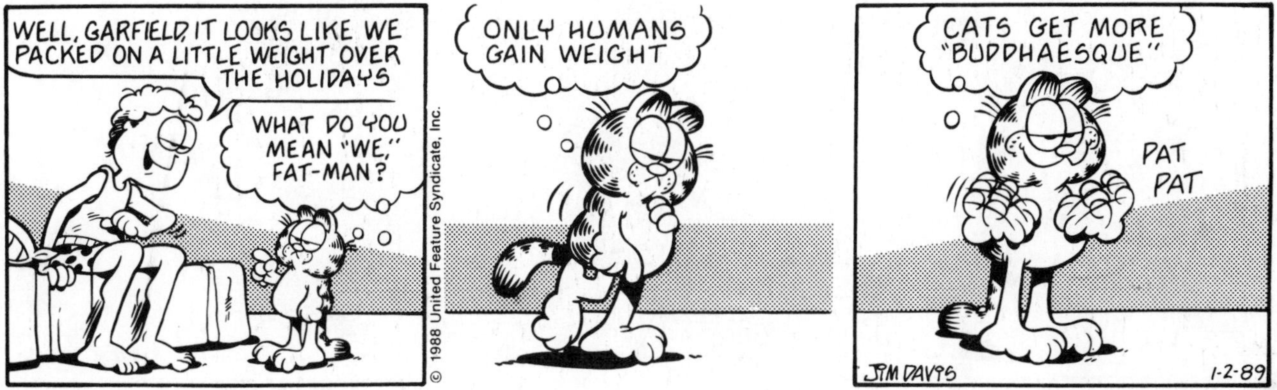
WELL, GARFIELD, IT LOOKS LIKE WE PACKED ON A LITTLE WEIGHT OVER THE HOLIDAYS
WHAT DO YOU MEAN "WE," FAT-MAN?
ONLY HUMANS GAIN WEIGHT
CATS GET MORE "BUDDHAESQUE"
PAT PAT
JIM DAVIS
1-2-89
© 1988 United Feature Syndicate, Inc.

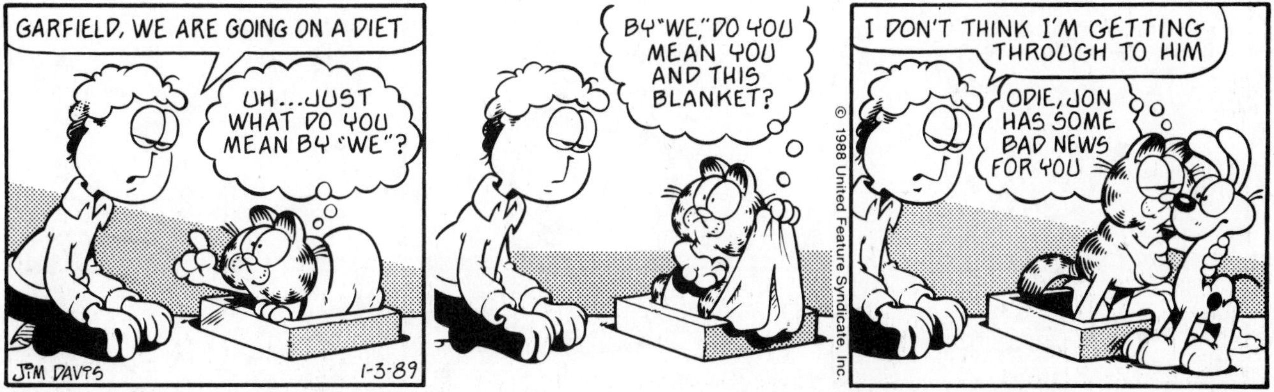
GARFIELD, WE ARE GOING ON A DIET
UH...JUST WHAT DO YOU MEAN BY "WE"?
BY "WE," DO YOU MEAN YOU AND THIS BLANKET?
I DON'T THINK I'M GETTING THROUGH TO HIM
ODIE, JON HAS SOME BAD NEWS FOR YOU
JIM DAVIS
1-3-89
© 1988 United Feature Syndicate, Inc.

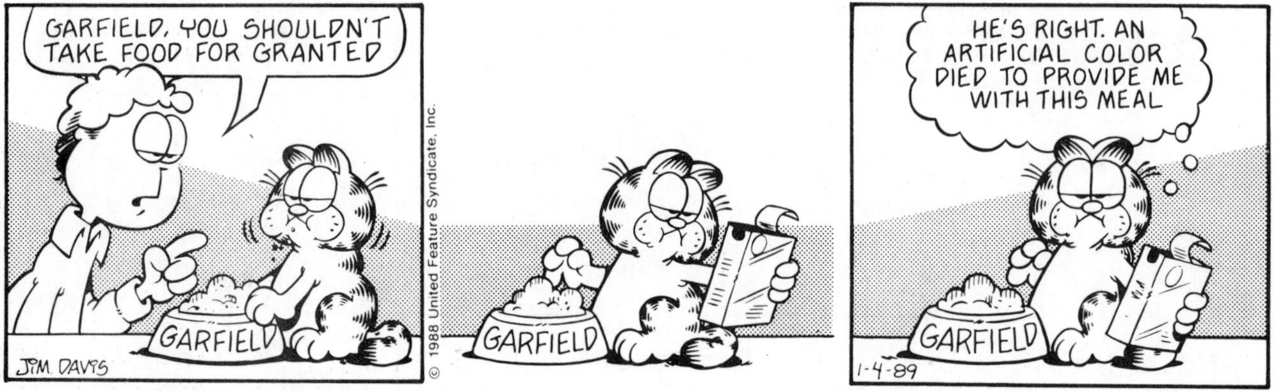
GARFIELD, YOU SHOULDN'T TAKE FOOD FOR GRANTED
GARFIELD
JIM DAVIS
© 1988 United Feature Syndicate, Inc.
GARFIELD
HE'S RIGHT. AN ARTIFICIAL COLOR DIED TO PROVIDE ME WITH THIS MEAL
GARFIELD
1-4-89

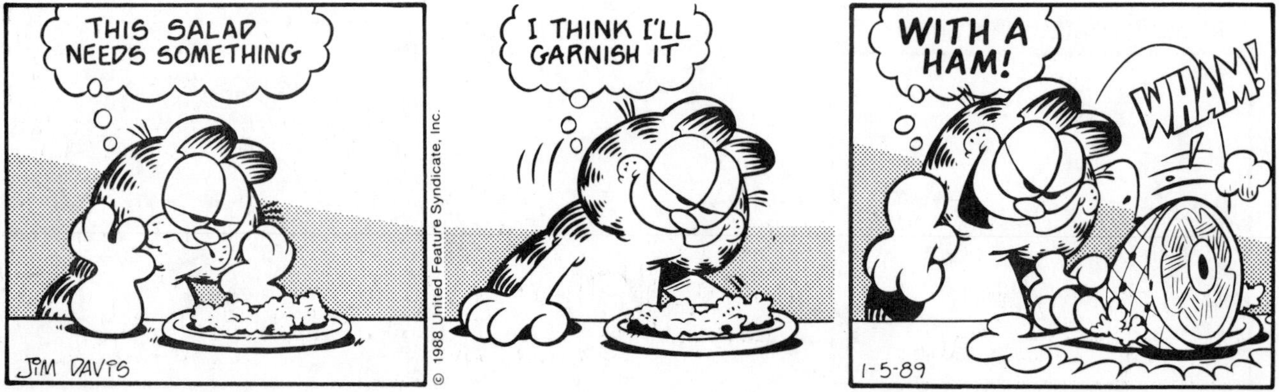
THIS SALAD NEEDS SOMETHING
JIM DAVIS
© 1988 United Feature Syndicate, Inc.
I THINK I'LL GARNISH IT
WITH A HAM!
WHAM!
1-5-89

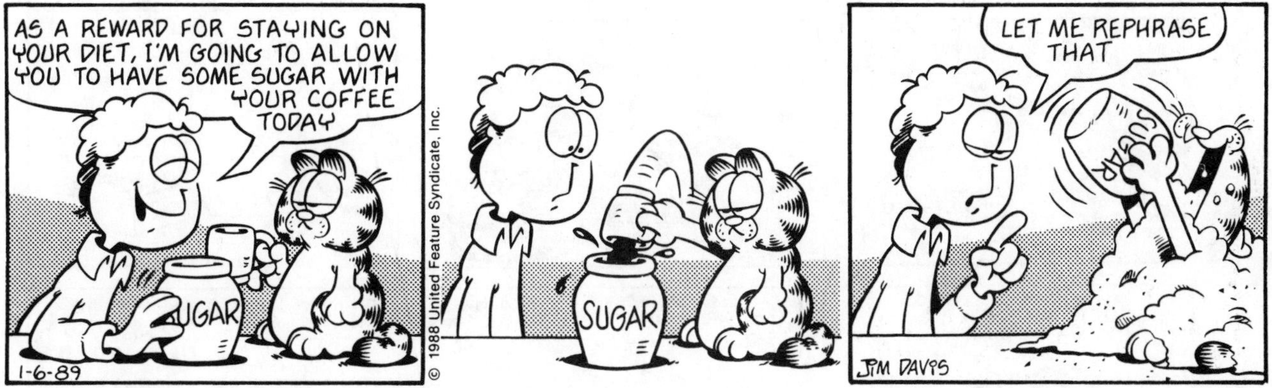
AS A REWARD FOR STAYING ON YOUR DIET, I'M GOING TO ALLOW YOU TO HAVE SOME SUGAR WITH YOUR COFFEE TODAY
SUGAR
1-6-89
© 1988 United Feature Syndicate, Inc.
SUGAR
LET ME REPHRASE THAT
SUGAR
JIM DAVIS

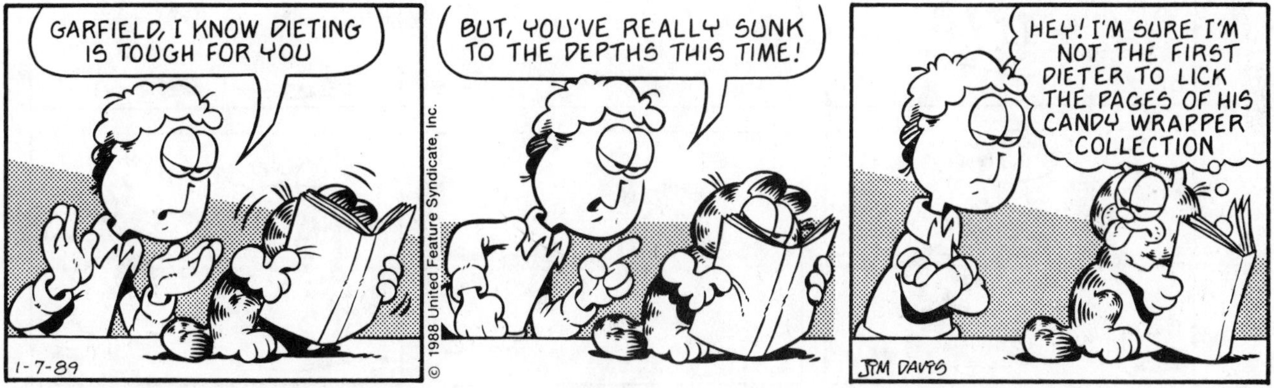
GARFIELD, I KNOW DIETING IS TOUGH FOR YOU
1-7-89
© 1988 United Feature Syndicate, Inc.
BUT, YOU'VE REALLY SUNK TO THE DEPTHS THIS TIME!
HEY! I'M SURE I'M NOT THE FIRST DIETER TO LICK THE PAGES OF HIS CANDY WRAPPER COLLECTION
JIM DAVIS

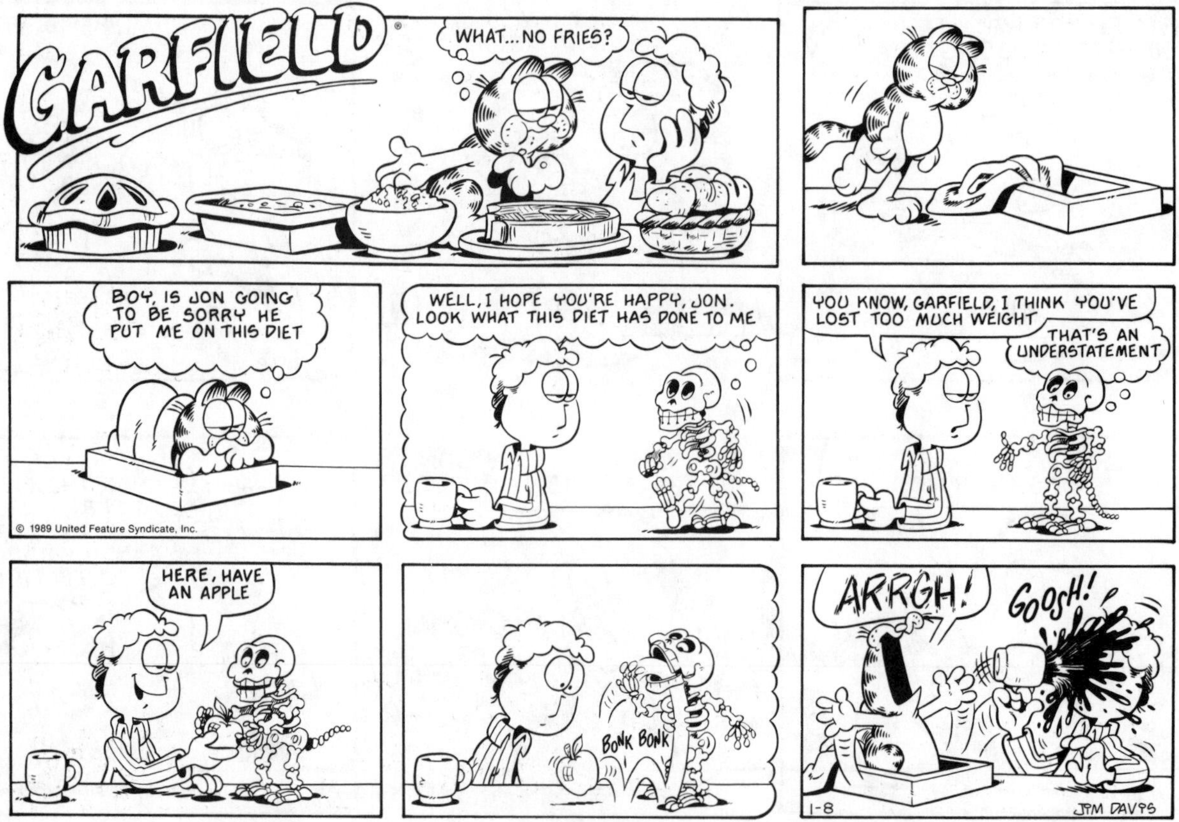
GARFIELD
WHAT... NO FRIES?
BOY, IS JON GOING TO BE SORRY HE PUT ME ON THIS DIET
WELL, I HOPE YOU'RE HAPPY, JON. LOOK WHAT THIS DIET HAS DONE TO ME
YOU KNOW, GARFIELD, I THINK YOU'VE LOST TOO MUCH WEIGHT
THAT'S AN UNDERSTATEMENT
HERE, HAVE AN APPLE
BONK BONK
ARRGH!
GOOSH!
1-8
JIM DAVIS

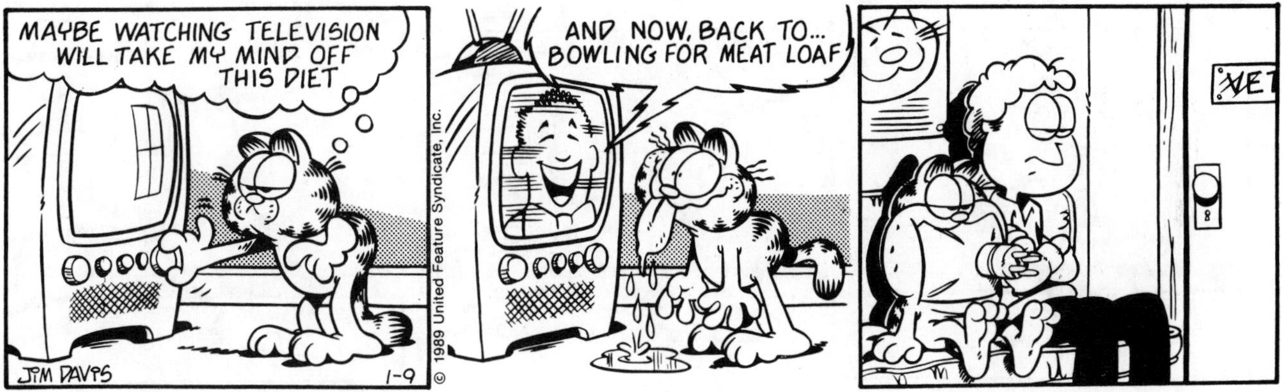
MAYBE WATCHING TELEVISION WILL TAKE MY MIND OFF THIS DIET
JIM DAVIS
1-9
© 1989 United Feature Syndicate, Inc.
AND NOW, BACK TO... BOWLING FOR MEAT LOAF
VET

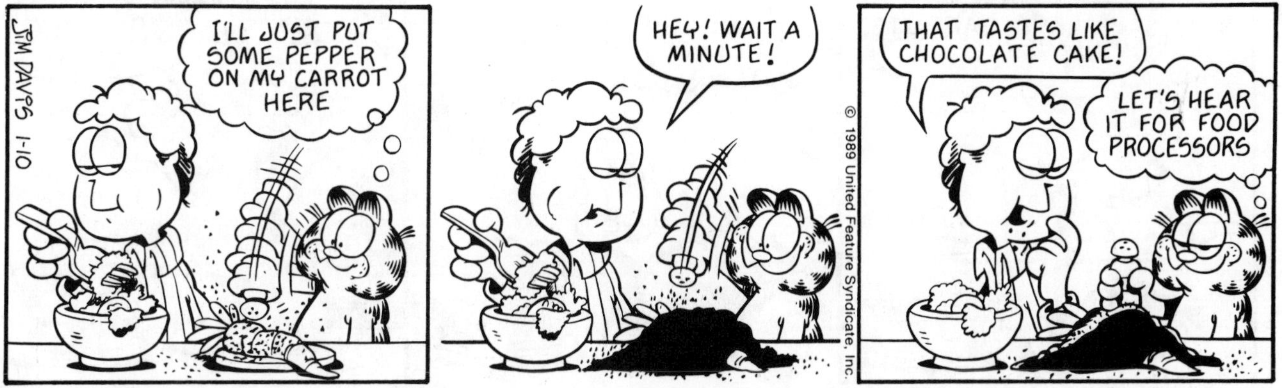
JIM DAVIS 1-10
I'LL JUST PUT SOME PEPPER ON MY CARROT HERE
HEY! WAIT A MINUTE!
© 1989 United Feature Syndicate, Inc.
THAT TASTES LIKE CHOCOLATE CAKE!
LET'S HEAR IT FOR FOOD PROCESSORS

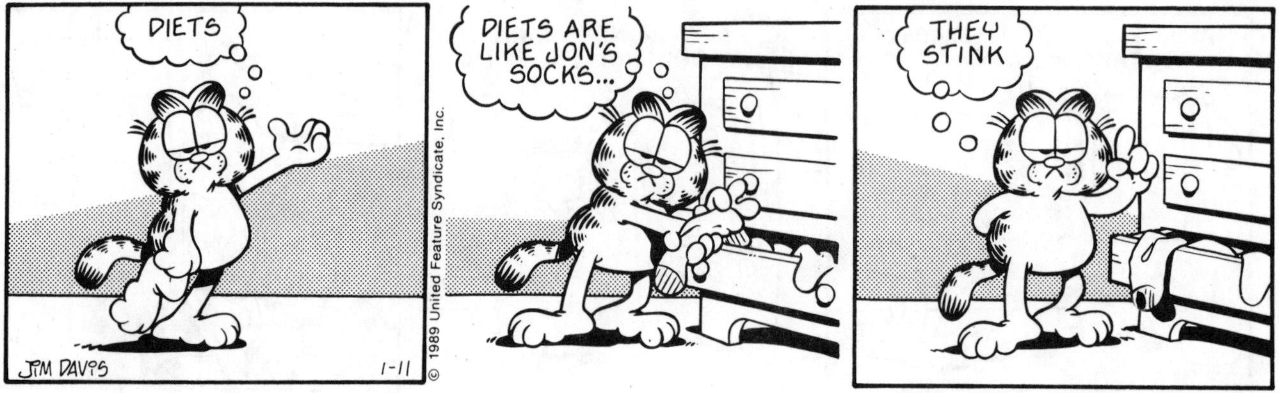
DIETS
DIETS ARE LIKE JON'S SOCKS...
THEY STINK
JIM DAVIS
1-11
© 1989 United Feature Syndicate, Inc.

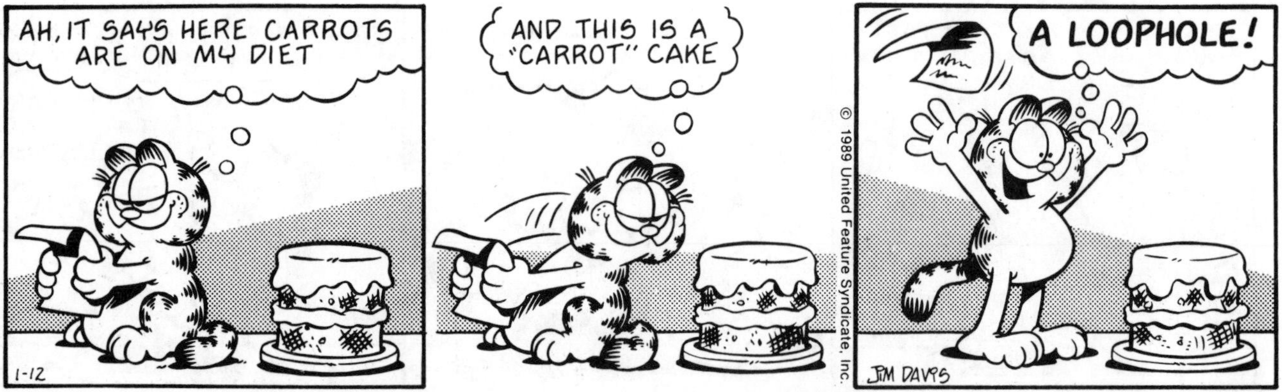
AH, IT SAYS HERE CARROTS ARE ON MY DIET
AND THIS IS A "CARROT" CAKE
A LOOPHOLE!
1-12
JIM DAVIS
© 1989 United Feature Syndicate, Inc.

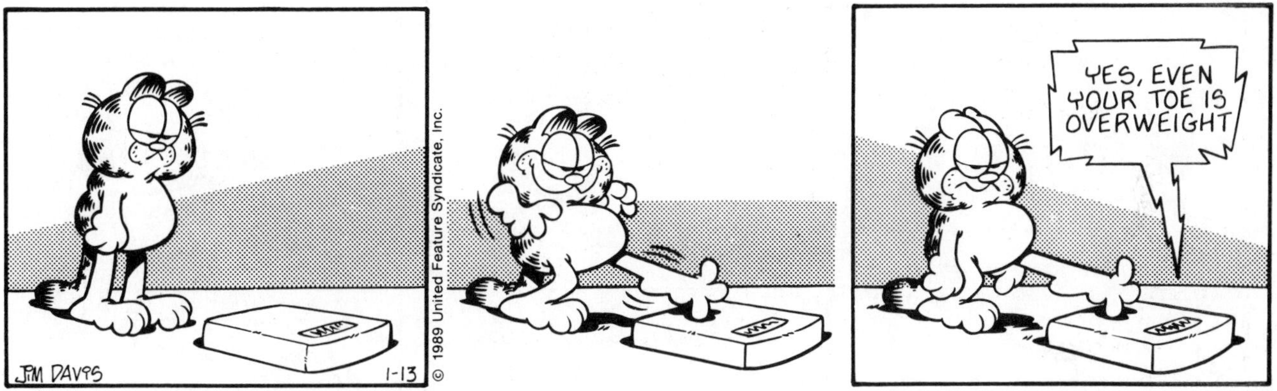
JIM DAVIS
1-13
© 1989 United Feature Syndicate, Inc.
YES, EVEN YOUR TOE IS OVERWEIGHT

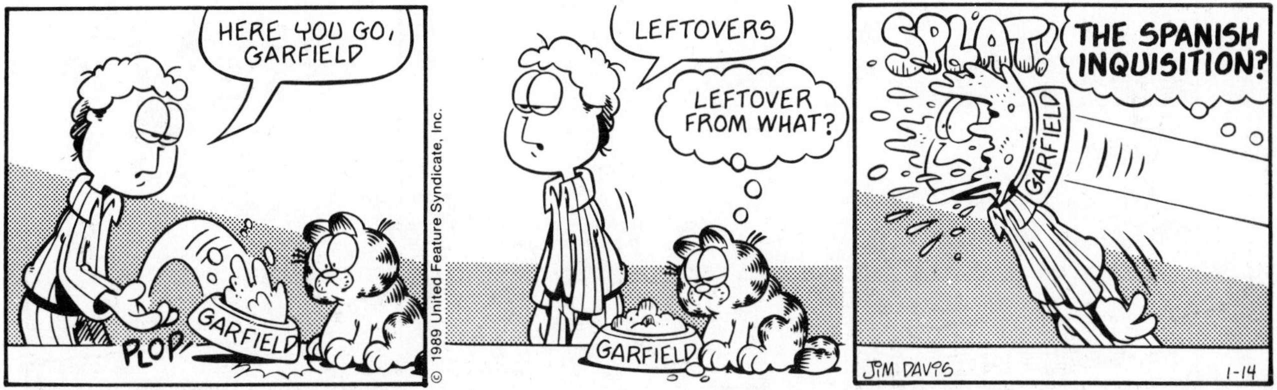
HERE YOU GO, GARFIELD
PLOP!
GARFIELD
© 1989 United Feature Syndicate, Inc.
LEFTOVERS
LEFTOVER FROM WHAT?
GARFIELD
SPLAT!
THE SPANISH INQUISITION?
GARFIELD
JIM DAVIS
1-14

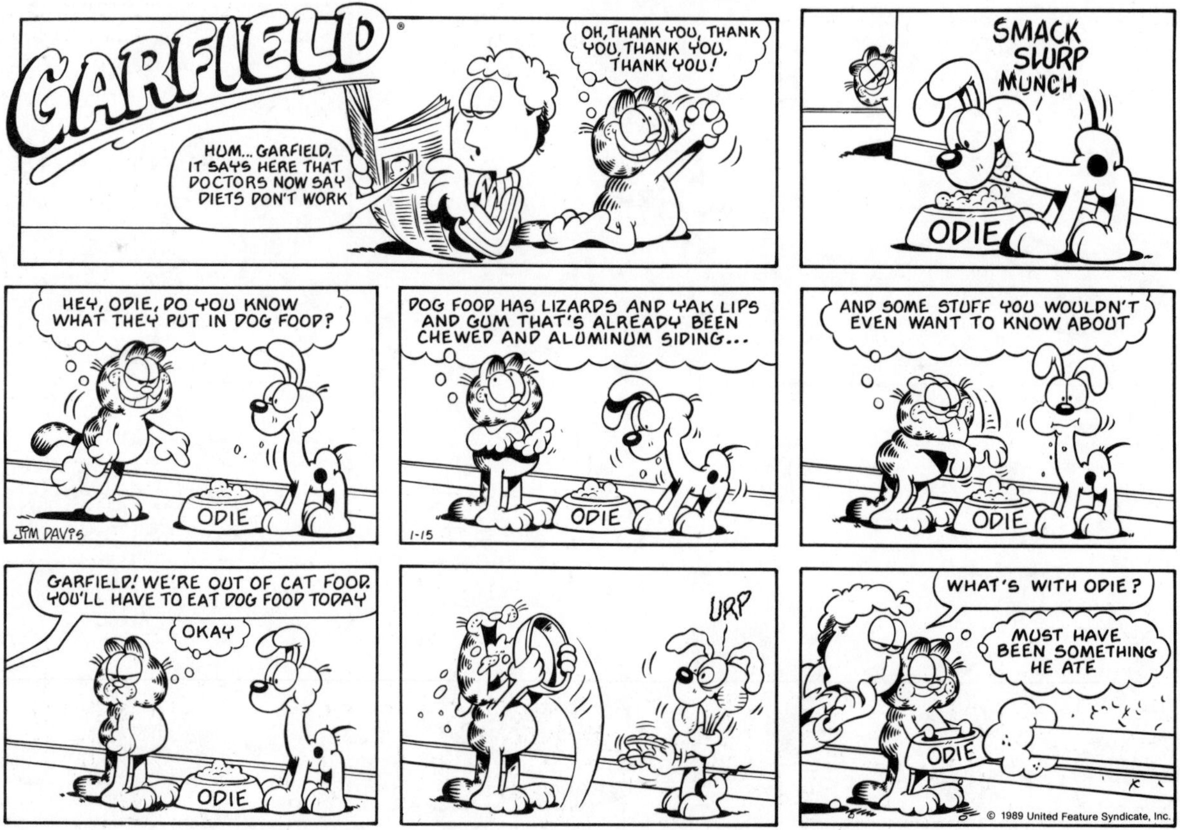
GARFIELD®
HUM... GARFIELD, IT SAYS HERE THAT DOCTORS NOW SAY DIETS DON'T WORK
OH, THANK YOU, THANK YOU, THANK YOU, THANK YOU!
SMACK SLURP MUNCH
ODIE
HEY, ODIE, DO YOU KNOW WHAT THEY PUT IN DOG FOOD?
ODIE
JIM DAVIS
DOG FOOD HAS LIZARDS AND YAK LIPS AND GUM THAT'S ALREADY BEEN CHEWED AND ALUMINUM SIDING...
ODIE
1-15
AND SOME STUFF YOU WOULDN'T EVEN WANT TO KNOW ABOUT
ODIE
GARFIELD! WE'RE OUT OF CAT FOOD. YOU'LL HAVE TO EAT DOG FOOD TODAY
OKAY
ODIE
URP
WHAT'S WITH ODIE?
MUST HAVE BEEN SOMETHING HE ATE
ODIE
© 1989 United Feature Syndicate, Inc.

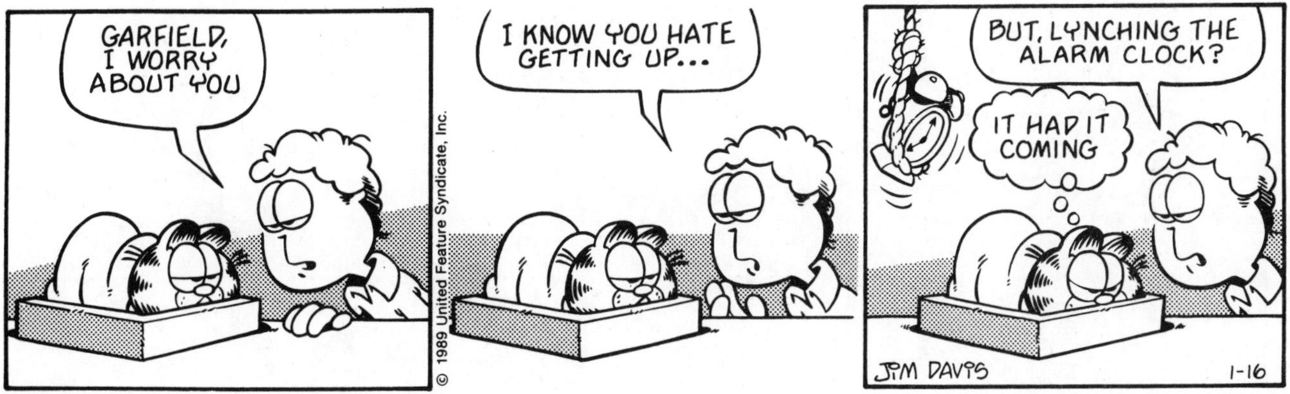
GARFIELD, I WORRY ABOUT YOU
© 1989 United Feature Syndicate, Inc.
I KNOW YOU HATE GETTING UP...
BUT, LYNCHING THE ALARM CLOCK?
IT HAD IT COMING
JIM DAVIS
1-16

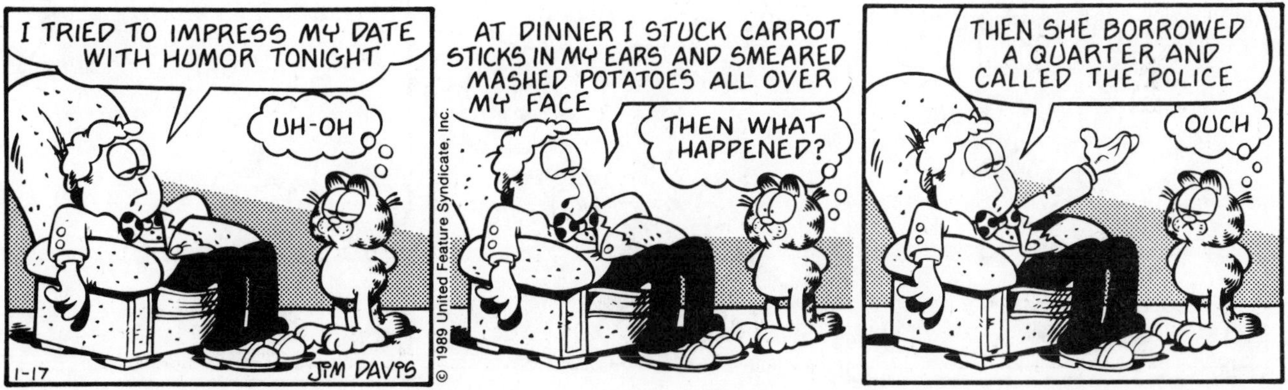
I TRIED TO IMPRESS MY DATE WITH HUMOR TONIGHT
UH-OH
1-17
JIM DAVIS
© 1989 United Feature Syndicate, Inc.
AT DINNER I STUCK CARROT STICKS IN MY EARS AND SMEARED MASHED POTATOES ALL OVER MY FACE
THEN WHAT HAPPENED?
THEN SHE BORROWED A QUARTER AND CALLED THE POLICE
OUCH

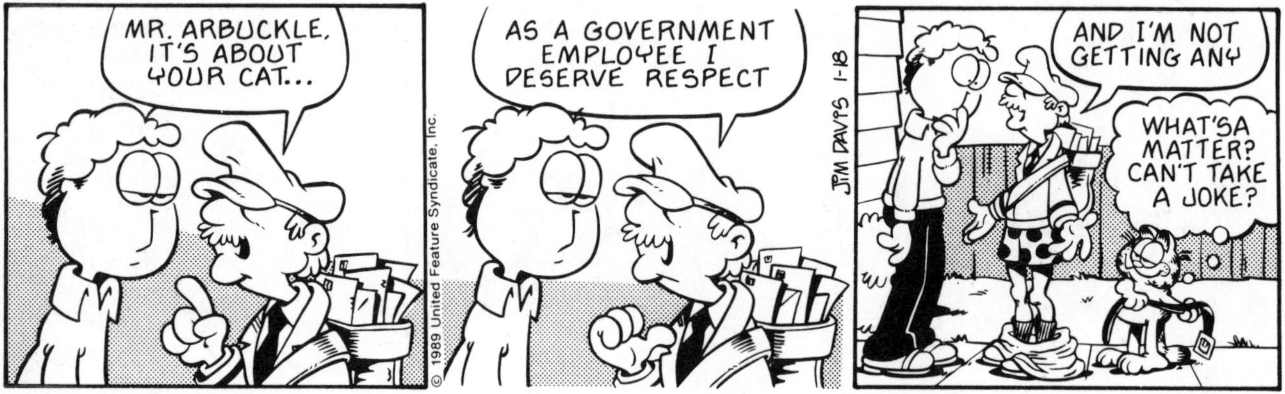
MR. ARBUCKLE, IT'S ABOUT YOUR CAT...
AS A GOVERNMENT EMPLOYEE I DESERVE RESPECT
© 1989 United Feature Syndicate, Inc.
JIM DAVIS 1-18
AND I'M NOT GETTING ANY
WHAT'SA MATTER? CAN'T TAKE A JOKE?

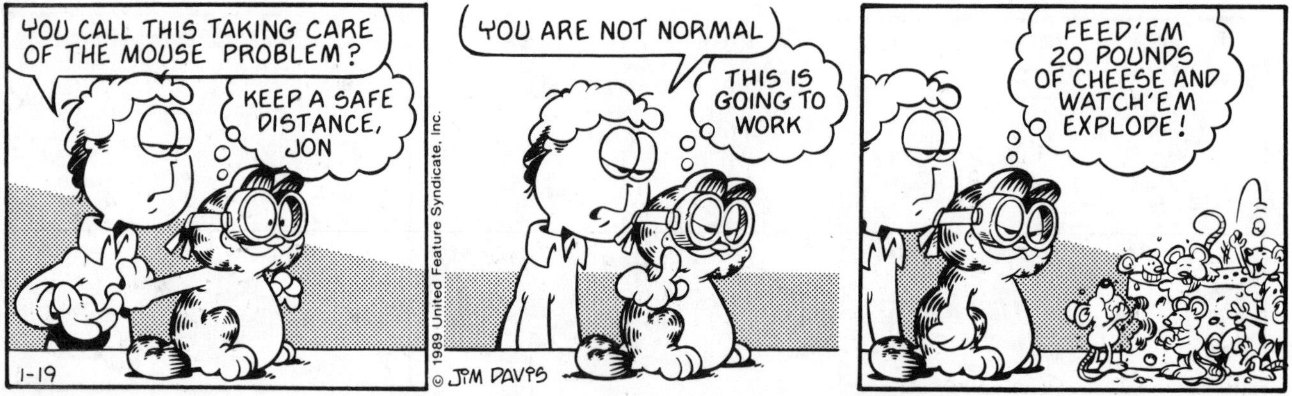
YOU CALL THIS TAKING CARE OF THE MOUSE PROBLEM?
KEEP A SAFE DISTANCE, JON
1-19
© 1989 United Feature Syndicate, Inc.
YOU ARE NOT NORMAL
THIS IS GOING TO WORK
© JIM DAVIS
FEED'EM 20 POUNDS OF CHEESE AND WATCH'EM EXPLODE!

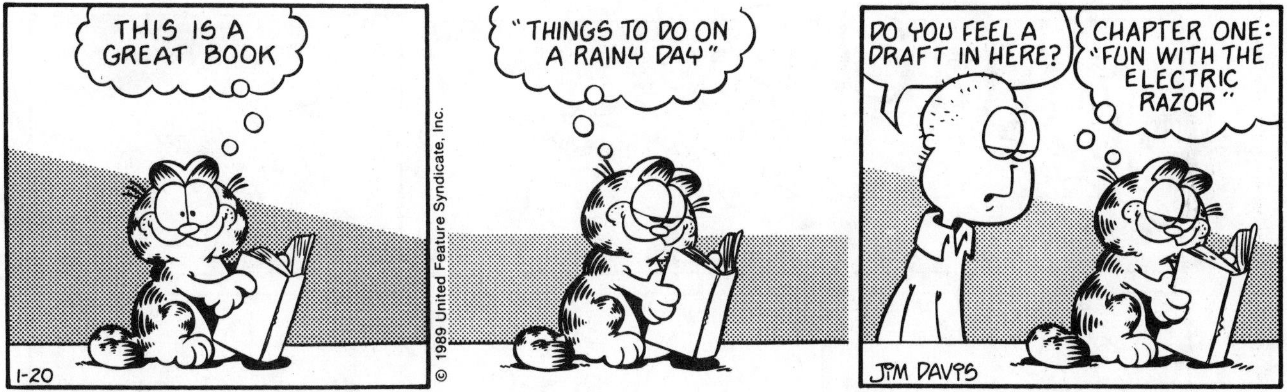
THIS IS A GREAT BOOK
"THINGS TO DO ON A RAINY DAY"
DO YOU FEEL A DRAFT IN HERE?
CHAPTER ONE: "FUN WITH THE ELECTRIC RAZOR"
JIM DAVIS
1-20
© 1989 United Feature Syndicate, Inc.

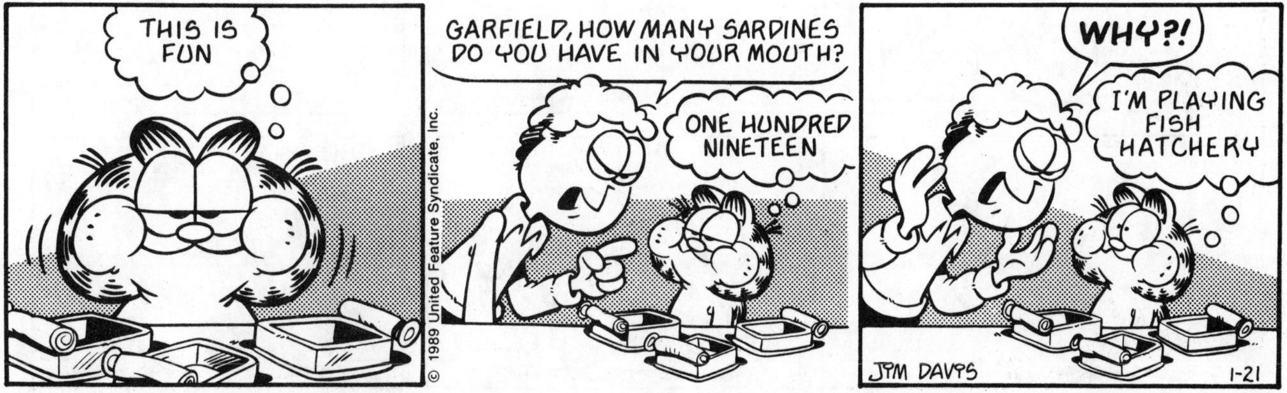
THIS IS FUN
GARFIELD, HOW MANY SARDINES DO YOU HAVE IN YOUR MOUTH?
ONE HUNDRED NINETEEN
WHY?!
I'M PLAYING FISH HATCHERY
JIM DAVIS
1-21
© 1989 United Feature Syndicate, Inc.

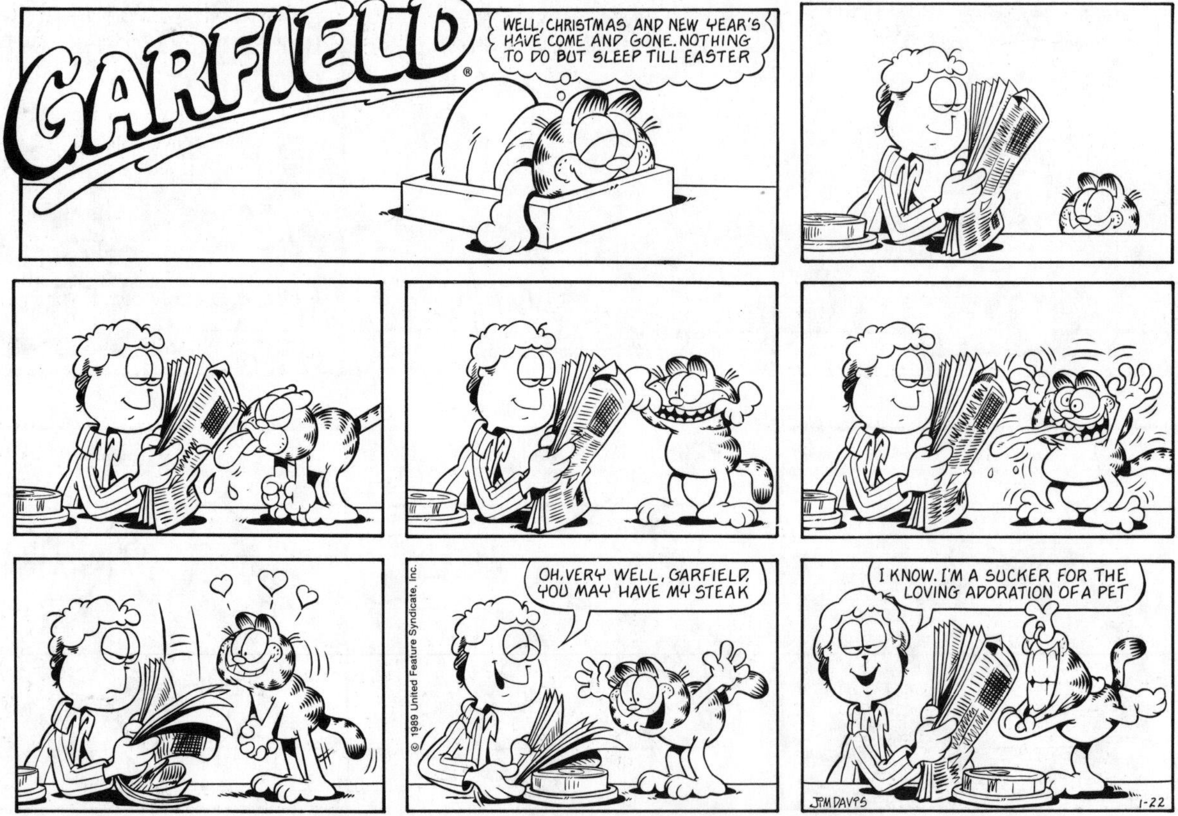
GARFIELD®
WELL, CHRISTMAS AND NEW YEAR'S HAVE COME AND GONE. NOTHING TO DO BUT SLEEP TILL EASTER
OH, VERY WELL, GARFIELD, YOU MAY HAVE MY STEAK
I KNOW. I'M A SUCKER FOR THE LOVING ADORATION OF A PET
JIM DAVIS
1-22

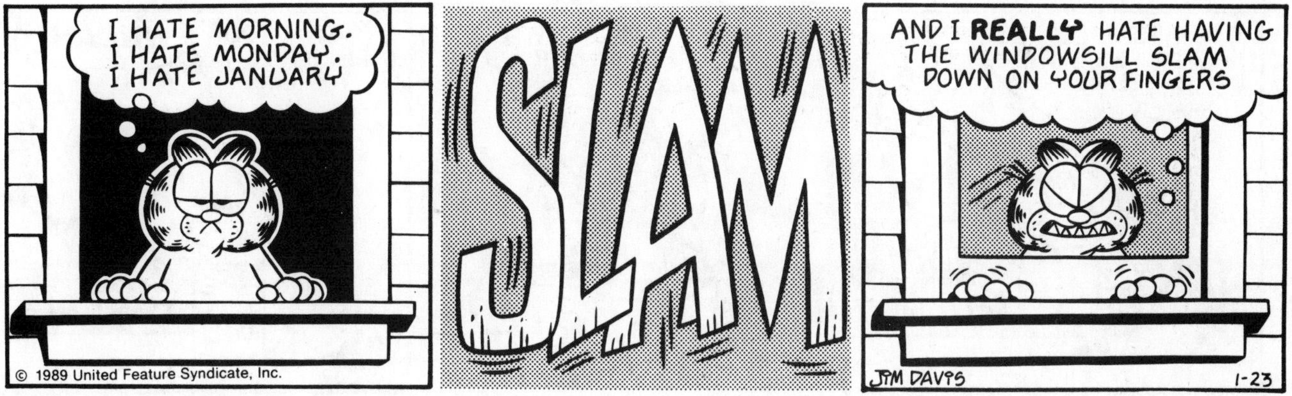
I HATE MORNING. I HATE MONDAY. I HATE JANUARY
SLAM
AND I **REALLY** HATE HAVING THE WINDOWSILL SLAM DOWN ON YOUR FINGERS
© 1989 United Feature Syndicate, Inc.
JIM DAVIS
1-23

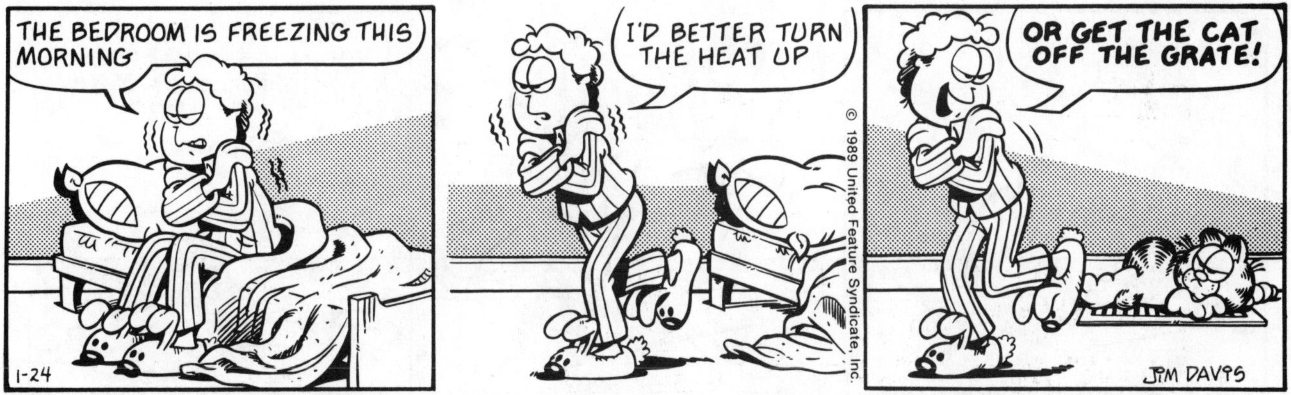
THE BEDROOM IS FREEZING THIS MORNING
1-24
I'D BETTER TURN THE HEAT UP
© 1989 United Feature Syndicate, Inc.
OR GET THE CAT OFF THE GRATE!
JIM DAVIS

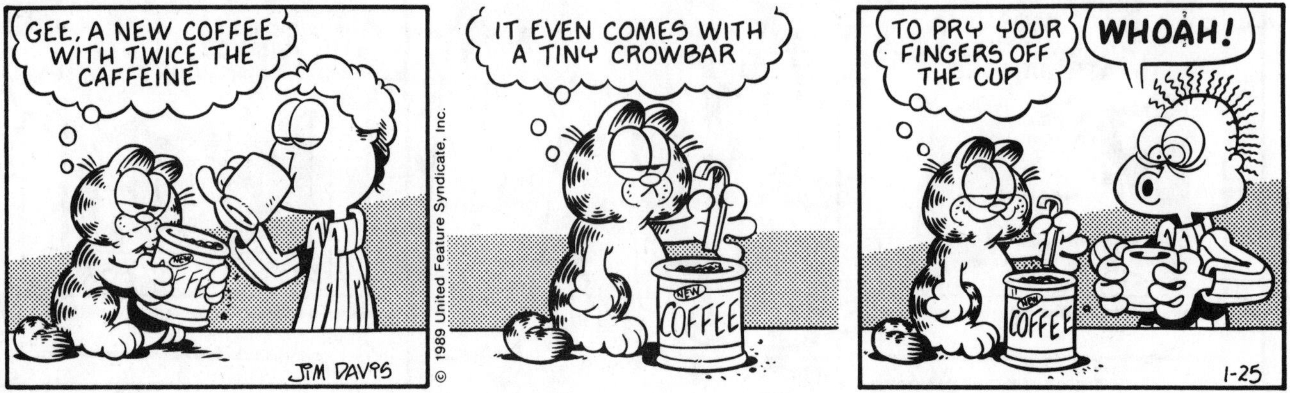
GEE, A NEW COFFEE WITH TWICE THE CAFFEINE
NEW
FFE
JIM DAVIS
© 1989 United Feature Syndicate, Inc.
IT EVEN COMES WITH A TINY CROWBAR
NEW
COFFEE
TO PRY YOUR FINGERS OFF THE CUP
WHOAH!
NEW
COFFEE
1-25

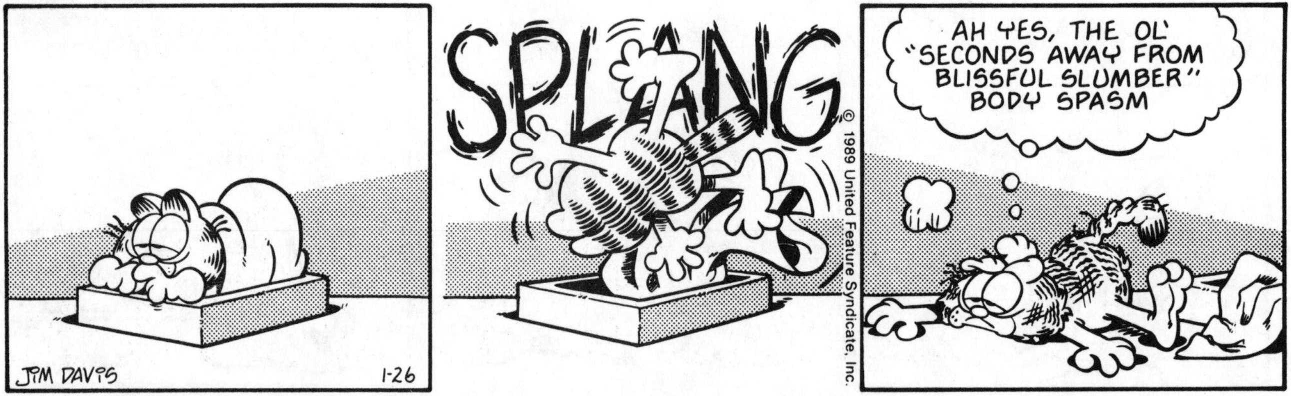
JIM DAVIS
1-26
SPLANG
© 1989 United Feature Syndicate, Inc.
AH YES, THE OL' "SECONDS AWAY FROM BLISSFUL SLUMBER" BODY SPASM

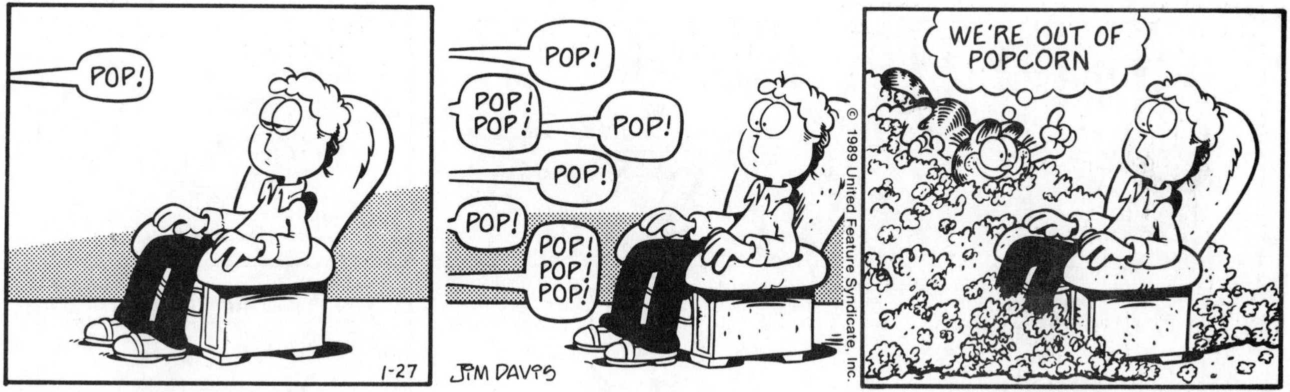
POP!
POP!
POP! POP!
POP!
POP!
POP!
POP! POP! POP!
WE'RE OUT OF POPCORN
1-27
JIM DAVIS
© 1989 United Feature Syndicate, Inc.

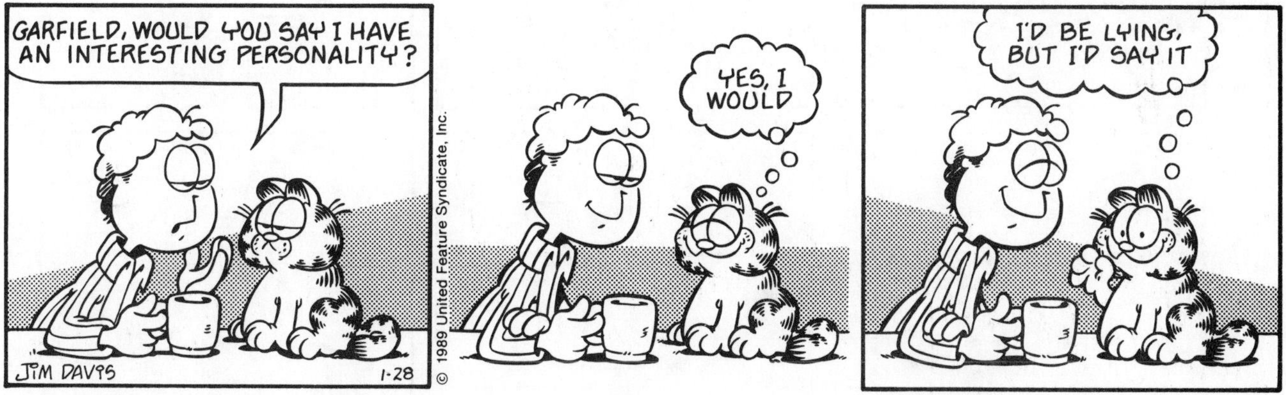
GARFIELD, WOULD YOU SAY I HAVE AN INTERESTING PERSONALITY?
YES, I WOULD
I'D BE LYING, BUT I'D SAY IT
JIM DAVIS
1-28
© 1989 United Feature Syndicate, Inc.

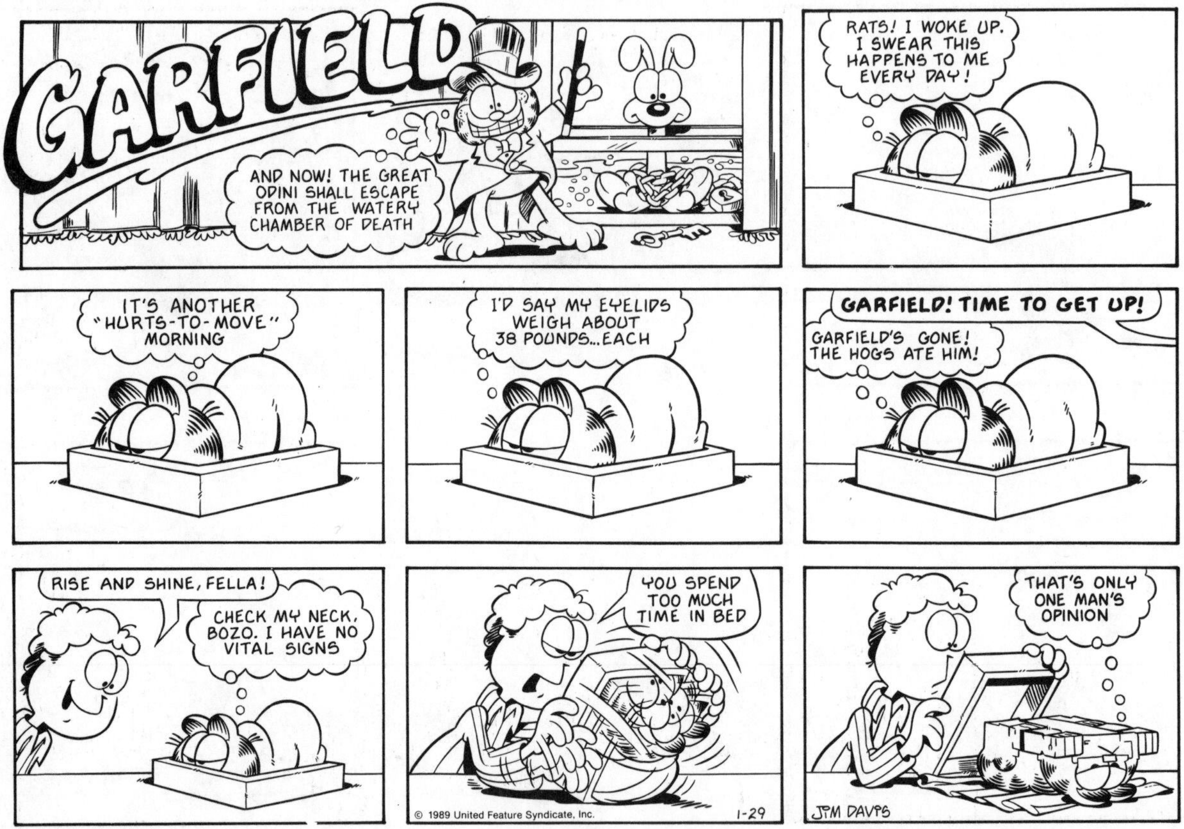
GARFIELD
AND NOW! THE GREAT ODINI SHALL ESCAPE FROM THE WATERY CHAMBER OF DEATH
RATS! I WOKE UP. I SWEAR THIS HAPPENS TO ME EVERY DAY!
IT'S ANOTHER "HURTS-TO-MOVE" MORNING
I'D SAY MY EYELIDS WEIGH ABOUT 38 POUNDS...EACH
GARFIELD! TIME TO GET UP!
GARFIELD'S GONE! THE HOGS ATE HIM!
RISE AND SHINE, FELLA!
CHECK MY NECK, BOZO. I HAVE NO VITAL SIGNS
YOU SPEND TOO MUCH TIME IN BED
© 1989 United Feature Syndicate, Inc.
1-29
THAT'S ONLY ONE MAN'S OPINION
JIM DAVIS

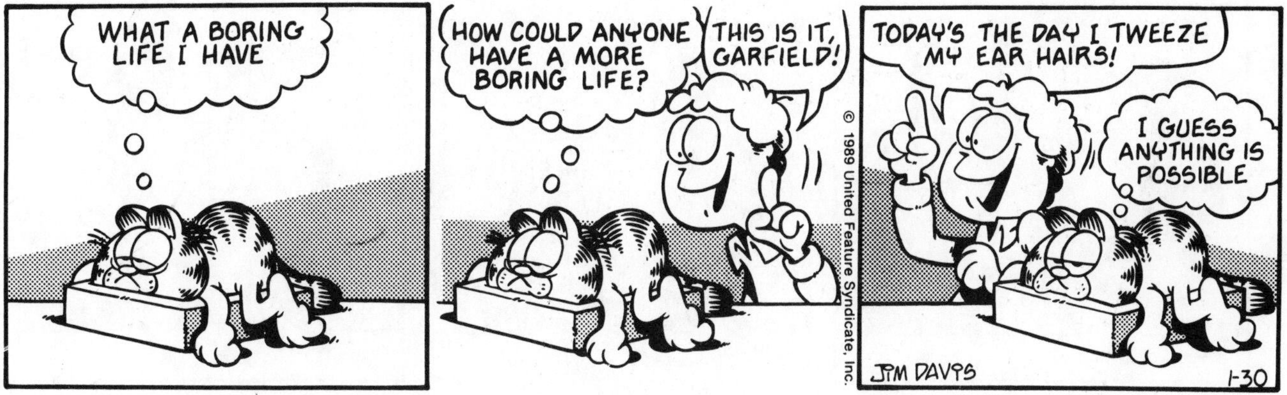
WHAT A BORING LIFE I HAVE
HOW COULD ANYONE HAVE A MORE BORING LIFE?
THIS IS IT, GARFIELD!
TODAY'S THE DAY I TWEEZE MY EAR HAIRS!
I GUESS ANYTHING IS POSSIBLE
© 1989 United Feature Syndicate, Inc.
JIM DAVIS
1-30

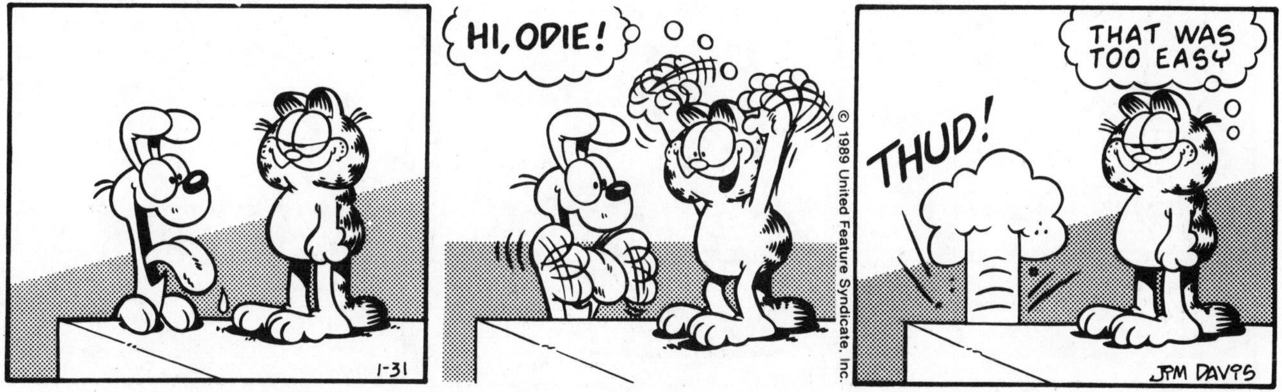
1-31
HI, ODIE!
© 1989 United Feature Syndicate, Inc.
THUD!
THAT WAS TOO EASY
JIM DAVIS

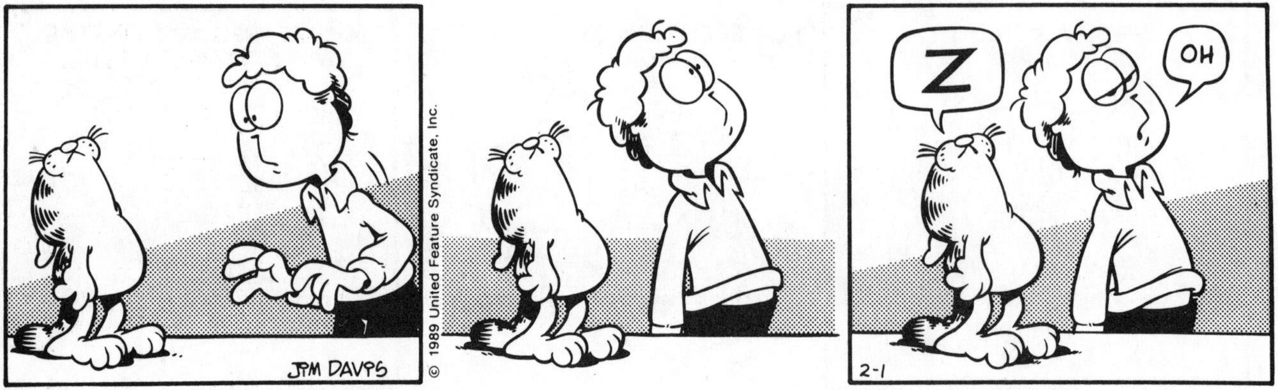
Z
OH
JIM DAVIS
© 1989 United Feature Syndicate, Inc.
2-1

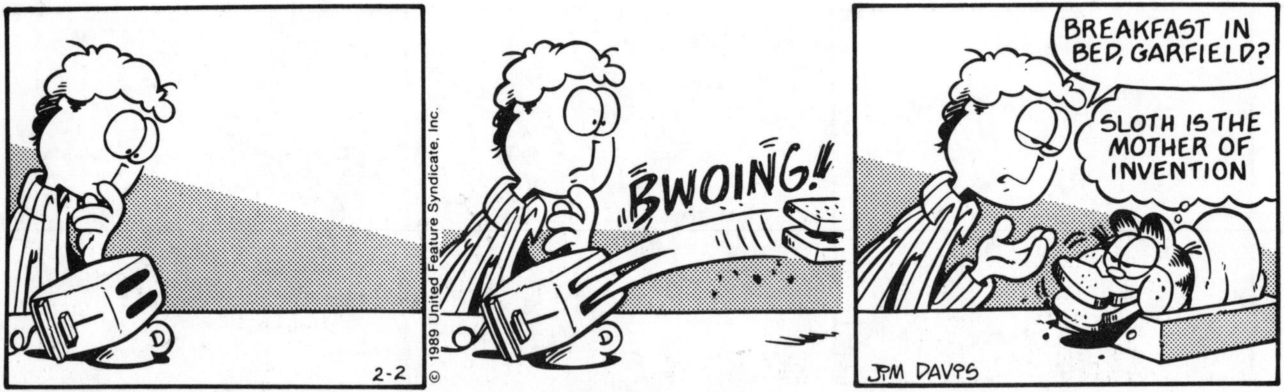
BWOING!!
BREAKFAST IN BED, GARFIELD?
SLOTH IS THE MOTHER OF INVENTION
JIM DAVIS
© 1989 United Feature Syndicate, Inc.
2-2

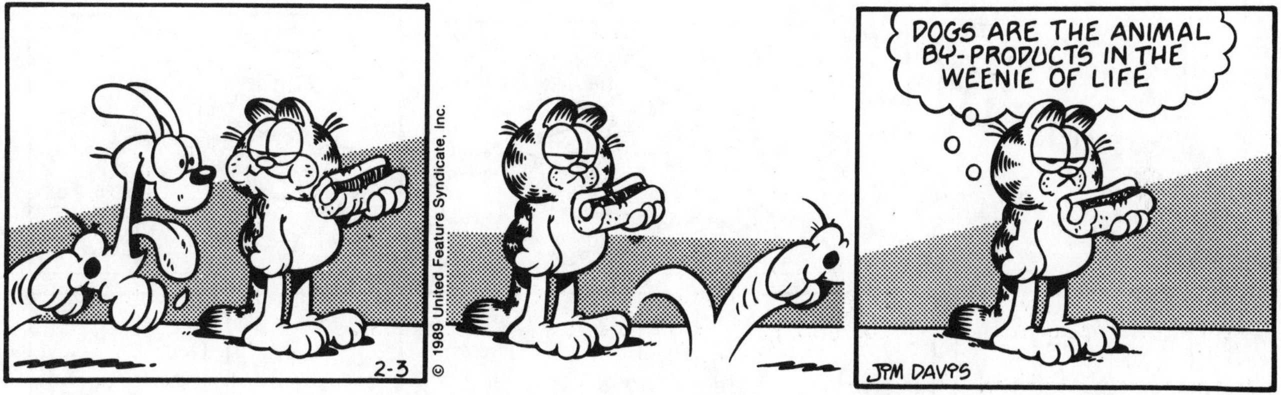
2-3
© 1989 United Feature Syndicate, Inc.
DOGS ARE THE ANIMAL BY-PRODUCTS IN THE WEENIE OF LIFE
JIM DAVIS

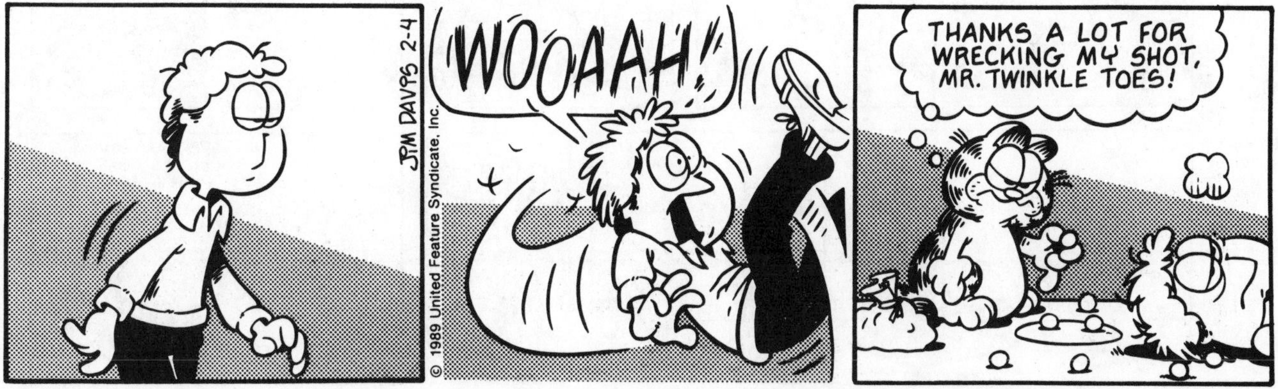
JIM DAVIS 2-4
© 1989 United Feature Syndicate, Inc.
WOOAAH!
THANKS A LOT FOR WRECKING MY SHOT, MR. TWINKLE TOES!

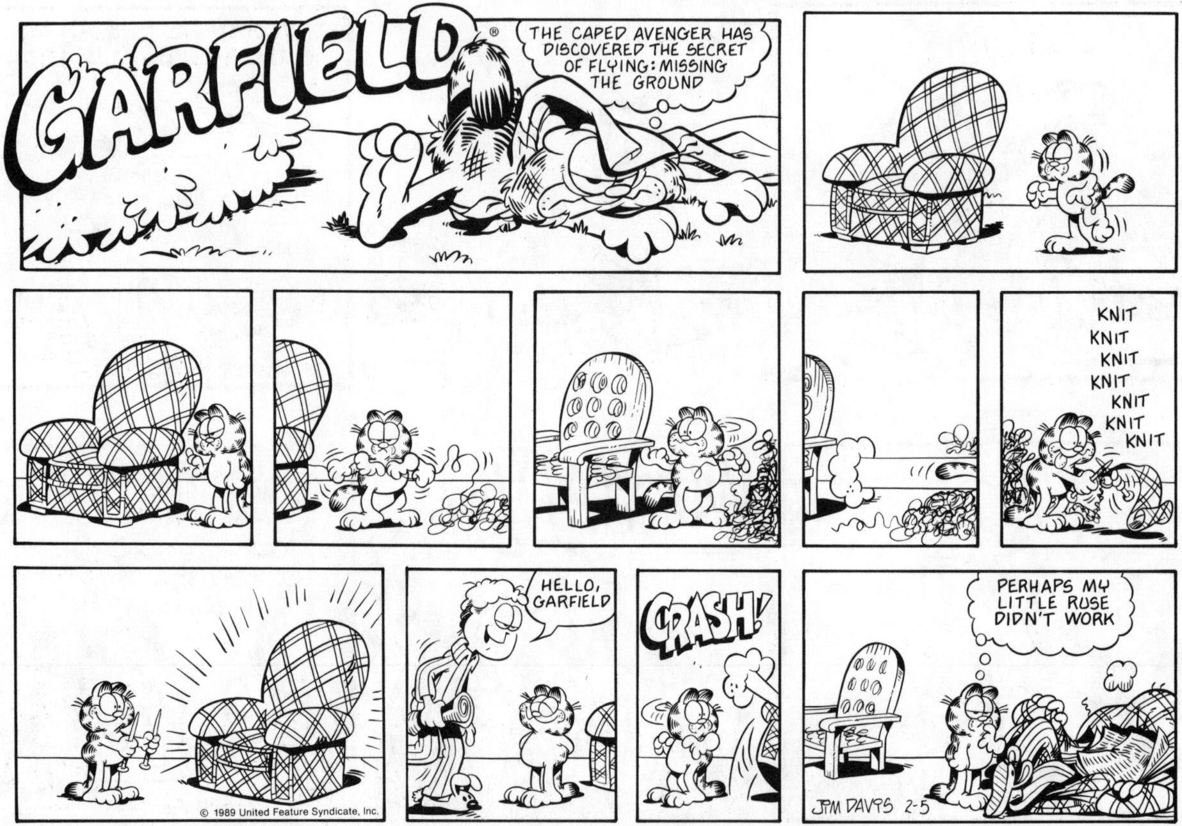
GARFIELD®
THE CAPED AVENGER HAS DISCOVERED THE SECRET OF FLYING: MISSING THE GROUND
KNIT KNIT KNIT KNIT KNIT KNIT KNIT
© 1989 United Feature Syndicate, Inc.
HELLO, GARFIELD
CRASH!
PERHAPS MY LITTLE RUSE DIDN'T WORK
JPM DAVIS 2-5

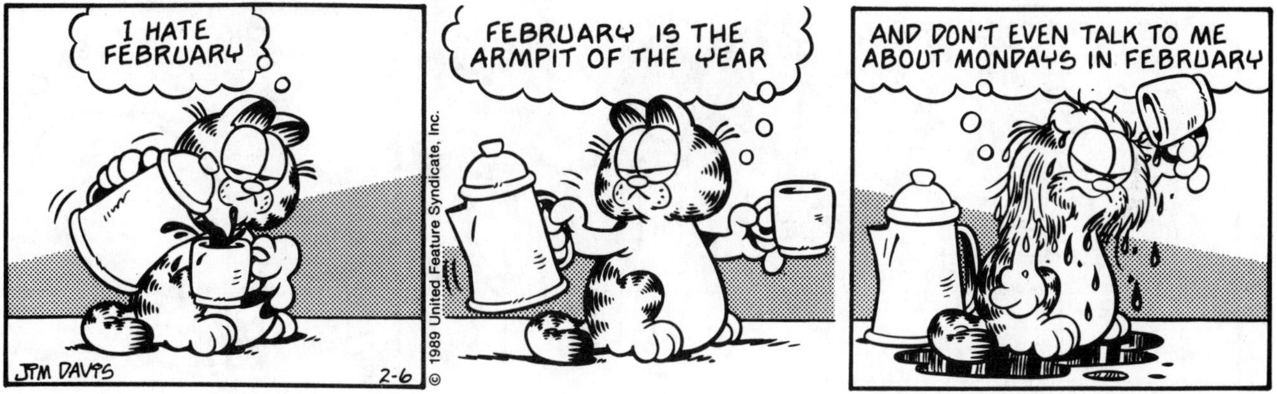
I HATE FEBRUARY
FEBRUARY IS THE ARMPIT OF THE YEAR
AND DON'T EVEN TALK TO ME ABOUT MONDAYS IN FEBRUARY
JIM DAVIS
2-6
© 1989 United Feature Syndicate, Inc.

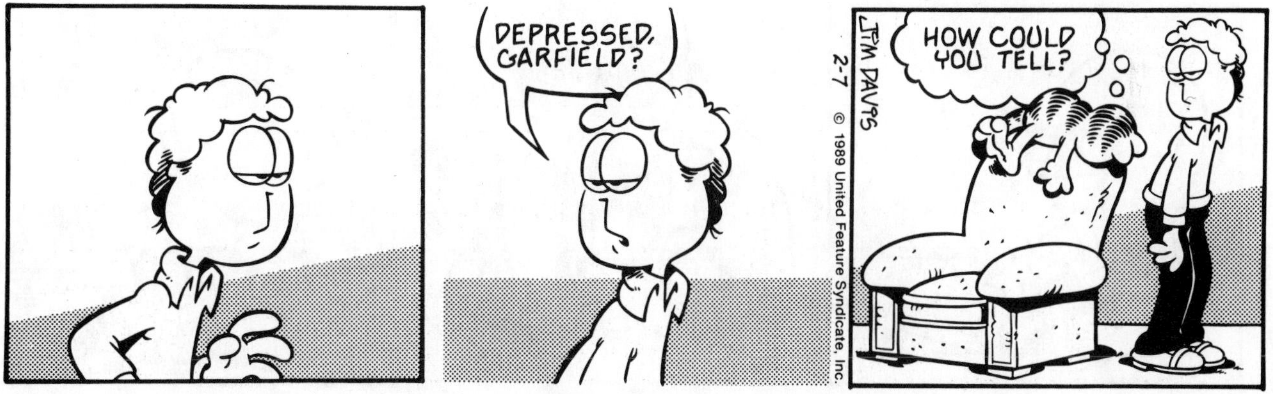
DEPRESSED, GARFIELD?
HOW COULD YOU TELL?
JIM DAVIS
2-7
© 1989 United Feature Syndicate, Inc.

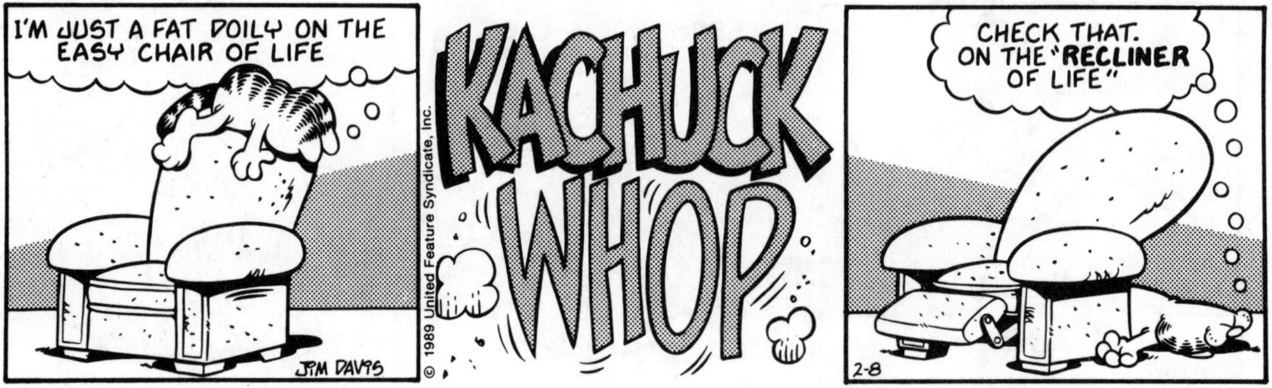
I'M JUST A FAT DOILY ON THE EASY CHAIR OF LIFE
JIM DAVIS
© 1989 United Feature Syndicate, Inc.
KACHUCK
WHOP
CHECK THAT. ON THE "RECLINER OF LIFE"
2-8

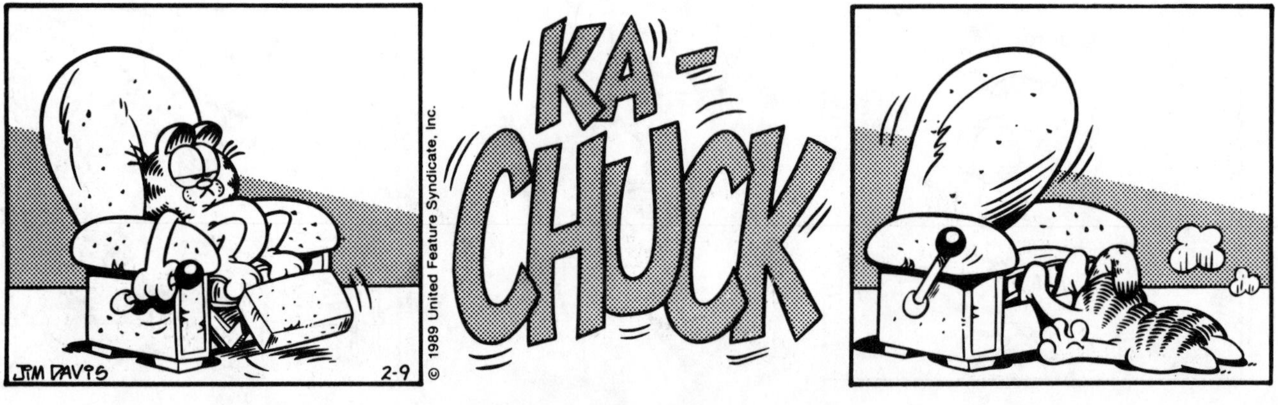
JIM DAVIS
2-9
© 1989 United Feature Syndicate, Inc.
KA-
CHUCK

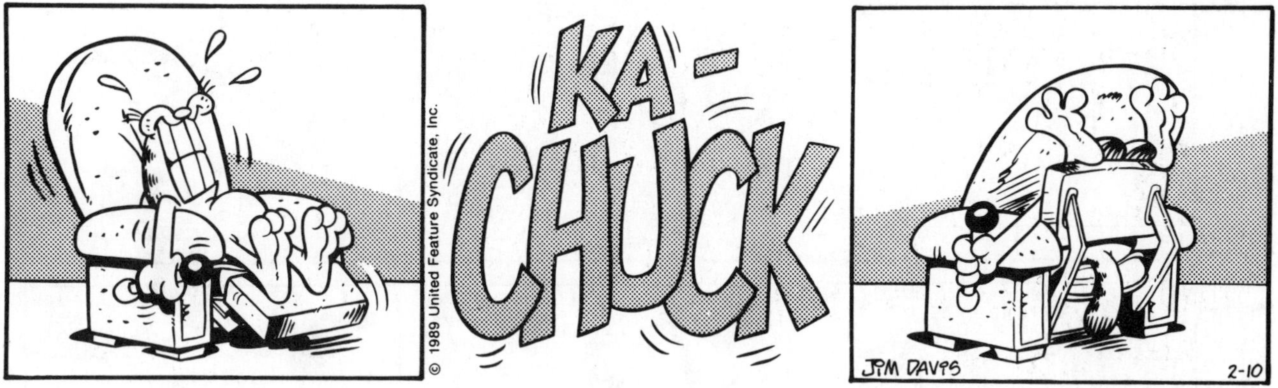
KA-CHUCK
© 1989 United Feature Syndicate, Inc.
JIM DAVIS
2-10

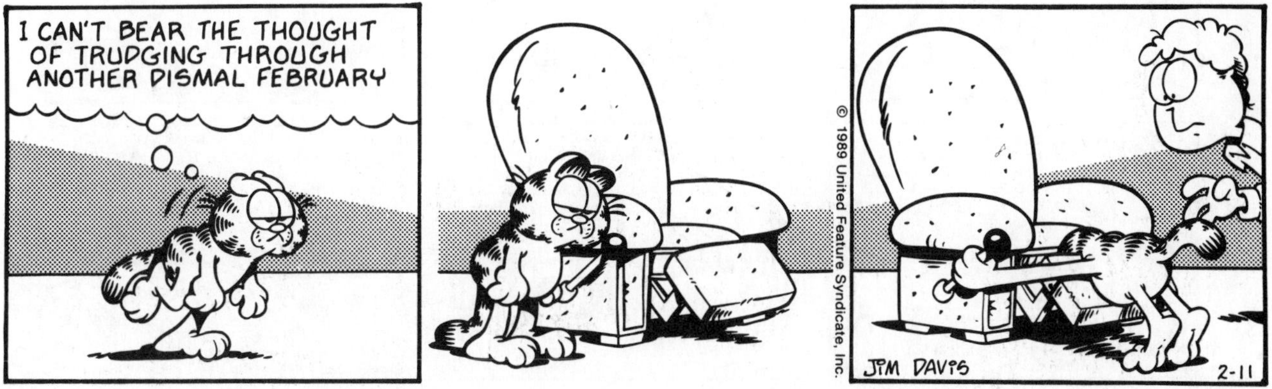
I CAN'T BEAR THE THOUGHT OF TRUDGING THROUGH ANOTHER DISMAL FEBRUARY
© 1989 United Feature Syndicate, Inc.
JIM DAVIS
2-11

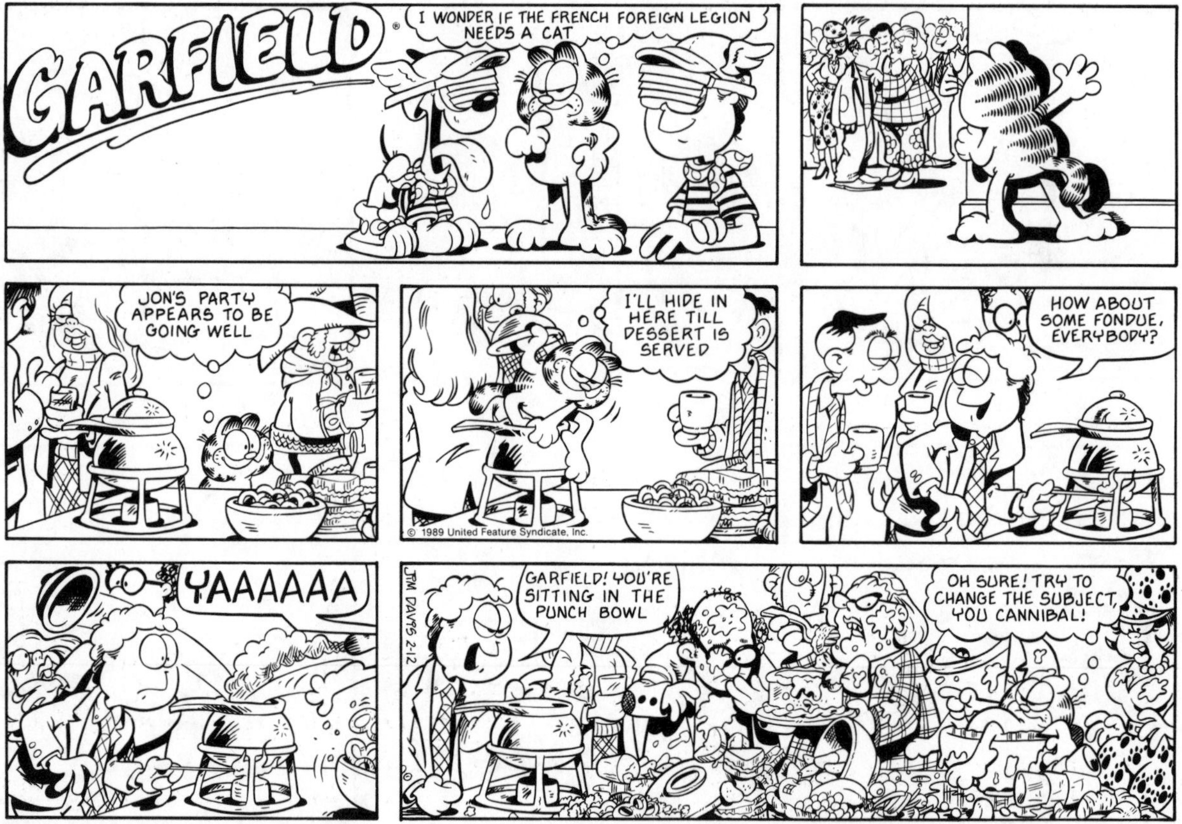

GARFIELD
I WONDER IF THE FRENCH FOREIGN LEGION NEEDS A CAT
JON'S PARTY APPEARS TO BE GOING WELL
I'LL HIDE IN HERE TILL DESSERT IS SERVED
© 1989 United Feature Syndicate, Inc.
HOW ABOUT SOME FONDUE, EVERYBODY?
YAAAAAA
JIM DAVIS 2-12
GARFIELD! YOU'RE SITTING IN THE PUNCH BOWL
OH SURE! TRY TO CHANGE THE SUBJECT, YOU CANNIBAL!

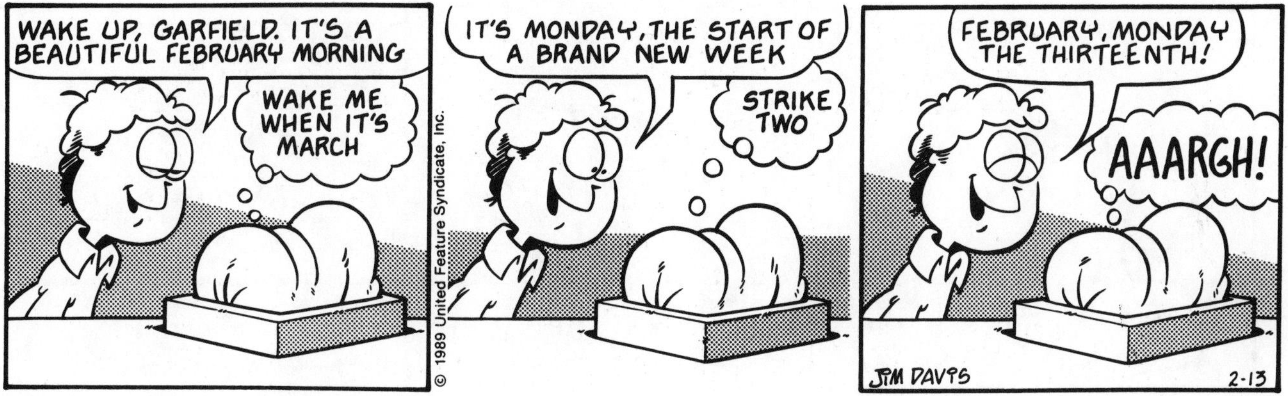
WAKE UP, GARFIELD. IT'S A BEAUTIFUL FEBRUARY MORNING
WAKE ME WHEN IT'S MARCH
IT'S MONDAY, THE START OF A BRAND NEW WEEK
STRIKE TWO
FEBRUARY, MONDAY THE THIRTEENTH!
AAARGH!
© 1989 United Feature Syndicate, Inc.
JIM DAVIS
2-13

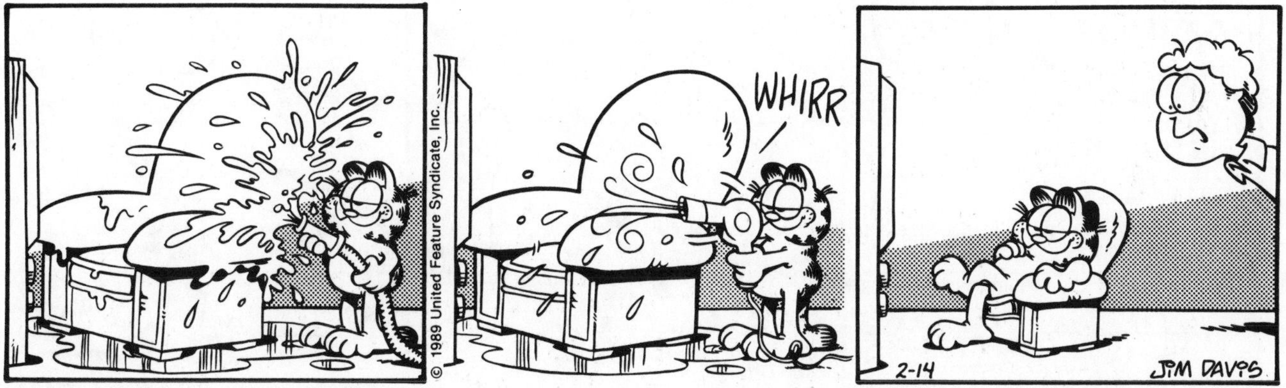
© 1989 United Feature Syndicate, Inc.
WHIRR
2-14
JIM DAVIS

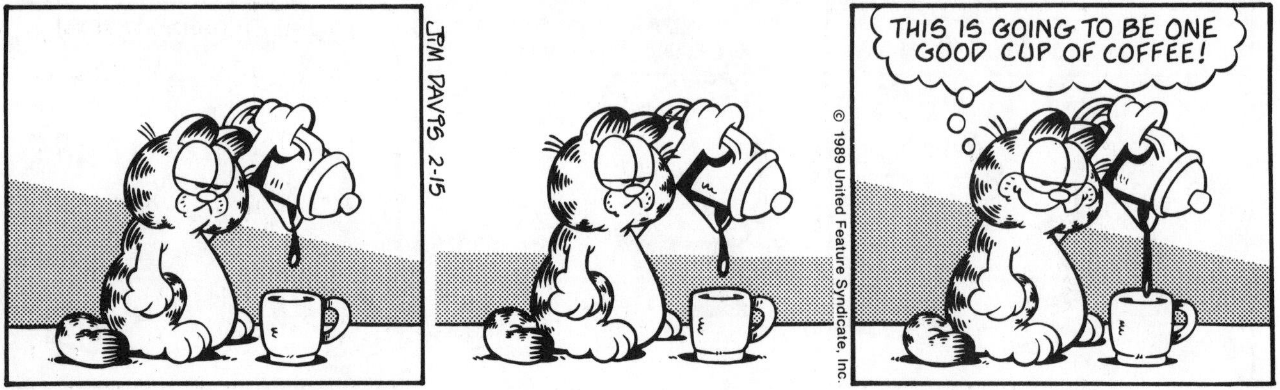
JIM DAVIS 2-15
© 1989 United Feature Syndicate, Inc.
THIS IS GOING TO BE ONE GOOD CUP OF COFFEE!

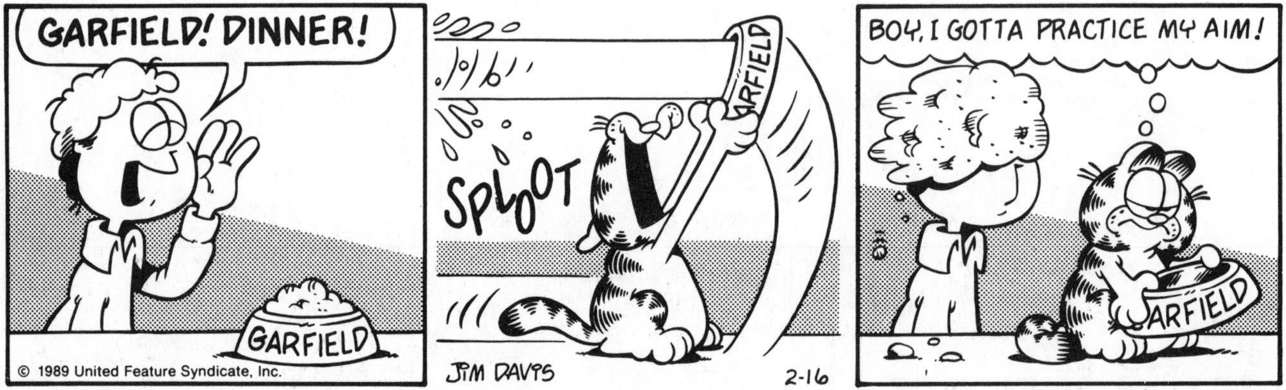
GARFIELD! DINNER!
GARFIELD
© 1989 United Feature Syndicate, Inc.
SPLOOT
GARFIELD
JIM DAVIS
2-16
BOY, I GOTTA PRACTICE MY AIM!
GARFIELD

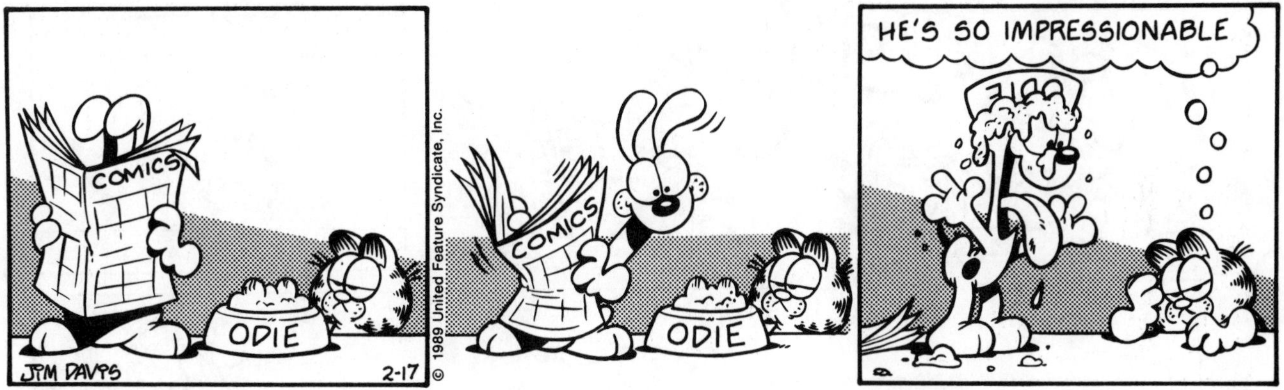
COMICS
ODIE
JIM DAVIS
2-17
© 1989 United Feature Syndicate, Inc.
COMICS
ODIE
HE'S SO IMPRESSIONABLE
ODIE

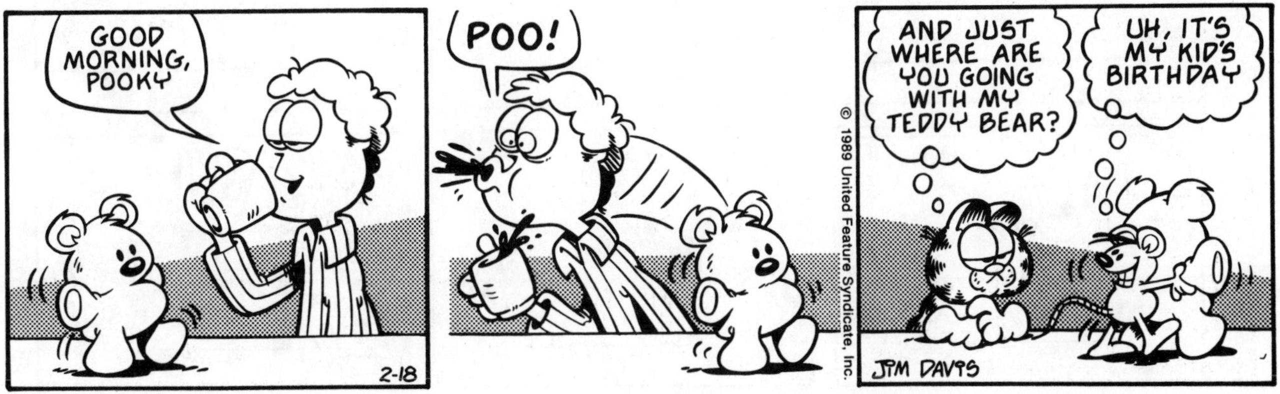
GOOD MORNING, POOKY
2-18
POO!
© 1989 United Feature Syndicate, Inc.
AND JUST WHERE ARE YOU GOING WITH MY TEDDY BEAR?
UH, IT'S MY KID'S BIRTHDAY
JIM DAVIS

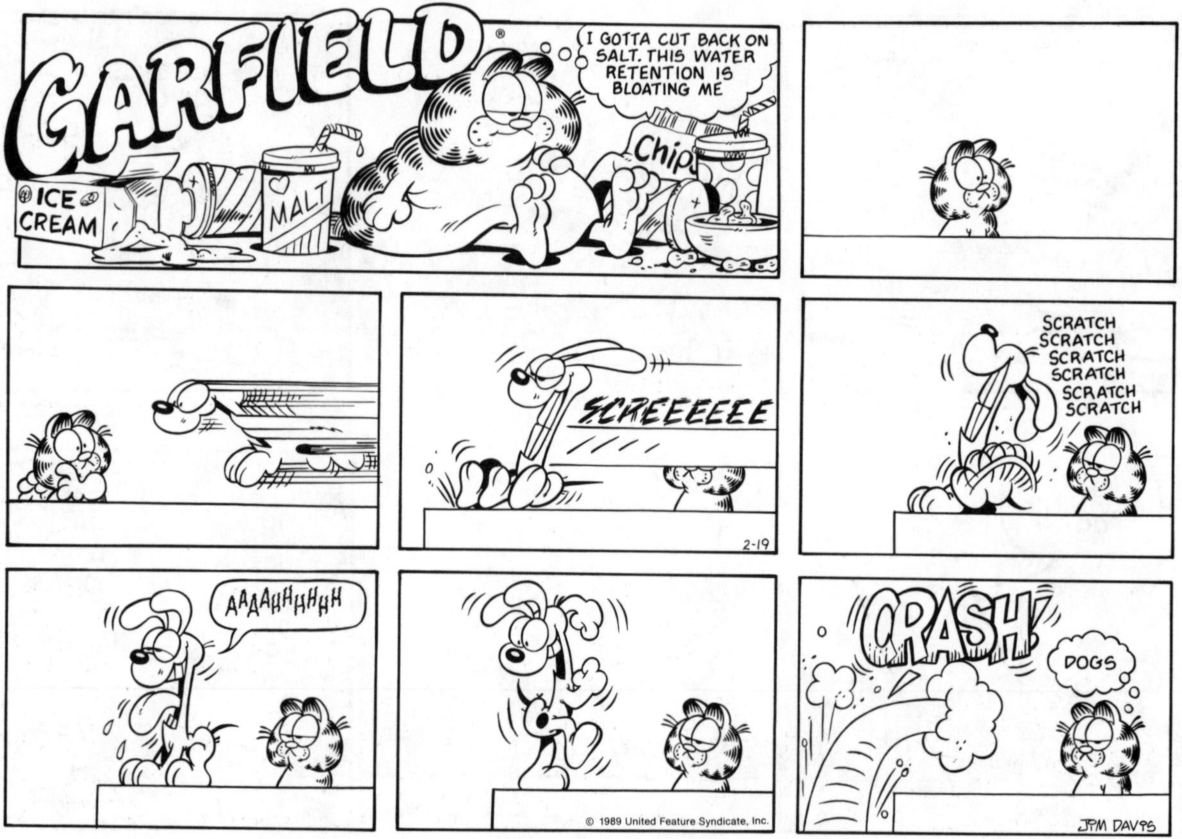
GARFIELD
I GOTTA CUT BACK ON SALT. THIS WATER RETENTION IS BLOATING ME
ICE CREAM
MALT
Chips
SCREEEEEEE
2-19
SCRATCH SCRATCH SCRATCH SCRATCH SCRATCH SCRATCH
AAAAHHHHHH
© 1989 United Feature Syndicate, Inc.
CRASH
DOGS
JIM DAVIS

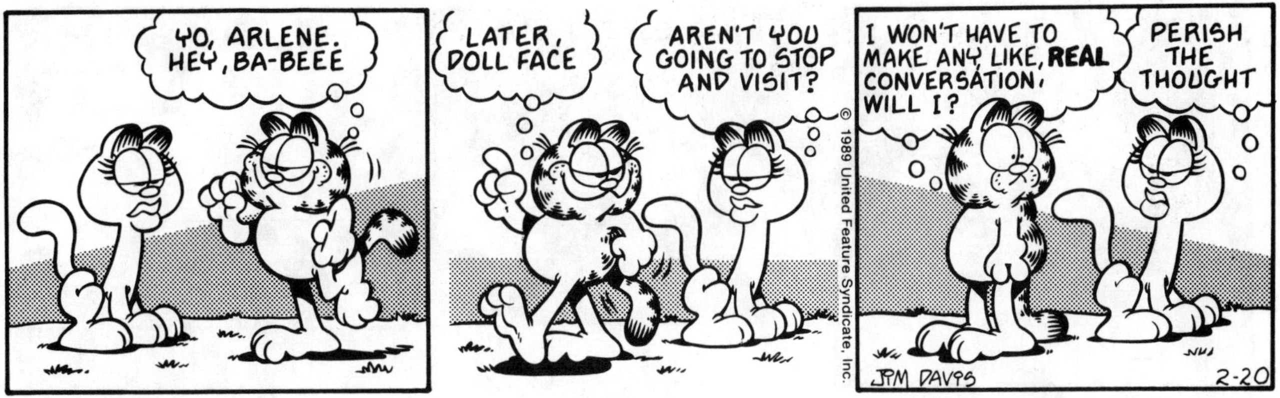
YO, ARLENE. HEY, BA-BEEE
LATER, DOLL FACE
AREN'T YOU GOING TO STOP AND VISIT?
I WON'T HAVE TO MAKE ANY LIKE, **REAL** CONVERSATION, WILL I?
PERISH THE THOUGHT
JIM DAVIS 2-20
© 1989 United Feature Syndicate, Inc.

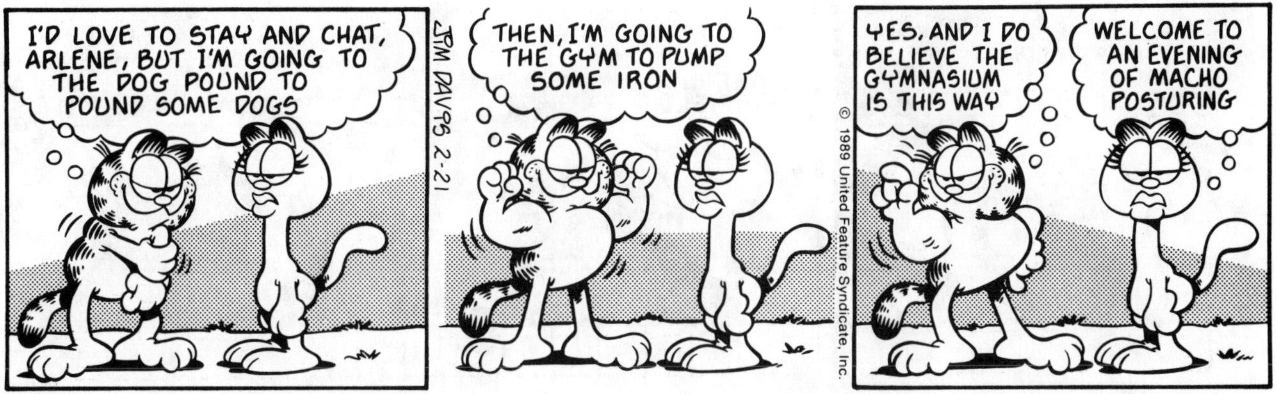
I'D LOVE TO STAY AND CHAT, ARLENE, BUT I'M GOING TO THE DOG POUND TO POUND SOME DOGS
JIM DAVIS 2-21
THEN, I'M GOING TO THE GYM TO PUMP SOME IRON
YES, AND I DO BELIEVE THE GYMNASIUM IS THIS WAY
WELCOME TO AN EVENING OF MACHO POSTURING
© 1989 United Feature Syndicate, Inc.

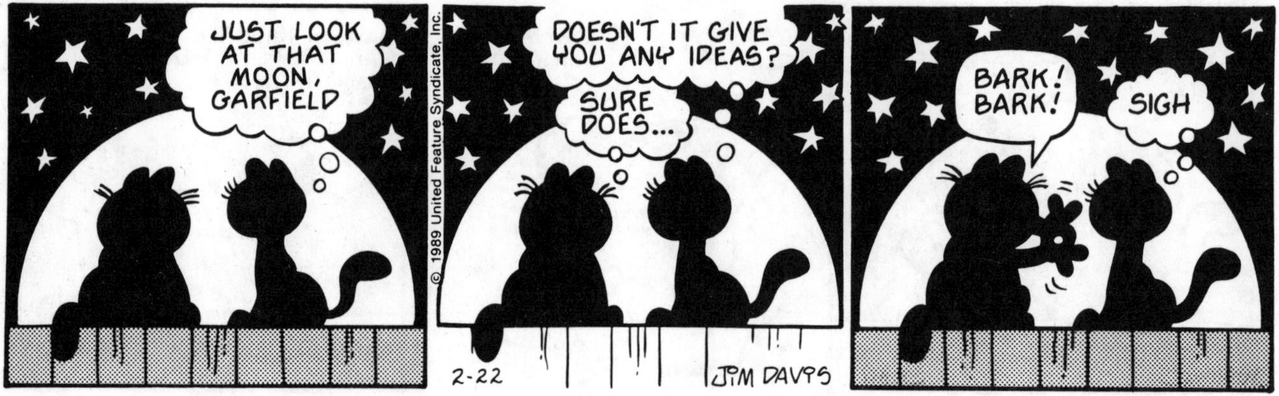
JUST LOOK AT THAT MOON, GARFIELD
DOESN'T IT GIVE YOU ANY IDEAS?
SURE DOES...
BARK! BARK!
SIGH
© 1989 United Feature Syndicate, Inc.
2-22
JIM DAVIS

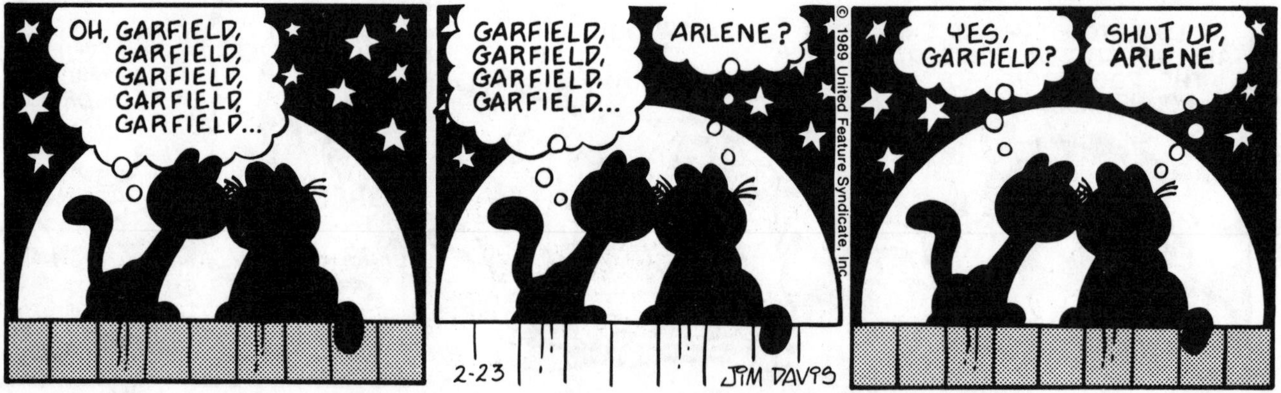
OH, GARFIELD, GARFIELD, GARFIELD, GARFIELD, GARFIELD...
GARFIELD, GARFIELD, GARFIELD, GARFIELD...
ARLENE?
YES, GARFIELD?
SHUT UP, ARLENE
© 1989 United Feature Syndicate, Inc.
2-23
JIM DAVIS

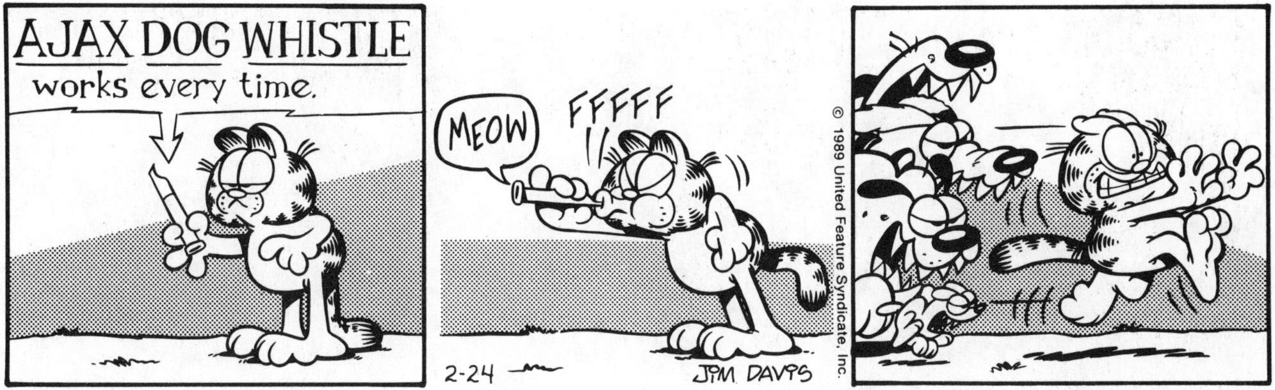
AJAX DOG WHISTLE
works every time.
MEOW
FFFFF
2-24
JIM DAVIS
© 1989 United Feature Syndicate, Inc.

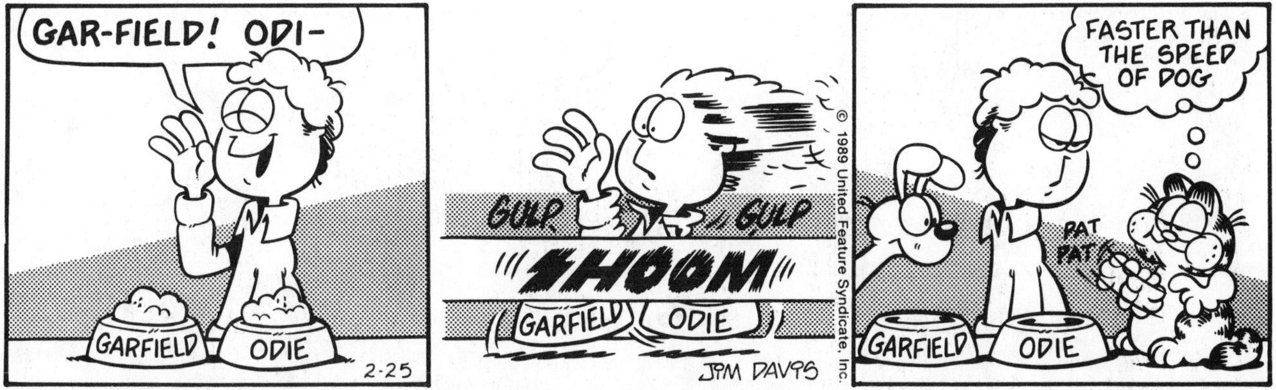
GAR-FIELD! ODI-
GARFIELD
ODIE
2-25
GULP
GULP
SHOOM
GARFIELD
ODIE
JIM DAVIS
© 1989 United Feature Syndicate, Inc.
FASTER THAN THE SPEED OF DOG
PAT
PAT
GARFIELD
ODIE

GARFIELD: a rare look behind the scenes

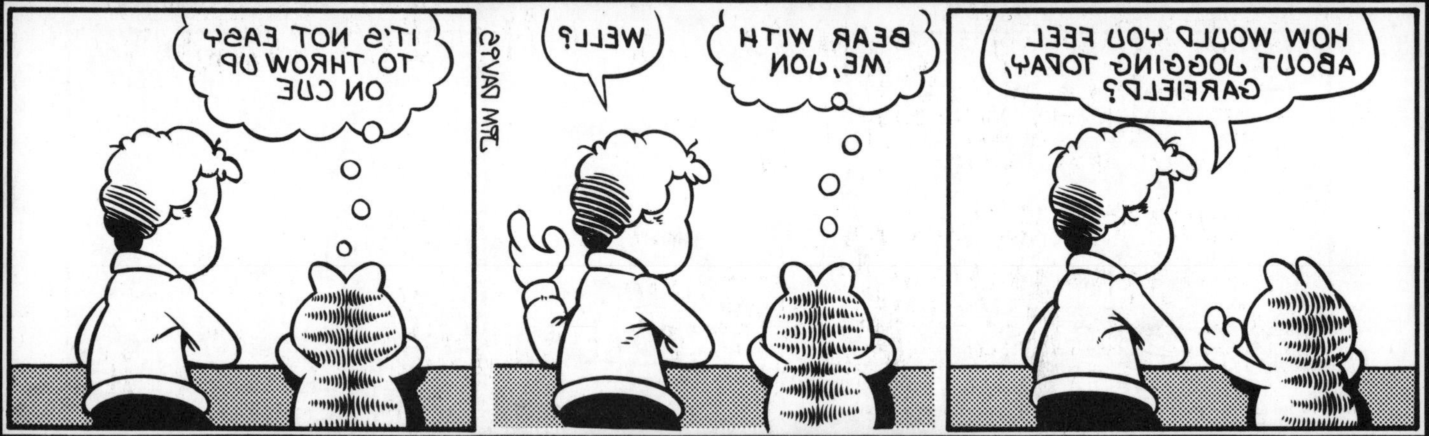
HOW WOULD YOU FEEL ABOUT JOGGING TODAY, GARFIELD?
BEAR WITH ME, JON
WELL?
IT'S NOT EASY TO THROW UP ON CUE